A Cloud
of Witnesses

Sermon Illustrations and Devotionals
from the Christian Heritage

from the library of
JIM BARNETTE

A Cloud
of Witnesses

Sermon Illustrations and Devotionals
from the Christian Heritage

C. Douglas Weaver

Smyth & Helwys Publishing, Inc.
Macon, Georgia

ISBN 1-880837-21-8

A Cloud of Witnesses
Sermon Illustrations and Devotionals from the Christian Heritage
By C. Douglas Weaver
Copyright © 1993
Smyth & Helwys Publishing, Inc.
Macon, Georgia 31207 USA
All rights reserved.
Printed in the United States of America.

The paper used in this publication meets the minimum requirements of
American National Standard for Information Sciences—
Permanence of Paper for Printed Library materials, ASI Z39.48-1984.

Library of Congress Cataloging-in-Publication Data

Weaver, C. Douglas.
A cloud of witnesses : sermon illustrations and devotionals from the
Christian heritage / C. Douglas Weaver.
xiv+206pp.   6x9" (15x23cm.)
Includes indexes.
ISBN 1-880837-21-8 (alk. paper)
1. Homiletical illustrations. 2. Baptists—Prayer-books and
devotions—English. I. Title.
BV4225.2.W43 1993
251'.08—dc20   93-34392
CIP

Contents

Fifth Century

Sixth Century

Seventh Century

Eighth Century

Tenth Century

Eleventh Century

Twelfth Century

Thirteenth Century

Fourteenth Century

Fifteenth Century

Sixteenth Century

Seventeenth Century

Eighteenth Century

Nineteenth Century

Twentieth Century

Indexes

Preface

In recent years there have been numerous calls for Christians, Baptists in particular, to remember their heritage. As the conventional wisdom goes, we have forgotten or distorted our roots. When we do remember it, we either feel superior to it or do not fully appreciate the hardships, commitment, witness, and faith of those who have gone before us, especially those with different beliefs or traditions.

Ministers and teachers should be about the task of increasing our understanding of our past. This book of sermon illustrations and devotionals is a practical attempt to help them begin to fill the gap in our appreciation of the Christian heritage. The material included communicates our Christian heritage in a variety of methods: stories, anecdotes, sayings by influential leaders and biographical sketches. Some of the subjects are well known, like Augustine and Martin Luther, while others, like Lioba and Macrina, will be new to most readers. Ministers can teach Christian history in a variety of ways. They can teach in their preaching by the use of illustrations. They also can focus their devotionals on specific events or persons that have made up our past cloud of witnesses. Some of the biographical sketches in the book can easily be used as the basis for historical sermons, an excellent way to demonstrate how the biblical witness has been lived out in the Christian pilgrims of our past.

The authors that have contributed to this work have made it an exciting book to edit. Many authors are distinguished church historians and are recognizable names in scholarly and Baptist denominational circles. Bill Leonard and Timothy George have contributed their stories, with only slight variations, from previous works. Leonard drew on his *Word of God Across the Ages: Using Christian History in Preaching* by Smyth & Helwys Publishing, Inc., and Timothy George drew on his *Theology of the Reformers*, published by Broadman Press. All the authors have academic expertise in the field of church history and/or have made the effort to use the Christian heritage in their preaching. The material on Augustine by Penrose St. Amant is unique in that it not only provides some illustrative material but is often devotional material directed at ministers themselves. A particularly attractive feature of the work, I think, is its gender inclusiveness, both in authorship and content. Some of the best women historians in Baptist life have made superb contributions. It is time that we realize that our heritage has many important contributions from women down through the centuries. I hope this book will help further that process of revision.

To aid the reader, several indexes have been included. In addition to ministers, this book can also be used by the laity in their devotional time and even as a "backroad" popular storytelling of the history of Christianity. I also think the book will prove an effective tool for use by students in church history classes. I have included a small sample of devotionals by my students to demonstrate how faith and academic discipline can be integrated in the classroom.

> Therefore since we are surrounded by so great *a cloud of witnesses*, let us lay aside every weight and the sin that clings so closely, and let us run with perseverance the race that is set before us, looking to Jesus the pioneer and perfecter of our faith. (Heb 12:1-2)

C. Douglas Weaver
Brewton-Parker College
Mt. Vernon, Georgia

Contributors

W. Loyd Allen, Chairman, Department of Religion, Mississippi College, Clinton, Mississippi

Penrose St. Amant, Senior Professor of Church History, The Southern Baptist Theological Seminary, Louisville, Kentucky

Rosalie Beck, Assistant Professor of Religion, Baylor University, Waco, Texas

Carolyn D. Blevins, Associate Professor of Religion. Carson-Newman College, Jefferson City, Tennessee

William R. Estep, Jr., Distinguished Professor of Church History, Emeritus, Southwestern Baptist Theological Seminary, Fort Worth, Texas

Timothy George, Dean, Beeson Divinity School, Birmingham, Alabama

D. Leslie Hollon, Pastor, Wornall Road Baptist Church, Kansas City, Missouri

E. Earl Joiner, Retired Chairman, Department of Religion, Stetson University, Deland, Florida

Deirdre Madison LaNoue, Ph.D. Candidate, Baylor University, Waco, Texas

Bill J. Leonard, Chairman, Department of Religion, Samford University, Birmingham, Alabama

Andrew M. Manis, Assistant Professor of Religion, Averett College, Danville, Virginia

Phyllis Rodgerson Pleasants, Registrar and Assistant Professor of Church History, Northern Baptist Theological Seminary, Lombard, Illinois

Walter B. Shurden, Callaway Professor of Christianity and Chairman, Roberts Department of Christianity, Mercer University, Macon, Georgia

Michael A. Smith, Pastor, New Hope Baptist Church, Nashville, Tennessee

Students of Brewton-Parker College
Anthony L. Chute, 1993
Gregory J. Carroll, 1992
Terri Farless, 1991
A. Randy Niswonger, 1992
Clarice K. Poland, 1992

C. Douglas Weaver, Barney Averitt Assistant Professor of Christianity and Chairman, Division of Religious and Philosophical Studies, Brewton-Parker College, Mt. Vernon, Georgia

James A. Weaver, Pastor, First Baptist Church, Madisonville, Kentucky

Danny M. West, Pastor, Litz Manor Baptist Church, Kingsport, Tennessee

First Century

001   **Nero.** *Roman Emperor* (37–68). According to Tacitus, when
Rome was burned in the first century, many people believed that
the fire was the result of an order from Nero. Tacitus reports that
Nero, thinking that many people would believe any kind of
gossip, spread a counter rumor that the burning of Rome was
done by a group already hated by many, the Christians. Subsequently, Nero rounded up a large group of those who confessed
that they were Christians and had them convicted not of burning
the city but of hating humanity. Some of those convicted were
torn by dogs, others were crucified, and some were burned to
provide light for the evening circus performances. Indeed, gossip
and lying can be deadly.[1] (Matt 5:10; 1 Tim 4:2; Jas 4:6-12)
(Gossip, Lies, Persecution) (EEJ)

Second Century

101   **Didache.** *Early Christian Writing* (2d cent.). The *Didache*, or
Teaching of the Twelve Apostles, is an important, early Christian
writing, probably of the early second century. Syria has been
suggested as the place of writing, and the influence of the Gospel
of Matthew, especially the Sermon on the Mount, is evident in
the ethical teachings. Admonitions include to turn the other cheek
and to pray for one's enemies—often considered some of Jesus'
most challenging teachings. The author of the *Didache* outlines
a way of life to follow and a way of death to avoid. At the
conclusion of this section of demanding morality, however, he
allows for a surprising compromise with Jesus' ideal to be perfect
as our Father in Heaven is perfect: "For if thou art able to bear
the whole yoke of the Lord, thou shalt be perfect; but if thou art
not able, do that which thou art able."

Such teaching resulted in the church setting up different
classes of Christians. The elite (clergy) were to keep the whole
yoke of the Lord; ordinary Christians had lesser expectations,
less responsibility, and less access to God. But we are all
ministers with equal responsibilities. We are *all* called to take on
the whole yoke of the Lord. The moral teachings of Jesus apply
to all of us. We compromise and conform all too easily to a

watered-down version of the gospel.[2] (Matt 5:48; 1 John 2:5) (Compromise, Ethics, Spiritual Perfection) (CDW)

102A **Ignatius**. *Bishop of Antioch* (35–107). Church history reveals a frightening propensity by Christians to resort to revenge and an "eye for an eye, tooth for a tooth" philosophy. The spirit of non-violent resistance was embodied by Jesus. The early Christian martyrs attempted to face persecution and the trials and tribulations of pagan culture with a witness that imitated Christ. Ignatius, the influential Bishop of Antioch, was arrested for his faith. Enroute to Rome to face a martyr's death, he wrote to fellow Christians at Ephesus.

> Pray continually for the rest of mankind as well, that they may find God, for there is in them hope for repentance. Therefore allow them to be instructed by you, at least by your deeds. In response to their anger, be gentle; in response to their slander, offer prayers; in response to their errors, be "steadfast in the faith;" in response to their cruelty, be gentle; do not be eager to retaliate against them. Let us show ourselves their brothers by our forbearance, and let us be eager to be imitators of the Lord, to see who can be the more wronged, who the more cheated, who the more rejected in order that no deed of the devil might be found among you, but that with complete purity and self-control you may abide in Christ Jesus physically and spiritually.[3]

(Isa 53:1-12; Luke 22:49-53; 23:34) (Non-violent Resistance, Persecution, Witness) (MAS)

102B One of the biggest ethical problems of the Church today is the integrity of its ministers. We are all familiar with the expression, "practice what you preach." The advise has been around a long time. Ignatius, Bishop of Antioch, at the turn of the second century, imitated the Apostle Paul and gave wise counsel to other church leaders. To the Ephesians he preached, "It is better to be silent and be real, than to talk and to be unreal. Teaching is good, if the teacher does what he says."[4] (Matt 5:14-16; Titus 2:7) (Integrity, Ministry, Leaders) (MAS)

103   **Jews and Early Christians**. (2d cent.). One of the major issues in the era of the Apostolic Fathers was the relationship of the Jews and Christians. Early Christian writers often demonstrated a love/hate attitude. As the church moved away from its Jewish roots and more into the Gentile mileu, Ignatius, Bishop of Antioch at the turn of the second century, said, "It is monstrous to talk of Jesus Christ and to practice Judaism." Ignatius said that he found inspiration "through the Hebrew prophets" but he considered Jewish teaching to be "strange doctrine and ancient fables."

The intensity of anti-Jewish feeling can be seen in the *Epistle of Barnabas*. This letter was written around A.D. 130, in Alexandria, Egypt, a city with a strong Jewish contingent. The author told the Jews that he was "one of yourselves and especially loving you above my own life." On the other hand, he called the Jews "wretched men" and told them that the Son of God became incarnate in order to "bring to summation the total of sins of those who persecuted his prophets to death." Furthermore, the Jews had completely misinterpreted God's intention for the concept of circumcision. According to Barnabas, an evil angel had led Jews to believe literally what should have been read allegorically as a circumcision of the ears and heart.

Christians often interpret the Bible in ways that will support their prejudices against others. We make it say what we want it to say. While not the only example, anti-semitism has been one of the worst.[5] (Matt 27:25; Acts 10:24; Jas 2:9) (Anti-Semitism, Biblical Interpretation, Prejudice) (CDW)

104A   **Justin Martyr**. *Early Christian Apologist* (ca. 100–165). Justin Martyr was the most famous apologist of the second century. In his defense of the faith to the Greek intelligentsia, Justin sought to prove that Christianity was the one true philosophy. Followers of Plato and other philosophers had some partial truth, but Jesus was the complete truth. At the heart of the matter, however, was not assent to minute theological formulae understood solely by scholars but the simplicity and profundity of faith and trust: "See Socrates," exclaimed Justin, "no one trusted in him so as to die for his doctrine, but in Christ . . . not only philosophers and scholars believed but also artisans and people illiterate."[6] (2 Cor 5:7; Gal 2:16; Heb 11:1) (Faith, Trust, Doctrine) (CDW)

104B Christianity has sometimes been labeled anti-intellectual and afraid of truth. Great thinkers throughout the ages, however, have affirmed that Jesus Christ is truth, and truth found in any field of knowledge has its source in him. Justin Martyr, the great apologist of the second century, was the first to argue that the true philosophy of life is Christianity. According to Justin, the ability to use reason or to speak what is true is rooted in Jesus the Living Word, whether the person recognizes it or not. Justin declared:

> Whatever has been uttered aright by any men in any place belongs to us Christians; for, next to God, we worship and love the reason (Word) which is the unbegotten and ineffable God; since on our account he has been made man, that being made partaker of our sufferings, he may also bring us healing. For all the authors were able to see the truth darkly, through the implanted seed of reason (the Word) dwelling in them.[7]

(John 8:31-32; 16:13; Phil 4:8) (Culture, Truth) (MAS)

105 **Pliny.** *Roman Governor* (ca. 112). Many Church historians belive that by the time of Pliny, governor of Bithynia at the turn of the second century, it was illegal in the Roman empire to profess Christianity. Since as far as he could tell, the Christians did not seem to be bad people, Pliny was a bit uncertain as to how far he should go in enforcing the law. Thus, he wrote to Emperor Trajan seeking his advice. Trajan's advice was that Pliny should not go out of his way to look for Christians. If they were brought to him, however, and they denied being Christian, they should be pardoned. They could demonstrate their innocence by paying tribute to the Roman gods. Pliny reported in his correspondence that he had already punished some (which likely means execution), and had others who reported that they were Roman citizens sent to Rome. He also reported that some had first confessed that they were Christians, but then denied it under threat of punishment. He added that despite his efforts to stop the spread of Christianity, it was still spreading, though he was optimistic that the movement could be stopped. Thanks be to God, he was wrong, but he calls attention to the fact that the faithfulness of a few can make a difference.[8] (Prov 28:20; Rev 2:10) (Faithfulness, Persecution) (EEJ)

106 **Polycarp.** *Bishop of Smyrna* (ca. 59–ca. 155). One of the most famous early Christian martyrs was Polycarp, Bishop of Smyrna and traditionally known as a student of the Apostle John. After a long life of eighty-six years, Polycarp was called upon to die or "swear by the genius of Caesar." He answered his prosecutor: "If you vainly suppose that I will swear by the Genius of Caesar, as you request, and pretend not to know who I am, listen carefully: I am a Christian. Now if you want to learn the doctrine of Christianity, name a day and give me a hearing."[9] (Exod 20:3; Dan 3:8-30; 6:6-23; Acts 4:18-20) (Christian Identity, Church and State, Faithfulness, Martyrdom, Temptation, Witness) (MAS)

Third Century

201 **Clement.** *Bishop of Alexandria* (153–217). Clement of Alexandria was one of the famous teachers of the early church. While not as prominent as his pupil, Origen, Clement wrote several important works. In the book, *The Instructor*, he gave advice to Christians on practical Christian living. One problem that has plagued the church throughout the centuries is a double standard when it comes to the obedience and virtue of men and women. Clement has a word for us regarding our equal privileges and responsibilities before the Lord:

> Let us, then, embracing more and more this good obedience, give ourselves to the Lord, clinging to what is surest, the cable of faith in Him, and understanding that the virtue of man and woman is the same. For if the God of both is one, the master of both is also one; one church, one temperance, one modesty; their food is common, marriage an equal yoke; respiration, sight, hearing, knowledge, hope, obedience, love all alike.[10]

(Gal 3:26-29; Eph 2:11-22; 5:22-33) (Double Standard, Equality, Ethics, Unity, Women's Right's) (MAS)

202A   Cyprian. *Bishop of Carthage* (200–258). Cyprian was Bishop of Carthage, North Africa, during the intense persecution of the church by the Roman emperor Decius in the year 250. The Church sent him into hiding, but during this time he wrote them many letters, never ceasing to exhort them to Christian living. In the midst of the anxieties of persecution, Cyprian admonished his people to remain firm in their faith. This was possible only through diligent prayer. Cyprian exhorted:

> Let us urgently pray and groan with continual petitions. For know, beloved brethren, that I was not long ago reproached with this also in a vision, that we are sleepy in our prayers, and did not pray with wakefulness. . . . Let us therefore strike off and break away from the bonds of sleep and pray with urgency and watchfulness, as the Apostle Paul bids us, saying, "Continue in prayer, and watch in the same."[11]

Wise words for us all amidst our anxieties. (Acts 6:4; Eph 6:18; 1 Thess 5:17) (Prayer) (MAS)

202B   One of the major schisms of the early church occurred when Novation, passed over in an election for the bishop's office in Rome, left to organize his own church. Novation accused the newly elected bishop, Cornelius, of compromising himself during the persecution of the emperor Decius in A.D. 250. Novation believed that his communion was the one true holy church because his followers had not compromised the faith during the persecution.

Cyprian, Bishop of Carthage, would have nothing to do with Novation's movement. Cyprian believed in holiness, but leaving the Church was not a holy act. Rather, Cyprian thought that Novation's split was really caused by the destructive power of personal jealousy over not being elected as the Roman bishop. He lamented,

> But what a gnawing worm of the soul is it, what a plague-spot of our thoughts, what a rust of the heart, to be jealous of another, either in

respect of his virtue or of his happiness; that is . . . to make other people's glory one's own penalty . . . such . . . are ever sighing, and groaning, and grieving; and since envy is never put off by the envious, the possessed heart is rent without intermission day and night. Other ills have their limit; and whatever wrong is done, is bounded by the completion of the crime. . . . Jealously has no limit; it is an evil continually enduring, and a sin without end.[12]

(Exod 20:17; 1 Cor 13:4) (Covet, Envy, Jealousy, Rivalry) (MAS)

202C There are many interpretations of the meaning of the Lord's Supper among the divisions of the church. Some speak of the real body and blood of Christ being present in the elements; others speak of the spiritual presence of the Lord during the observance of the Supper; others partake of the bread and cup as a memorial in remembrance of Jesus' death on the cross.

In the early Christian centuries, Christians affirmed the real presence of the Lord in the Supper (Eucharist). Technical theories of transubstantiation or consubstantiation were not invoked; believers simply believed that Christ's literal body and blood were present. Consequently, the Supper was an important event with implications for salvation. In the opinion of Ignatius, Bishop of Antioch, the Supper was "the medicine of immortality."

During the persecution of the church by the Emperor Decius in the middle of the third century, masses of believers renounced their faith. When many sought repentance and a return to the church, they faced a traditional part of the penalty of excommunication by the church—exclusion from participation in the Eucharist. But Cyprian, Bishop of Carthage, began to question the practicality of denying the Supper forever even to the worst of sinners. Indeed, the Eucharist was "spiritual food" that gave needed strength to believers for daily living. When a new persecution came, Cyprian wondered, how could penitent believers even attempt to resist forsaking the faith again without the nourishment of Christ's body and blood?

According to Glenn Hinson, in the early church era, Christians believed that they were engaged in a cosmic battle. When baptized, they enlisted and were initiated into the army of Christ.

Their task was to fight on God's behalf against the army of Satan. Like any army, the combatants needed to rearm themselves constantly. The Lord Supper was this rearming for the battle of daily Christian living.[13]

We don't have to affirm the "real presence" of Christ in the elements in order to experience the powerful spiritual presence of God in our observation of the Supper. We can experience the nourishment of "spiritual food" as we gain strength in the sharing of the bread and cup together. As we remember Christ's death, we can fellowship and rejoice in our unity in Christ. As we partake of communion, we can renew ourselves for the daily tasks of Christian living. Indeed, the early church reminds us that the Supper is a powerful symbol of the spiritual presence of Christ in our lives. (1 Cor 11: 20-34) (Lord's Supper) (CDW)

203A **Perpetua and Felicitas.** *Early Christian Martyrs* (d. 203). What does total allegiance to God mean? Both Mark and Luke record that following Jesus would cost the disciple everything, including family relationships. In a society where identity was found in the family, not the individual, Jesus was relating the truth of a sacrifice, the dimensions and ramifications of which are not appreciated usually by us today. Jesus said that in the conflict that would ensue from a total commitment of one's self to God, family members would turn against each other. He also promised that this extreme sacrifice would not go unnoticed by God. One group of Christians who clung to these scriptures to validate their lives were the martyrs.

At the beginning of the third century in North Africa, persecution of Christians broke out in Carthage. One of the catechumens taken into custody was Perpetua, a noblewoman still nursing her son. When she was first incarcerated, her father came to her begging her to renounce her faith for the sake of her family, for him, and for her infant son. In the midst of his begging, Perpetua pointed to a pitcher and said, "Father, do you see this vessel lying here to be a little pitcher, or something else?" He replied that it was a pitcher, of course. Then Perpetua responded, "Can it be called by any other name than what it is?" When he said "No," she continued, "Neither can I call myself anything else than what I am, a Christian." At that point her father was so enraged he fell on her as if to tear her eyes out, then went away. In spite of the anguish that she experienced over the violent upheaval in her family, and the obvious anguish of her father, Perpetua remained firm in her faith, ready to suffer anything, to serve as a witness to the living God as revealed in Jesus Christ by the Holy Spirit. Three more times he came to her begging her to renounce her faith, refusing to let her nurse her son, and forcefully trying to prevent her from going before the judge to profess her faith in Christ. Each time she was deeply troubled by her father's inability to see the truth, but strengthened in her determination to witness to her Lord even unto death.

How easy we have it! There is no emperor persecuting us, demanding the sacrifice of our lives!! It is difficult for us to understand how literally early Christians understood scripture and the allegiance they knew being a Christian entailed. Perhaps that is our persecution. Indifference to the claim of God on our lives, indifference to the demands of allegiance will do what no persecution ever could—kill us. May we be jolted out of our indifference to examine anew God's claim on our lives and our allegiance to God.[14] (Mark 10:28-30; 13:9-13; Luke 18:28-30; 21:12-19) (Indifference, Martyrdom, Persecution, Sacrifice) (PRP)

203B   Vibia Perpetua gave new meaning to the idea of being faithful to Christ. Jailed by the Roman governor of Carthage around A.D. 202 for being a Christian, she would not deny her faith. As she waited for her execution, she recorded her thoughts in an autobiography, providing one of Christianity's oldest and most vivid accounts of martyrdom.

Perpetua recorded that loved ones pled with her to recant her faith and be free. But she refused to do anything that she felt dishonored God. She sent each one away, affirming that her faith in God did not depend on external circumstances, such as freedom or imprisonment. She even refused to obey her father's command to give up Christianity and ignored his pleas to come home and take care of her infant son.[15]

During her imprisonment, Perpetua maintained a strong spirit. Eventually, the prison warden and many of the soldiers who dealt with her became believers. The account of her death, provided by a member of the church in Carthage, begins, "The day of their victory dawned, and with joyful countenances they marched from the prison to the arena as though on their way to heaven."[16] In the arena, Perpetua finally had to direct the tip of the soldier's sword to her own throat so he could make a clean stroke. He shook so badly he could not aim for himself. So Perpetua died in the arena of Carthage, proclaiming her faith in God.

Perpetua clearly saw her duty to God and did it with thanksgiving and joy because she was true to her commitment and faith. The account of her death ends with words that, God willing, are true today:

> . . . that even in our day the same Holy Spirit is still efficaciously present, along with the all powerful God the Father and Jesus Christ our Lord, to whom there will always be glory and endless power. Amen.[17]

(Ps 28; 31; Isa 40:27-41; Rom 12:1-2; Jas 1:1-8; 1 Pet 1:3-9) (Courage, Faithfulness, Martyrdom, Perseverance) (RB)

203C Felicitas was eight months pregnant. She knew she could not go with her friends to the forum to experience the second baptism of martyrdom unless she delivered her child before the day set for their trials. The group of Christians gathered around her to pray. They had been jailed together, condemned together, and had nurtured each other in the faith through all of this. Now they wanted to die together. So they prayed. In the fervor of their praying, labor began. Such pain! Even with this group bonded by suffering gathered around, nothing could take away the excruciating pain of childbirth on the prison floor. In the midst of her crying out, one of the jailers derided her: "You who are in such suffering now, what will you do when you are thrown to the beasts, which you despised when you refused to sacrifice?" Felicitas returned the taunt with the strength of her conviction. "Now it is I that suffer what I suffer; but then there will be another in me, who will suffer for me, because I also am about to suffer for him." A child of God! An heir! This woman, through her courage, claimed the promise *before* her death of sharing in Christ's glory because she willingly chose to share in Christ's suffering.

Felicitas gave up her daughter and then her life in order to share in Christ's suffering. As Christ suffers in the oppressed, the homeless, the hungry, the imprisoned, the ill; as Christ suffers with those who have been so battered by life they believe their horizon *excludes* God; as Christ suffers today, what are we willing to give up to share in Christ's suffering? Our position of privilege? Our comforts? Our need to stand on top of someone else in order to feel successful? Are we indeed heirs who share in Christ's suffering or are we faking it, hoping no one, —especially God—will notice?[18] (Rom 8:17-19) (Persecution, Suffering) (PRP)

204 **Tertullian.** *Bishop of Carthage* (145–220). Tertullian, Bishop of Carthage and the father of Latin theology, held an uncompromising view toward accommodating the Christian faith to the paganism of Roman culture. He is famous for the line, "What has Athens to do with Jerusalem, the Academy with the Church?" In his estimation, the sin of this world has a singular root: idolatry. Tertullian began his treatise *On Idolatry* with these solemn words:

> The principle crime of the human race, the highest guilt charged upon the world, the whole procuring cause of judgment, is idolatry. For, although each single fault retains its own proper feature, and although it is destined to judgment under its own proper name also, yet it is marked off under the general account of idolatry.[19]

(Exod 20:3; Hos 2:1-13; Matt 22:34-40) (Idolatry, Judgment, Sin) (MAS)

Fourth Century

301 **Ambrose.** *Bishop of Milan* (ca. 339–397). In the fourth century, shortly after ordering the massacre of seven thousand citizens of

Thessalonica, the emperor Theodosius traveled to Milan and proceeded to the church of Bishop Ambrose for communion. Ambrose intercepted the emperor at the door with the declaration, "You cannot enter here with hands soiled by human blood." Theodosius averred that if he had been guilty of murder, so had King David, the man after God's own heart. Ambrose unwaveringly replied, "You have imitated David in his crime, imitate him in repentance." The emperor had to promise not to execute any sentence of death until forty days after the offense, and he did penance before being admitted to communion.[20] (2 Sam 12:1-15; Luke 3:7-14) (Repentance, Sin) (JAW)

302   **Anthusa.** *Mother of John Chrysostom* (d. 384). People who might otherwise never doubt Holy Scripture begin to have problems with Proverbs 22:6 when they become the parents of teenagers. The proverb sounds so nice and neat, so confident of positive results, the way platitudes are supposed to sound. "Train you child and she/he will not depart from it" is usually the way we hear this passage. It sounds so hollow when your own flesh and blood rebel against everything you ever believed and taught! What we usually don't hear is the qualifying phrase "and when she/he is old," which is when the "not departing from it" is promised. Not even Holy Scripture predicts what will happen in the interim!! Parenting is an act of faith, not management by objectives. Parenting is lived out in unknowing, not in engaging in certain behaviors because of the predictability of successful results.

Yet there is hope. Stories of parents in Christian history permit us to hope in God's presence in the midst of our unknowing. Anthusa was a single parent in fourth century Antioch who had been widowed shortly after her son was born. Sons were considered a greater anxiety than daughters at that time in the Roman Empire because they would grow up to have the freedom to get into more trouble and because they were so much more expensive to educate and prepare for favorable positions in society. Anthusa wanted the very best for her son. As he grew up, he brought her great joy because she could look on him and see the image of her deceased love. She was a devout Christian, embracing widowhood rather than re-marrying. Single, female parents in the fourth century were a rarity, and Anthusa struggled to learn how to run her household, fend off those who would seduce her for the bit of property she inherited, engage in business, and be respected as a person of authority. She sacrificed economically in order for her son's inheritance from his father to remain intact for him to claim upon coming of age. In every way, she saw to it that her son received the best education available in Antioch both from the rhetorician, Libanius, and from the church. She did not make him take care of her, but instead handled all business matters herself, leaving her son free to immerse himself in his studies. As she described it, "For could you say that 10,000 loved you, yet no one will afford you the enjoyment of so much liberty, seeing there is no one who is equally anxious for your welfare."

Anthusa and John experienced conflict. At first, there was no guarantee he would become a Christian. The influence of his non-Christian teachers was strong. Once John committed his life to Christ, his youthful enthusiasm ignited in him the desire to be a hermit. The anguish Anthusa expressed! Her only son a hermit! Her only son renouncing everything she had struggled and sacrificed in order to provide him the very best life possible. What anguish she felt as she begged him not to desert her and "widow" her again. How she must have felt that everything she had done was in vain whether he was a Christian or a believer in the ancient gods of Rome. In the midst of all of this, Anthusa remained faithful in devotion to her God and devotion to her son. She provided John the space to deepen his devotion to Christ, even when she was uncertain how she would be affected by it.

In her struggles as a single parent and in conflict with her son, Anthusa had no idea she would be remembered by her son as an example of Christian devotion. She did not know that when John told Libanius about her, the great believer in the ancient gods would exclaim, "Heavens! What women there are among the Christians." Anthusa had no way of knowing that the way she taught her son Bible stories would one day find its way into his writings as the model for Christian parenting. In the midst of her unknowing, Anthusa provides hope for all parents. Her faithfulness in spite of no guaranteed results is a living witness to the presence of God in the midst of struggle and conflict even with those we love the most. Because of her faithfulness, space was provided for those she loved to encounter the living God and respond on their own to the claim of that God on their lives. She trained up her child in the way he should go and his affirmative response to the living God he encountered in that training meant that when he was old he did not depart from the way, even when it resulted in his own death. Thanks be to God for God's presence in our unknowing![21] (Prov 22:6) (Parenthood) (PRP)

303A   **John Chrysostom.** *Bishop of Constantinople* (ca. 347–407). "Another sermon on giving! And that passage about being cheerful—AGAIN! Can't preachers be creative? Try a new angle? See if they can convince me to be cheerful about being asked for money for the umpteenth time, from the umpteenth source, when I don't have enough to begin with!" Stewardship emphases in churches all over the world provoke such negative reactions. Some people hate to preach on stewardship because they know that no matter what they say, people hear them begging for money. Some preachers wear themselves out thinking of the newest gimmick to boost giving. Congregants resisting pleas to give of themselves, their time, and their money to support ministry is nothing new. Perhaps we can learn from those who faced this resistance in the past.

In the fourth century, John Chrysostom, one of the great preachers of the early church, was famous for his emphasis on charitable giving and love for humanity as definitive characteristics of Christians. He was also criticized for "harping" on these themes. His response was to work the complaints into a sermon. Repeating the criticism that he preached *every* day on giving and love, John declared that he would not cease doing so either. If his auditors had attained perfect lives defined by giving and love then, John said, he could not cease preaching about it for fear they would fall away from the life they were living. He had to exhort them continually for their own good. However, John observed, his congregants had not come even half-way close to living lives defined by giving and love. Therefore he had to encourage them continually to strive towards the ideal. If they didn't like it, they should complain to themselves for not living in such a manner that would permit him occasionally to relax his exhortations. He slyly suggested, "For indeed you do the same in blaming me, as if a little child, hearing often of the first letter of the alphabet and not learning it, were to blame its teacher, because the teacher is continually and forever reminding the child about it." John insisted that Christians would give willingly and gleefully if they would ever take seriously Jesus' words, "For as much as you have done it unto the least of these, you have done it unto me."[22] "Therefore, let us give as if giving to Christ" was John's clarion call, not only to his own congregation, but to each one of us. Recognizing the presence of the living God in our lives allows us to give ourselves, our time, our resources to Christ. Come! Let us give to Christ even now, in this hour, in this place. (Matt 25:31-46; 2 Cor 9:7) (Giving, (Stewardship) (PRP)

303B   Holy Scripture is witness to the light of God that arises in the midst of the deepest darkness to illumine the darkness. Scripture is not witness to the light taking away the darkness or exempting people from confronting the darkness in which they live. John Chrysostom in his sermon on Matthew 4 pointed out that the light springs up on its own accord. No amount of human seeking will summon the light of God's presence into existence. The light dawns. It bursts forth when we are enveloped in darkness. God seeks us, comes to us, and breaks into our darkness as only God can. We cannot summon the sunrise. We can wait and allow the light to illumine our very being as it dawns.[23] (Matt 4:12-17) (Light of God) (PRP)

303C   John Chrysostom was introduced to me in my early courses in church history as a golden-tongued orator who defended the faith, condemned the immorality of the rich, and gave generously to the poor. Philip Schaff says of him that none of the eastern church fathers left a better reputation. What is incredible is that Schaff and many church historians make only passing vague references or none at all to the horrible statements Chrysostom made about the Jews. While exaggerations were part of the oratorical styles of the time and regarded as part of the language of an eloquent speaker, we have to say that in his zeal for God, Chrysostom said things about the Jews that were not so true and contributed to the poisoning of relations between Jews and Christians that continues to the present day. He had, indeed, a zeal for God, but it was not all according to knowledge. There are still many people in the church like that. We can share their wisdom, but must learn not to drink their poison.[24] (Rom 10:2) (Knowledge, Zeal) (EEJ)

304A **Diocletian.** *Roman Emperor of Great Persecution* (303). Paulus Orosius, the fifth century church historian, popularized the notion that early Christianity experienced persecutions from ten Roman emperors, a fate similar to the Hebrews experiencing the ten great plagues in Egypt before the Exodus. Actually, the persecutions were sporadic and often local. But two persecutions, including the final one at the hand of emperor Diocletian in A.D. 303, were empire-wide and aimed at destroying Christianity by destroying the scriptures.

Some people handed over their copies of scripture to the authorities and saved their lives. Others kept their scriptures and suffered the consequences. One believer was brought before a government official and was told to read from the Gospels he illegally kept. He read, "Blessed are those who are persecuted for righteousness' sake, for theirs is the kingdom of heaven" (Matt 5:10). Finishing that verse he read again, "If any man will come after me, let him deny himself, and take up his cross and follow me" (Matt 16:24).

Pagan opponents believed that the defeat of the Christian faith was based on destroying the scriptures. But martyrs kept the faith revealed in the holy writings. The scriptures are our sole authority for our faith and practice. They are the Word of God and bear witness to Jesus, the Living Word. Let us not destroy our faith by destroying the scriptures through lack of use, bibliolatry or handing them over to the pagan gods of the present age.[25] (Matt 5:10; 16:24) (Bible, Martyrdom) (CDW)

304B   In the fourth century, during the persecution begun by En.
Diocletian, a young Roman army officer who was a member ᵥ
the court of Galerius, Diocletian's son-in-law, was impressed by
the courageous faith of the Christians in Nicomedia. He, too,
became a believer. When the Christians were next interrogated,
this young officer stepped forward and identified himself as one
of the followers of Christ. "Are you mad?" asked Galerius. "Do
you wish to throw away your life?" "I am not mad," the officer
responded, "I was mad once, but am now in my right mind."[26]
(Rom 12:1-2; Eph 4:22-24; Phil 2:5) (Conversion, Martyrdom,
Mind) (JAW)

305A   **Egyptian Desert Monks** (4th cent.). Too often we confuse our
self-will with temptations from the Evil One. The early Christians
living in the Egyptian deserts of the fourth century knew that we
must first learn self-control before we can confront the evil that
surrounds us. The following story about an experienced desert
prayer-warrior and a novice in the life of faith makes this point
clearly:

> Abba Abraham, who was a disciple of Abba Agatho once asked Abba
> Poeman: "Why do the demons attack me?" And Abba Poeman said
> to him: "Do the demons attack You? The demons do not attack us
> when we follow our self-wills, because then our wills become demons
> and themselves trouble us to obey them. If you want to know the kind
> of people with whom the demons fight, it is Abba Moses and men
> like him."[27]

"Abba Moses and people like him" are Christians who have
through disciplined obedience to some extent both tamed and
learned their own desires. We must be careful to distinguish
between the failure that is a result of our own lack of discipline
and the temptations that are beyond our control. (Rom 12:2-3)
(Discernment of Spirits, Evil, Pride, Temptations) (WLA)

305B   The tension between prayer and work, contemplation and action,
is a vital one in Christian maturity. The believer must never lose
sight of the balanced life of faith. Our religious activities can
become an excuse not to face our responsibilities to our

neighbors. The fourth century monks of Egypt, desert prayer-warriors, have left us a good example of how even the most religious among us need to be reminded of this truth.

> A brother came to Abba Silvanus on Mount Sinai. And when he saw the brothers working he said to the old man: " 'Labor not for the meat which perisheth' (John 6:27): and 'Mary hath chosen the best part (Luke 10:42).' " And the old man said to his disciple: "Call Zacharias, and put this brother in a cell where there is nothing." And when three o'clock came he kept looking at the door, to see when they would send someone and summon him to eat. But no one spoke to him. So he rose and went to the old man and said: "Abba, do not the brethren eat today?" And the old man said: "Yes, they have eaten already." And the brother said: "Why did you not call me?" And the old man answered: "You are a spiritual person and do not need food. We are earthly and since we want to eat, we work with our hands. But you have chosen the good part, reading all day, and not wanting to take earthly food." When the brother heard this he prostrated himself in penitence and said: "Forgive me, Abba." And the old man said: "I think Mary always needs Martha, and by Martha's help Mary is praised."[28]

Those who neglect their own basic needs or their responsibility to their community in the name of religion may be poor models of true Christianity. (Luke 10:38-42; 2 Thess 3:11-13) (Christian Maturity, Prayer, Works) (WLA)

305C The Bible must be used in order to be useful to the Christian. Every generation is tempted to believe it is practicing the faith when it is really only preserving its past. The fourth century Christians of the Egyptian deserts gave us fair warning about this temptation. Listen to the words, still relevant for us, of an ancient Christian:

> The prophets wrote books. Our fathers came after them, and worked much at them, and then their successors memorized them. But this generation has come, and it copies them on papyrus and parchment and leaves them unused on the window-ledge.[29]

The Bible may be the most purchased book in the English language, but if it remains unread, unapplied, we have failed to be faithful Christians. (2 Tim 3:16-17) (Bible) (WLA)

305D   Abbess Syncletice was a fourth-century female desert monk, one of church history's prayer-warriors whose wisdom about the life of prayer has sustained Christianity ever since. She said something worth remembering about the relationship of body and spirit:

> Everything that is extreme is destructive. So do not suddenly throw away your armor, or you may be found unarmed in the battle and made an easy prisoner. Our body is like armor, our soul like the warrior. Take care of both and you will be ready for what comes.[30]

We cannot expect to be spiritually strong if we ignore our physical needs or abuse our bodies, whether the abuse is by drugs, overwork, or overeating. (Rom 12:1-2; 1 Cor 6:19-20) (Body and Spirit, Gluttony, Prayer) (WLA)

305E   True interpretation occurs, our enemy faces defeat, when the Spirit within the inspired scripture leaves the printed page and enters the life of the believer. The desert Christians of fourth-century Egypt left us a vivid image of this in the following description of sacrificial love:

> Abba Evagrius said that there was a brother who had no possessions but a Gospel, and he sold it to feed the poor. And he said a word that is worth remembering: "I have even sold the word that commands me to sell all and give to the poor."[31]

(Luke 18:18-25; 2 Tim 3:16-17) (Bible, Love, Materialism) (WLA)

305F   The Bible is no passive object of worship, but an active weapon for waging Christian peace. The fifth-century monk Cassian recognized this. He stated that whoever practices the study of scripture "as the *summum bonum* (supreme good) and not as means will use them in vain. He possesses the tools of the trade but has no idea what they are for." Once in the deserts of ancient Egypt, a young Christian came to an old desert prayer-warrior and told him that he had recited the whole Bible from memory. "You have filled the air with words" was the old man's response. Another came saying he had written all Scripture in his own hand. "You have filled a window-ledge with manuscripts," said the old man.[32] Christians are not to be like gun collectors who fill their houses with weapons but never fire a shot. Scripture must be practiced in striving for the kingdom of God. (Heb 4:12) (Bible, Faith and Works) (WLA)

306   **Eusebius and King Agbar**. *Early Christian Historian* (c. 260–c. 340). Eusebius, the famous fourth-century historian, recorded a legend about Agbar the Black who lived and ruled in Edessa, part of the kingdom of Oshoene outside the boundaries of the Roman Empire. Having heard of Jesus' miraculous healing power, the king wrote Jesus and requested healing. Jesus wrote back and said his mission in Palestine must first be fulfilled but after his ascension, a disciple would come and heal the King and give life to him and his people.[33]

Christianity is a missionary faith. While a legend, the story of King Agbar reveals the concerns of the earliest Christians for sharing the gospel beyond the reaches of their everyday world, the Roman Empire. They knew they were to be witnesses to the uttermost part of the earth. (Matt 28:18-20; Acts 1:8) (Missions) (CDW)

307   **Forty Martyrs of Sebaste**. (ca. 320). Basil of Caesarea and Gregory of Nyssa, two of the famous Cappodocian brothers, narrated in their writings the story of the forty martyrs of Sebaste in Lesser Armenia. There were forty soldiers of the Twelfth Legion of Rome's imperial army who were Christians. Their captain announced to them that the Emperor Licinius had issued an edict that required all soldiers to offer sacrifice to the pagan gods. These forty soldiers replied, "You can have our armor and even our bodies, but the allegiance of our heart belongs to Jesus Christ."

It was mid-winter, A.D. 320. The captain had the men march out to a frozen lake. Their clothes were stripped off of their backs, and they were told either to renounce Christ or to die. There were baths of hot water on the banks of the lake as a temptation to apostasize. Throughout the night, the men huddled together and sang "forty martyrs for Christ, forty martyrs for

Christ." Unrelentingly, the frigid air took its toll. One by one, the soldiers fell in death.

Finally, only one soldier remained alive. But his courage failed, and he stumbled to the shore, renouncing his faith in Christ. The officer of the guard had been watching this drama of sacrifice and now defection. Secretly he had come to believe in Christ. When he saw the fortieth man come to the shore, the officer walked out onto the frozen lake, disrobed, and confessed that he also was a Christian. As dawn broke the next morning, there were forty bodies on the ice.[34] Tertullian, the great defender of the faith from North Africa, was right: "We multiply whenever we are mown down by you; the blood of Christians is seed."[35] (Mark 8:34-38; Acts 7:54-8:4; Rom 12:1-2) (Evangelism, Martyrdom, Self-Sacrifice) (JAW)

308   **Julian**. *Pagan Roman Emperor* (332–363). Yet we have not emptied the cloud of witnesses. There is one more in particular who haunts me. Look! Can't you see him? Of all the people from the fourth century I have met, I am haunted by the Emperor Julian. He was the most ethical, deeply religious emperor of the Roman Empire in that century. Pious to a fault, he was also the last Roman Emperor to try to wipe out Christianity. Julian should haunt each of us, for you see, he would have been a Christian had it not been for the Christians he knew. It was the Christians who murdered his father and brothers, kept him in confinement and isolation, force-fed him scripture so that even the joining of heaven and earth in the liturgy could not erase the bitterness and sorrow he had experienced.[36]

Perhaps we would all do and be church differently if we realized every time we gather, we are joined both by those who unite their praise and prayers to ours **and** by those who are waiting, longing, for the Christians to be Christian, to offer the world something the world does not already have, so they, too, can listen, learn, be drawn in, and, one day, join the Alleluia! (Heb 12:1) (Christian Lifestyle, Witness) (PRP)

309   **Macrina**. *Early Christian Teacher* (327–379). Born in Cappadocia in 327, Macrina was the oldest of ten children.[37] She is

credited by three of her brothers, who became great bishops of
the early church, with instilling in them the desire to study the
Bible and to serve God. She received an excellent secular and
theological education. Macrina loved God with her mind and
took great joy in teaching others about the Lord.[38]

But Macrina did not just love God, she also loved others.
She founded a hospital for the needy and established the first
religious community for women in Pontus. Professor Loops
wrote of Macrina that she made the convent a "school of earnest
Christianity" in which she educated both men and women.[39] The
humility with which she lived her life radiated. When her brother
Basil became the Bishop of Caesarea, she advised him to remain
humble. Her brother Gregory visited her, distraught because he
had angered a church leader and was exiled to be the Bishop of
Nyssa, a small, unimportant town. She counseled him that God
had something important for him to do and that he needed to be
about the Lord's business and quit worrying about positions.
Peter, Bishop of Sebaste, credited her with raising him in the
Lord.[40]

She died showing her concern and love for others. Gregory
remained with Macrina until she died, and he was appalled to
find that she did not have a decent robe in which to be buried.
She had given all her clothes to the poor. But Gregory purchased
a beautiful wedding gown for her, and Macrina was buried as the
bride of Christ. In life she gave all she had to others, in death
she was with Christ.[41] Macrina lived the Greatest Commandment
and gave to the Christian world an example of what it means to
love God and others truly. (Ps 136:1-3; Prov 22:6; Amos 6:4-7;
Matt 25:31-46; Luke 10:38-42; Acts 16:1-5) (Bible, Humility,
Self-Sacrifice, Service, Teaching) (RB)

310   **Martin of Tours.** *Bishop of Tours, Patron Saint of France* (d.
397). Martin of Tours was a missionary to France in the fourth
century. A soldier who had not yet become a Christian, Martin
encountered one day a man scantily clothed. Martin only had a
single garment himself, but he cut it in two and gave a half to
the poor beggar. In a dream that night Martin saw Christ himself
wearing the half of the garment he had given to the man. Martin

became a Christian, left the army, became a monk, and then a bishop, through whom many accepted the gospel.[42] (Matt 25:31-45) (Salvation, Social Gospel) (JAW)

311A   **Monica.** *Mother of Augustine* (c. 331–387). For centuries, scholars (especially Christian scholars) have studied and appreciated the writings and teachings of Augustine, the great fourth-century thinker. His contributions to Christianity are unmatched. Many forces shaped Augustine's life and thinking. One of the unquestionable influential forces in his life was his mother, Monica.

Monica believed in the power of prayer and was deeply committed to it. Monica's life seemed to be full of people to pray for: a pagan husband, a critical mother-in-law, and a wild son named Augustine. Her husband, Patricius, was an irritable man known for his violent temper. The salvation of Patricius was of utmost concern to Monica when she prayed. Before his death her pagan spouse became a Christian.

In the meantime, Augustine stumbled through the stupidities of adolescence into young manhood. Monica warned her son about the folly of premarital sexual relations. Nothing Monica could say to Augustine seemed to alter his behavior. (Later Augustine acknowledged that God was speaking to him through Monica, but both voices were ignored at the time.) At sixteen, Augustine committed theft, took a mistress, and had a son. He seemed to give his mother plenty to pray for. But Monica refused to quit praying for her rebellious son. In his *Confessions*, written later, Augustine described how God rescued his soul from its darkness because of his mother's prayers.

The faithful prayers of one woman in north Africa changed the radical behavior of a defiant son. God used that changed son to shape the doctrine of western Christianity.

Never underestimate the power of a person committed to prayer.[43] (Phil 4:6; 1 Thess 5:17; Jas 5:16-18) (Prayer) (CDB)

311B   One of the most important things parents can give to their children is unconditional love. Even when the parent is immature and the child does not respond the way the parent expects or desires, unconditional love makes an impact. When Augustine decided to go to Rome, his mother begged him either not to go or to take her with him, but he deceived her and went to Rome without her. Still, as he reflected on his decision, he recognized in retrospect that parental love is a powerful force. It still is.[44] (Prov 22:6) (Parenthood) (EEJ)

312A **Olympias.** *Noblewoman of Constantinople* (b. 368). In responding to those who were trying to trap him about allegiance to Caesar, which is the issue behind paying taxes, Jesus provided more than a cagey answer. He stunned his listeners then and now with his bold challenge to their, and our, understanding of how we express allegiance to God. Allegiance to God is more than what we do with our money. Allegiance to God demands our whole life.

One woman who accepted Jesus' challenge was Olympias, fourth century noblewoman in Constantinople. Both by birth and marriage Olympias had contact with the court of the Emperor Theodosius. An only child who was widowed shortly after she was married, Olympias was a very wealthy woman from the consolidated inheritances. She was also a rigorously devout Christian who perceived virginity and the solitary life as God's claim on her. She was determined to be true to her Christian calling regardless of the opposition she faced. And there was opposition—first of all from the Christian Emperor. Theodosius wanted Olympias to marry his relative, Elpidius. When she refused, he tried to coerce her. In response to the Emperor's threats, Olympias responded, "If my King desired me to live with a male, He would not have taken away my first husband." She went on to say that God, through the death of her husband, "had freed me from subjection to a man while He laid on me the gentle yoke of chastity." In the Greek language, Olympias was making a play on words, since she used the word *basileus,* (king) which Christians used to refer both to the Emperor and to God. The boldness of telling the Emperor that her ultimate allegiance was not to him but to another *basileus* was not without a price. Theodosius ordered all her property confiscated, denied her access to any bishop, and forbade her to attend church, all of which was carried out with a vengeance by the prefect of

Constantinople egged on by Elpidius. The reasoning was that out of boredom Olympias would prefer marriage. Rather than caving in to the coercion, Olympias thanked the Emperor for relieving her of her property that could have interfered with her relationship with God by tempting her to pride. Then she directed him to distribute it to the poor for the salvation of his own soul. Never did she consider marrying Elpidius or surrendering her God-given vocation to any imperial demand. Her prayer was, "Let me not be so seduced by earthly things so as to lose the soul's true riches."

Olympias knew full well what Jesus meant when he said, "Give to Caesar what is Caesar's, and to God what is God's." Caesar could have her wealth. What could never be surrendered was God's claim on her life and the way God directed her to live out that claim.[45] (Matt 22:15-22) (Obedience, Wealth) (PRP)

312B One can only imagine that in the political/ecclesiastical crisis in which she found herself, Olympias remembered Jesus' words—a *lot*. Those who were really Jesus' disciples would hold on to his teaching and then they would know the truth that would set them free. She had been set free, too. She was free of any attachment to her wealth. Her fortune had been confiscated by the Emperor and then restored when she would not submit to his wishes. She then chose to give it to the church as patron of many bishops who depended on her support for their ministry. She was free from fear of imperial decrees and imperial officials, too. In her youth, she had not hesitated to challenge the Emperor and prove her allegiance was first to God and God's claim on her life. She was free from any desire for physical comfort because she practiced the most rigorous asceticism as the way of purifying her desire for God and deepening her life in God.

Now she was older. She was the head of a convent attached to the cathedral. She served with the bishop as an instructor of catechumens. She oversaw significant ministry to the poor, both in Constantinople and in far away lands. She had proven herself as God's servant, was established and highly respected. Now this! The bishop whom she loved with the holy love that forms from shared ministry and shared ideals had been exiled!! A new bishop, more submissive to imperial whim, was installed, and the Emperor was especially concerned that those who were loyal to the former bishop prove their allegiance to the new one by receiving communion from him. Once again, she was hauled into court, this time before an imperial functionary instead of the Emperor. There were charges brought against Olympias and the women who served the church with her concerning their loyalty to the former bishop. These charges were met with resistance. Finally, the prefect said the women could repent, accept communion from the new bishop, and be set free. The other women complied with the prefect, fearful he really did have the power to bind them or set them free. Olympias knew a different freedom over which the prefect had no control. She rebutted, "I will not hold communion with those from whom I ought to secede, nor consent to anything that is not lawful to the pious."

As in her confrontation with the Emperor in her youth, a price was exacted for her courage. The prefect summoned her again and levied a severe fine against her, but as before, the loss of her property had no effect on her. She then exiled herself and lived away from Constantinople until her death. Olympias was a follower of Christ, a true disciple who held to his teaching, thereby knowing the truth that set her free. She was free indeed! Thanks be to God![46] (John 8:31-32) (Courage, Freedom, Obedience) (PRP)

313   **Paula**. *Early Christian Ascetic* (347–404). Paula was a Roman noblewoman who became a Christian after the death of her husband around A.D. 380. Although her life had previously been devoted to family and wealth, her conversion caused a radical change so that she devoted herself to asceticism, generosity to the poor, and the support of the work of Jerome, a Christian scholar.[47]

Paula studied the Scriptures and followed the austerities being popularized by Paul the Hermit and others who were fleeing into the deserts of North Africa to devote themselves to God. She never entered a bath, except when seriously ill. She slept on the ground, covered only with a mat of goat's hair. She spent many nights in prayer instead of sleeping.[48]

Paula and her daughter, Eustochium, used their wealth to establish a monastery in Bethlehem that Jerome directed, as well as three convents for women that Paula supervised. They also built a guest house for the sick, the elderly, orphans, and any others who were needy. She was said to have owned most of the city of Nicopolis, but she gave all of her wealth away in order to do good works and build the institutional church.

Another way in which Paula gave of herself was in her assistance to Jerome. Jerome's great work was translating into Latin the Septuagint. This work was called the Vulgate. Paula not only provided Jerome's living expenses but also purchased all of the manuscripts and supplies needed for his work. Paula was quite a scholar herself and often contributed to his work with her intellectual stimulus and critical response.[49]

Paula gave everything she had, as well as herself, to the work of the church in the fourth century. Nothing the world had provided for her in noble heritage mattered or compared to the surpassing greatness of knowing her Lord and serving Him. (Luke 9:23-24; 2 Cor 9:7) (Generosity, Piety, Self-Sacrifice, Stewardship) (DML)

Fifth Century

401A **Augustine.** *Bishop of Hippo* (354–430). Augustine was struggling in perplexity about the matter of the trinity. One day as he was contemplating the question, he was walking along the ocean shore. He noticed a little boy who was playing. The young fellow had dug a hold in the sand with a sea shell, and he was going back and forth to the ocean, filling the shell with water and then emptying it into the hole.

Augustine asked the boy what he was doing, and the lad answered, "I am putting the ocean in this hole."

Augustine laughed and realized the lesson before him to learn: "That is what I am trying to do; I see it now. Standing on the shores of time, I am trying to get into this little finite mind things that are infinite."[50] (Isa 55:8-9; Rom 11:33-36) (God's Nature, Trinity, Wisdom) (JAW)

401B   In the history of Christianity, perhaps no one has so vividly
written on the depths of sin as Augustine. He believed that the
fundamental sin of pride ever hounds us. Our only escape is utter
dependence upon the grace of God. In his *Confessions*, Augustine
wrote:

> But, O Lord, Thou alone Lord are without pride, because Thou art the
> only true Lord, who hast no lord; hath this third kind of temptation
> also ceased from me? To wish, namely, to be feared and loved of
> men. . . . Affrighted by my sins and the burden of my misery, I had
> cast in my heart, and had purposed to flee to the wilderness: but Thou
> forbadest me, and strengthenedst me, saying, Therefore Christ died
> for all, that they which live may no longer live unto themselves, but
> unto Him that died for them. See Lord, I cast my care upon Thee,
> that I may live, and consider wonderous things out of Thy law. Thou
> knowest my unskilfulness, and my infirmities; teach and heal me.[51]

(Rom 7:14-25) (Dependence on God, Grace, Prayer, Pride, Sin)
(MAS)

401C   The process by which Augustine came to know God was long
and not without a spiritual, intellectual, and moral struggle every
step of the way. One of his greatest problems was his enslave-
ment to sexual lust. He had taken a mistress when he was sixteen
years old, and she had borne him a child. Even though he
became conscience-stricken, sent her back to Africa, and agreed
to a marriage arranged by his mother, he was unable to keep his
vow. Although he liked the girl, she was too young, and he was
asked to wait two years before marriage. Having prayed "Lord
give me chastity, but not yet," he took another mistress, but was
still in misery. Then one day when he was meditating in a garden
with a friend, he opened the Bible and read the first thing he
saw, which was a passage in Paul's letter to the Romans: "not in
rioting and drunkenness, not in chambering."[52] That ended his
conflict. (1 Kgs 20:40; Matt 6:34; Rom 7:19; 8:11-14) (Conflict,
Procrastination, Repentance) (EEJ)

401D   Shortly after his conversion, Augustine was confronted on the
street by a former mistress. He saw her and turned to walk in the
opposite direction. The woman cried out with surprise,

"Augustine, it is only I." As he kept walking, Augustine called back, "Yes, but it is not I." (2 Cor 5:17; 1 Pet 1:13-16) (Holiness, New Creation) (JAW)

401E When Augustine went to stage plays in Rome and Milan, he watched the effects of the drama on the audience as much as he did the players. He was particularly intrigued by the way many people seemed to enjoy watching suffering on the stage. After some reflection, he concluded the reason was that these people could sympathize with human suffering without having to do anything about it.[53] (Jas 2:14-17; 1 John 3:16-17) (Faith and Works, Sympathy) (EEJ)

401F Christian ministry must take the long view. Augustine is counted among the three or four most influential Christians since New Testament times. As he lay on his death bed in the North African town of Hippo in the year 430, all that he had worked for over a lifetime lay in ruins around him. Vandal invaders had devastated the countryside, burning church and home alike. Barbarians surged around the very walls of the city in which Augustine lay dying, a broken old man whose culture and country slumped in smoking wreckage all around him. The shadows of the Dark Ages were descending. If he had tried to accommodate the gospel to fit what he saw, what would he have left us? But praise be to God, Augustine always wrote and acted with his sights set on the final goal. By taking his perspective from eternity, he gave us a Christian theology and spirituality that has proven durable across all these centuries and among countless other cultures. Augustine ministered as if God were looking on. Christian ministry acts in the sight of God and does not lose heart. (2 Cor 4:1-6) (Faithfulness, Ministry, Perseverance) (WLA)

401G Augustine had a motto printed on the wall of his dining room: "He who speaks an evil word of an absent man or woman is not welcome at this table." (Eph 4:29; Jas 3:1-2; 4:11-12) (Evil Speech, Gossip) (JAW)

401H It is sometimes said that Augustine's *Confessions* are not an autobiography; but that depends upon what is meant by autobiography. The treatise called *Confessions* is an autobiography in the sense that the author wrote openly and succinctly about his heart and his feelings.[54] He looked at himself and the larger life of which he was a part *subjectively*—to use a word that fits into the jargon of our time. What we read in the *Confessions* is what Augustine *felt, saw,* and *believed.* He treated retrospectively his *personal spiritual pilgrimage* and his *conversion* from paganism to Christianity "as a clue to, and an illustration of, the universal situation of humanity in relation to God."[55] The emphasis on personal feelings is apparent from the outset of the book, where he commented concerning God: "Thou hast formed us for thyself, and our hearts are restless till they find their rest in thee."[56] At the age of seventy-four, Augustine was able to say that "the *Confessions* still move me when I read them now as they did when I first wrote them."[57]

The *Confessions* point to an "inner world," the large size of which inspired him but also made him anxious. Augustine wrote: "There is, indeed, *some light in men*; but let them walk fast, walk fast, *lest the shadows come.*"[58] Augustine was profoundly aware of the "dark night of the soul" as an ever present possibility. He believed in the goodness of the created order and also the human tendency to corrupt it. The only extant piece of poetry that he wrote reflects this dual (not dualistic) situation:

> Those things are yours, O God. They are good,
> Because you created them.
> None of our evil is in them. The evil is ours
> If we love them
> As the expense of yourself—these things
> that reflect your design.[59]

The evil that is ours is "a perversity of the will," Augustine said, a perversity that "turns [humanity] away from thee, O God."[60] Evil is to be "possessed by pride," to worship the "creature" rather than "the Creator," to be dominated by concerns for power, status, sex, and greed (cf. Rom 1:21-23). Augustine continued his litany of "the evil that is ours" by listing "the lust to dominate," "envy," "a denial of dependence upon God," "great pain," "pride" and "concupiscence." He softened his preoccupation with evil by saying that "much good still flows beside the evil."[61]

Augustine attributed evil to the fall, which cut off "direct awareness of God from human consciousness." This dislocation has "been mercifully bridged through the Bible."[62] The depth of divine revelation in scripture was the centerpiece of Augustine's concern. The "treasures" set forth therein formed a Christian culture, a *Doctrina Christiana*, in which Augustine engaged in a spirited dialogue with classical culture.

What does this issue in ancient culture have to do with preaching today? Briefly, I believe it helps to focus the contemporary issue of relating the Christian gospel to our secular world. My impression is that ours is a time of widespread biblical illiteracy that is more serious than we commonly realize. There are plenty of Bibles in our homes but the thrust of biblical faith in our daily lives seems to me to be woefully weak. There are, of course, exceptions to this generalization in our homes and churches. Yet my perception is that people tend to remember isolated biblical passages learned at home mainly from their mothers and are inclined to recall verses from Sunday School, sword drills, and B.Y.P.U. (that dates me!) and can quote them more or less correctly from memory (that's good) usually out of context (that's not good). A series of sermons dealing with the mighty and majestic meaning of the Bible, treating passages in context, in simple (not simplistic) language related to major cultural issues we face in America today would be salutary and, I believe, popular. A few suggested topics could be: "The Bible and Marriage;" "The Bible and the Single Adult;" "The Bible and the Sexual Revolution;" "The Bible and Career Choices;" "The Bible and the Loss of Precious Things." Basic biblical preaching with a hermeneutical thrust is perhaps the greatest need of the church today. By "hermeneutical" I mean taking the exegetical task seriously (what did the passage mean when it was written?) and then trying to set forth with the help of the Holy Spirit what the passage can mean today to those who hear us preach.

Let me repeat a point that our secular culture takes, if at all, "with a grain of salt." I speak again of the Fall, which took humanity away from the goodness of life to our love for things that divert us from the love of God. The human condition is a curious mixture of "original sin" and the "image of God." Therefore, our lives are sometimes ambiguous because "so much good" still flows beside the evil "as in a vast racing stream."[63] Augustine spoke of "the gratuitous accidents of daily life" and almost immediately mentioned the "sheer diversity and abundance of chirruping birds."[64] *Freakish accidents* and *chirruping birds* are symbols of what life is really like.

Let me give two personal examples of the mingling of great pain and genuine pleasure. In 1989, I was in Jewish Hospital in Louisville, Kentucky, for tests to determine the cause of excessive fluids in my system. I planned to be there one night but stayed two months. I got out of bed and carelessly caught my right foot on a leg of a table used to serve food to the patients. I was catapulted across the room and hit a concrete wall full force. The result was that the "ball" at the top of the thigh bone (the femur) shattered the receptacle (the acetabulum) in which the ball fits. A freakish accident like this is what Augustine spoke of as "gratuitous." That's life, but only a part of it. Life is sometimes tragic; life is sometimes good. We should not be cynical and pessimistic when things go wrong. We should not be sentimental and naive when things go right. Life is both a dull and also a joyous adventure.

The rest of the story is set not in a hospital with my right leg in traction. The second setting is "Treetops"—our home on a beautiful bayou in Mississippi. There I see the "sheer diversity of chirruping birds" with colors no artist could capture. There are several magnificent pileated woodpeckers and squirrels my wife feeds. These beautiful creatures are quick and full of life and grace as they play in the trees outside our picture windows, outdoing the most gifted trapeze artists with amazing dexterity.

Augustine was aware of a goodness in life that came from God, a goodness mingled with evil, much he attributed in a world made by a good God to a "derangement" that he did not define. He spoke also of some "unspeakable sin" as the chief source of human woe, which he also left undefined. Suddenly and unexpectedly, he tried to soften the intellectual puzzle and moral blow of the doctrine of original sin by writing, "yet so much good still flows beside the evil 'as in a vast racing river'." Augustine then went on to speak of "intellectual brilliance," "the play of light and color," "the scent's of flowers" and "the sea . . . as it slips on and off its many colors like robes."[65] These comments were intended to show the sheer goodness of life despite its tragedy.

Augustine indicated that people marvel at mountain tops, the vast expanse of the sky, the rivers flowing into the seas, the shining stars "and yet they leave themselves unnoticed; they do not marvel at themselves."[66] This failure he regarded as a tragedy because "God is deeper than my inmost being." A person is "driven" to flee "outwards" "to wander" far from one's true destiny and thus lose "touch with the real self." This "turning outwards" meant for Augustine "a loss of identity," a sense of isolation, a severing of existence that is "full of cares" because the self is cut off "from the whole."[67] This process of fragmentation propelled the young Augustine onto the surface of life with its superficial values, where earthly pleasures that seemed so alluring surfeited him and pagan philosophies that at first promised certainty and peace turned to skepticism. His immersion in classical literature and his extraordinary rhetorical skills did not fill the vacuum in his life. Peter Brown in his brilliant book, *Augustine of Hippo, A Biography*, speaks of these tendencies in Augustine's theology as "the Fall," "an agonizing weakness" that forced him to flee from himself and thus to "a wandering"[68] from the true home of his soul, an "agonized weakness,"[69] resolved only by God's grace and power that filled the void he could not fill as a "playboy," a gifted philosopher, and a noted rhetorician. Augustine's problems are also ours. Can we find rest in a restless world? He might preach to us, "You Can Go Home Again." (Gen 3; Matt 5:45; Rom 1:22-23; 7:14-25) (Ambiguities of Life, Evil, Goodness of Creation, Self-Identity, Sin) (PSA)

401I   Augustine's story is not his alone. It is the story of humanity in its struggle to find rest and peace in a restless world. One contemporary example comes to mind. Ralph Barton was a gifted writer and a master of caricature. His gifts left him unsatisfied. He made his living writing books about our human foibles with accompanying caricatures. He wandered over the world in a search for his illusive destiny. Alone in a second-rate and run-down hotel in Paris, he put a bullet in his brain. The note he left said: "I have had an exceptionally good life as life goes. The most charming and intelligent people I have known have liked me. But my life and my work have lost their meaning. I have run from country to country in a deliberate effort to escape from myself. I have done this because I am lonely and tired, tired of inventing devices for getting through twenty-four hours a day."

The stories of Ralph Barton and Augustine have certain parallels. Both were restless; both wandered looking for the illusive solution to life with its lights and shadows, births and deaths, tragedy and triumph. Both were writers, though Barton was, of course, a story teller and caricuratist and Augustine was one of the truly great theologians in the history of the church. Barton found only boredom and despair—and suicide. Augustine found God, and God found Augustine, whose wanderings led him to his Lord and whose restless heart found rest and gave him the courage to see it through with a prayer on his lips as he died at the age of seventy-five. A possible sermon topic could be, "Who Was Augustine and What Does His life Have to Do With Mine?"(text, Matthew 11:28) Hopefully you get my point. Wisdom was not born yesterday or today. There's a lot of it in Augustine.

It is repetitious, but it is true—ours is a restless time, somewhat similar to Augustine's era, a period in which people seek peace and contentment outside themselves, as the young Augustine tried to do. As a consequence, he could hardly bear to be alone. Alfred North Whitehead said that "religion is what we do with our solitude." That is a limited understanding of religion, but it raises the important question of solitude and what we do with it. Solitude can be a solace in life when the shadows come and words, simple or eloquent, do not help. In times like that, we need to be alone, to sort things out, to seek the healing and strength and guidance of God's Spirit. Solitude can accentuate our loneliness, however, and elicit unhealing introspection that magnifies our problems. A sermon topic on "solitude or loneliness" would seem fitting especially for older people who live alone (possible texts: Psalms 23; 46:10; Matt 28:19-20).

Society today is basically technologically and consumer oriented. The idea is widespread that if we can just accumulate enough things—houses, lands, stocks, and bonds—we shall find peace of mind and happiness amid the troubles of life. The search goes on, encouraged by a multitude of magazines and books that portray perpetually smiling people surrounded by the latest gadgets, elegant furniture, luxurious homes, clothes for every occasion, offices with deep carpets that match the drapes, and worry-free cruises to far-away places, where the smiling continues. Radio and television follow suit with advertisements (usually too loud) that virtually guarantee happiness if you buy this or that. Commercialism has invaded some religious radio and television programs, in which at times simplistic solutions— "spiritual prescriptions"—are offered as solutions to complex problems of finance, illness, grief, doubt, skepticism—these impersonal approaches, some well intended, do not really deal with the void in our souls, our "inner world," that God alone can fill. "It is man's tragedy," Augustine said, "that he should . . . lose touch with himself [and] wander far from his own heart."[70] This happened to the young Augustine, whose restlessness became a gate through which God came to bring salvation and peace. Ralph Barton's restlessness was not a gate but a wall. He could not penetrate with his unusual human ingenuity. The result was not a new life of hope but a sad event that brought a gifted life to a tragic conclusion.

In our noisy streets in the cities, people jostle each other trying to get here or there amid the rumble of traffic and constant talk, talk, talk about the stock market or this or that business deal or "I'd better hurry or" "I'll be late for this or that appointment." Recently a student came into my office to tell me that she was "burned out" listening to class lectures. And so it goes. All of us, at times, need retreats from the almost non-stop noise of traffic, of talk, of the thunder of jets, of television, of the tumult of the marketplace. Peace and quiet are in short supply in our mechanized world. A poem by Rupert Brooke points up the importance of quietness in the midst of the bedlam of today's world:

> Safe in the magic of my woods I lay
>   and watched the dying light
> Faint in the pale high solitudes
>   And washed by rain and veiled by night.
> Silver and blue and green were showing
>   and the dark wood grew darker still
> Wind was hushed and peace was growing
>   and *quietness* crept up the hill.
> I knew this was the hour of knowing.

There are some things we shall never know until we are quiet, until we listen to our hearts. Blaise Pascal (1623–1662), the French mystic and theologian, sounded the same note in his comments concerning the wisdom of the heart at a time when reason was held by some as the way to truth. He said, "The heart has its reasons that reason does not know."

No wonder Augustine's *Confessions* have been compared to Pascal's *Pensees* because their questions and answers to life's deepest issues were similar. Rousseau's *Confessions* appeal not to God who fills the void in our lives but to a "return to nature" and contrast sharply with Augustine's *Confessions* that are addressed to God. Rousseau's autobiography is the work of an eccentric genius who believed peace could be found by immersion in the alleged simplicities of nature; Augustine knew that the "heart finds no rest until it rests in God," not in nature, not in intellectual prowess.

Goethe's Faust, like Augustine, sought peace and truth in nature, philosophy, and divinity, only to end in despair, disillusionment, and the loss of "all peace of mind."

> Alas! I have explored
> Philosophy and law and medicine,
> And over deep divinity have poured,
> Studying with ardent and laborious zeal;
> and here I am at last, a very fool,

With useless learning cursed
No wiser than at first.
But I have lost all peace of mind
Whate'er I knew or thought I knew
Seems now unmeaning and untrue,
The fancy too has died away,—
The hope that I might in my day
instruct and elevate mankind.[71]

(Ps 23; 46:10; Matt 6:24; 11:28-30; 28:19-20; 1 Cor 1:18-28)
(Intellect, Materialism, Restlessness, Solitude) (PSA)

401J   Augustine was an uncommonly powerful preacher. Frequently his sermons were addressed to a wide spectrum of people of varied intellectual and religious tastes. They faced serious problems of Christian belief in an unsettled pagan society, where Manichaeanism, Neo-Platonism, and Skepticism were making inroads into Christianity. The people were also faced with a larger cultural problem: the collapse of Roman Africa that was on the horizon and the anxiety elicited by the barbarians, who were moving westward. Arian Christianity that questioned Christ's deity posed a major theological problem because it penetrated into most of the Germanic tribes.

Augustine was keenly aware that life is "tough" and often unfair. The death of his mother, Monica, at the age of fifty-six left its mark on him. He spoke of the "terrible day"[72] following that sad and unexpected event. He said, "She loved to have me with her . . . far more than most mothers." Monica died at Ostia, the port for Rome, at the beginning of their proposed trip back to Africa. "An immeasurable sorrow flowed up in my heart," he said as he made his way home, after an interval in Rome due to a blockade that delayed the departure. He was accompanied by a friend and Adeodatus, his son by a concubine, with whom, according to the fashion of his time, he lived for fourteen years during his early life. Adeodatus died at the age of seventeen shortly after their arrival in Africa, leaving Augustine alone.

Despite the loss of his mother, whom he adored, and his son on the verge of a promising manhood (and the "wicked ways" of his youth that he looked back upon with much regret), Augustine was not a morose man. There are unexpected and delightful places in his preaching where genuine humor related to the theme of his sermons suddenly appears (not jokes for their own sake to generate laughter). Preaching on one of the Psalms, he said: "Let me try to winkle (draw out?) the hidden secrets of this Psalm we have just sung and chip a sermon out of them to satisfy your ears and minds." In a sermon on the text, "Knock and it shall be opened unto you" (Luke 11:9), he said, "Knock by showing a keen interest; knock even for me by praying for me that I should extract something from it worth telling you."[73] No wonder he held his hearers spellbound. His allegorical method involved what has been described as "a mixture of intellectual excitement, sheer aesthetic pleasure [and] . . . a notable display of wit."[74]

Augustine's exegesis of a biblical passage was not a laborious exercise of grammatical and historical detail. He displayed the gift of dealing with a passage in such a way that his audience would listen to what he said and share in it. His rhetorical skills were merely means of eliciting a response that included doing something about what they heard. He sought to involve the audience in prayer for the preacher so that "something worthwhile would occur." The idea that preaching is an "event" that occurs here and now in the sermon and is not merely comments about the biblical past was an important aspect of his preaching. Augustine put it this way: "the thread of our speech comes alive through the very joy we take in what we are speaking about."[75] Rhetoric that was governed by self-conscious rules, of which he was a master, was subordinated to the basic issues his hearers faced so that he might communicate with them. Immediacy, not aesthetic grandeur, increasingly became Augustine's criterion as a preacher as the years passed. It has been suggested that "he lived through the emotions of which he spoke."[76] He abhorred style for its own sake and despised synthetic feeling that could be conjured up but which he did not really feel. Preaching for him was not role playing to please or shock the public but the authentic upsurge of the gospel from both his head and his heart.

Unless the people who hear us preach feel a sense of our own joy they will not be joyful. If we are not excited about the gospel, how can we expect those who hear us preach to be excited about it? The worst that can be said about a sermon is that it is uninteresting and boring. It may be eloquent, prepared with care, with attention to the nuances of good exegesis, but if it misses the genuine concerns of the people in their joys and sorrows, it is little more than an exercise in futility. Just as Augustine did not permit his rhetorical skills and eloquence to come between himself and those to whom he preached, we should not permit our learning and our way with words to build a wall between us and the people who come to church seeking hope, consolation, and a "lift" from the routines of their daily lives. Let our learning and our polished vocabularies be used as instruments for the proclamation that the Kingdom of God came with Christ (Matt 12:28), who has already put all things "under his feet," including "the last enemy that shall be destroyed, [which] is death" (1 Cor 15:26-27). Let us make it clear that Christ's victory over sin in the cross and over death in the resurrection was not his alone but is a victory in which we can share here and now by faith in Him as Savior and Lord. (Luke 4:16-20; Rom 10:14; 1 Cor 15:26-27, 50-57) (Preaching, Tragedy) (PSA)

401K The criteria of the Christian cannot be the criteria of contemporary society. Augustine was well aware of the impact that human custom and what he called "the chain of habit" can have on human life. "The habits of a life-time"[77] still trapped him somewhat but he found consolation and constant liberation in God, who filled the void in his soul with strength for his weaknesses and forgiveness for his sins. He sounds a lot like Paul on this point: "Do not be conformed to this world but keep on being transformed by the renewing of your mind so that you may discern [the] good and acceptable and mature will of God" (Rom 12:2).

Augustine's enormous power as a preacher is disclosed in his ability to link his feeling with those of his hearers. He did not stand in a pulpit above his seated listeners, who *stood* during the sermon, while Augustine *sat* in his *cathedra* (his bishop's chair). He looked at them squarely in the eye as he "fed" them. He said,

"I go to [get] feed so that I can give you to eat." I am "*the servant*, the bringer of food, *not the master* of the house." He once told Jerome, translator of the Latin Vulgate, that he could never be a "disinterested Bible scholar." What he gained through his assiduous study he "paid out immediately to the people of God."[78]

Augustine had found liberation from his past in Christ and sought in his preaching and in his life to break the shackles that bound his hearers. His preaching was primarily pastoral and was reflected in his life, which was an example of the liberating power of the Christian gospel. What he said and the way he lived were symbols of "good news" at a time when "bad news" was widely evident, especially during the last years of his career, when the Vandals were threatening Hippo. But he was free from fear.

For Augustine, the crucifixion of Christ was paradoxically "a solemn measured act of power" not the weakness and finality of death. He could have described the cross as "a solemn act of [liberation]." He spoke of the cross as "the sleep of a lion" about to awaken to be king of all he surveyed. Augustine "saw in the prophets . . . men like himself: men with a message to bring home to the . . . people—*a hammer shattering the stones*."[79]

Augustine made much of what he called the "inner world."[80] He spoke of it as "a source of anxiety" as well as a source of "strength," in which were hidden both "unexpected dangers" and a "self-awareness" that brought the "first shafts of light" that illuminated the dark shadows of the past. Perhaps today we would speak of Augustine's relentless search for "self awareness" or perhaps his struggle in the search for "self identity." In the *Confessions*, there is a constant probing of his "inner world," a search that today we might describe as a "therapy of self examination." He desired to know the truth in order that he might, as he said, "do the truth in [my] heart, before thee, by confession: with my pen, before many witnesses. . . . "[81] He was troubled by the enigma of *the world* that is *inside of humanity*, a badge of human *uniqueness*, but also a source of *guilt and pain*. No wonder he prayed: "I beseech you, God to show my full self to myself."[82] He thought the "inner world" was the locus where the real self resides. Both Augustine and the philosopher Plotinus believed that the "knowledge of God" could be found in the form of some "memory" of this inner world.[83] There is in Augustine's thought a very large place for a massive and illusive inner dimension in human nature of which we are for the most part unaware. Augustine was keenly aware of this ambiguous reality that he felt was "as much a source of anxiety as strength."[84] For Plotinus, it was "a reassuring continuity."[85]

Another author who regarded the "inner world" as a source of strength and hope was Rufus Jones, the Quaker scholar. He said, "our greatest task in life is to find the rest of ourselves." His statement suggests a sermon topic, "Finding the rest of ourselves." We are made in God's image—there are heights to which we may rise by tapping unused resources; there are depths to which we may sink by turning our backs upon our capacities and living largely for ourselves. What a pity it is to permit life's travail: to turn us away from the enjoyment of beauty, from the pursuit of truth, from a sense of compassion for those who are "hurt" in the struggle to survive. I think it was Baron von Hugel who said: "Caring is everything; nothing matters but caring." Perhaps that is a bit oversimplified—nevertheless if we really cared about what happened to others, many of our human problems could be solved.

In some measure, all of us face alternatives. What we do with our unused capacities is surely one of life's most important issues. There are indeterminate possibilities to which we may rise in our love, foreshadowing, though dimly, the sacrificial love of our Lord; there are also what Augustine called "an agonizing weakness [and] wandering" that leads to restlessness, loss of hope, and "a lamentable darkness." He also spoke of his own "latent possibilities" that were "hidden" from himself creating doubt that his mind could "trust its own report."[86] This brings us again to his doctrine of "original sin," an inevitable and inordinate self-love that separates us into our small and self-centered worlds and from God. It also creates the illusion of stability brought about by piling up power, money, and the fragile securities of this world. The "illusion" includes the idea that "great possessions" are the key to a really successful life.

Augustine and his clergy lived abstemious lives, using simple crockery for plates at their vegetarian meals as symbols of poverty. He once refused a silk robe because he felt it would "embarrass him" and it "would look strange" on his "old limbs" with "white hair."[87] The monks went too far in their lives of self denial, but surely they were closer to a proper Christian life-style than the "rich young ruler" and those like him who make "great possessions" selfishly used as the purpose of life.

The problem of the rich young ruler was not so much his possessions, but his illusion that what he had was the key to his fulfillment, that what he had overshadowed what he might have been. He lived on the surface of life, and, though he caught a glimpse of a new life lived for others, his possessions caused him to turn away in sorrow. What he possessed stood in the way of what he could have become if he had answered Christ's call to follow Him. Not money necessarily but the "love of money is the root of all evil," said Paul. (1 Tim 6:10; Titus 1:7)

This ancient story is also a contemporary story. Honors, position, power, money, and the glittering prizes of the world can stand in the way of full and meaningful lives. The "outer world" of which Augustine spoke, can overpower the "inner world" and limit our horizons as to what life can be. Indeed, we need to find the "rest of ourselves." As Christians "we are now the children of God and it does not yet appear what we shall be" (1 John 3:2) if we dare to follow our Lord. (Ps 42; 63:1; Matt 19:16-22; Rom 12:2; 1 Tim 6:10; Titus 1:7) (Cross, Human Nature, Imitation of Christ, Preaching, Self-Identity) (PSA)

401L   Destruction and chaos were evident in the Roman world after the sack of Rome by Alaric, the leader of the Visigoths, in 410. Augustine, then fifty-six years of age, was profoundly moved by this shattering event and what followed. Buildings were sinking gradually into ruins, money was in short supply, the great ampitheatres were crumbling. The world Augustine knew had grown old and uncertain. His youthful strength was ebbing away. Twenty years later in 430 came the final blow. Roman rule in Africa collapsed and Hippo was surrounded by the Vandals, who swept across the Iberian Pensinula into Africa. Augustine was an old man and the world also. Yet, in a way, Augustine was not really "old." After all, "old age" is not primarily a chronological measurement. Augustine was "youthful" to the end of his long life because he continued to *function* as a preacher, writer, and administrator. And his *consciousness* was clear to the end.[88]

Possidius, a contemporary, who wrote a *Life of Augustine*, made an acute comment about the Bishop of Hippo: "I think that those who gained most from him were those who had been able to see and hear him as he spoke in church and most of all those who had some contact with the quality of his life among men."[89]

In a sermon Augustine preached near the end of his life, when his health was failing, he spoke words of wisdom for his time and ours:

> You are surprised that the world is losing its grip? The world is old;
> it is full of tribulations. . . . Do not hold on to the old man, the
> world: do not refuse to regain your youth in Christ, who says to you,
> "the world is passing away, the world is losing its grip, the world is
> short of breath. Do not fear, '*thy youth shall be renewed as an
> eagle*'" (Ps 103:5).[90]

Let's not keep looking back. Things look better ahead. Leslie Weatherhead told this story: "I sat once on the bed of a man who was dying and His hand lay within my own. I must have gripped his hand more tightly than I thought, for he said a strange thing to me. 'Don't pull me back, it looks so wonderful further on.' "[91] (Ps 103:5; Isa 40:31; 1 Cor 15:50-57) (Death, Old Age) (PSA)

402 **St. Patrick**. *Patron Saint of the Irish* (ca. 390–ca. 460). St. Patrick had early in life been taken into slavery in Ireland. A traditional story recounts that one day he went back to the mountain where in servitude he had herded swine. He reflected on the unfathomable ways of God who had used his slavery as a stage in his life journey of becoming a missionary to the Irish people. As Patrick meditated, he sensed gathering around him the spirits of those who had preceded him in the service of Christ, and the spirits of those who would come after him. Patrick was alone, but not lonely, for he was surrounded by "so great a cloud of witnesses"[92] (1 Kgs 19:11-18; Heb 12:1-2) (Family of God, Heritage, Loneliness) (JAW)

Sixth Century

501A **Gregory I.** *Father of Medieval Papacy* (ca. 540–604). Gregory, who was to become pope, was appointed the abbot of the monastery of St. Andrew's in Rome in 586. A traditional story is that Gregory saw some beautiful English children being sold as slaves in the market of Rome. Intrigued by their appearance, he asked to know who they were. The reply was that they were Angles. Gregory responded, "Not Angles, but angels." That experience became the impetus for the mission to England.[93] (Mark 9:33-37; 10:13-16) (Children, Missions) (JAW)

501B In the sixth century, Pope Gregory I sent missionaries to the south of England. King Ethelbert of Kent, whose wife was already a Christian, received the missionaries, but only outside. He feared the magic that they might work indoors.

At least Ethelbert was gripped by a sense of awe at the wonderful, powerful mystery of God. There was for him no casual and easy familiarity with things holy. A marked contrast to Ethelbert is Simon, the magician who wanted to buy the Holy Spirit for his own.[94] (Acts 8:9-24) (God's Holiness, Holy Spirit, Sorcery) (JAW)

501C Gregory the Great was the first significant pope of the Middle Ages. He is known for providing stability for the church amidst the barbarian invasion, helping to define medieval Christian society. Gregory was also just the third major leader (Gregory of Nazienzan and John Chrysostom) in the history of Christianity to write on the nature of the ministerial office. In his *The Book of Pastoral Care*, he analyzed such topics as qualifications for church leadership, and he offered advice to ministers on how to counsel a variety of problems. His words about the dangers of insincerity and self deception are still relevant today:

The insincere are to be admonished to realize how burdensome is the business of duplicity that they guiltily bear. For in the fear of discovery, they ever try to defend themselves even dishonourably, and are ever agitated with fear and apprehension. Now, nothing is more safely defended than sincerity, nothing easier to speak than the truth. But when a man is forced to defend his deceit, his heart is wearied with the toilsome labour of doing so. . . . For commonly, though they are discovered in their fault, they shrink from being known for what they are, and they screen themselves under a vale of deceit. . . . The result is that often one who aims at reproving them . . . finds he has all but lost the certain conviction he has been holding concerning them. . . . They, poor fools, take delight in what is to their own harm.[95]

(Jer 17:9; 1 Cor 3:18; 1 John 1:8-9) (Lies, Pastoral Counseling, Self-Deception, Sin) (MAS)

Seventh Century

601 **Hilda of Whitby**. *English Abbess* (614–680). Hilda of Whitby, a relative of several English kings, committed her life completely to God at the age of thirty-three in A.D. 647. She wanted to live quietly in a French convent where her sister Hereswith lived. Before she could sail, Bishop Aidan, the head of the church in her area, told her he believed she should be an abbess and take responsibility for spiritually nurturing nuns and monks. She became the head of the most famous religious house in northeast England, the Abbey of Whitby,[96] where she supervised all the operations of the convent and monastery, from business to worship.

God gave her unique gifts in administration and leadership that the church needed. During the thirty-plus years she served as abbess, Hilda trained leaders who became five of the most important bishops in the English church, including Bosa, Archbishop of York.[97]

She loved the Bible and believed that each person should be able to read and understand it for themselves. Any person who came to one of her houses received an education so they could "rightly divide the Word of truth." Venerable Bede, the first English church historian, wrote of Hilda that "Those under her direction were required to make a thorough study of the scriptures and occupy themselves in good works."[98]

Hilda modeled the life of Christ to her people. Although she experienced great pain from illness during the six years prior to her death, she never ceased giving thanks to God, nor did she stop teaching the nuns and monks in her care. At the age of sixty-six, Hilda died after "an earthly life devoted to the work of heaven."[99] (Deut 11:18-25; Ps 119:33-40; Matt 5:13-16; 2 Tim 3:10-17; Titus 2:1-15) (Bible, Call, Discipleship, Faithfulness, Leadership) (RB)

Eighth Century

701   **Boniface.** *Apostle of Germany* (680–754). Medieval Europe was made Christian by a variety of means, some good and some bad. Moral persuasion was the ideal, but coercion was often the end result. Missionaries often confronted barbarian tribes who sacrificed animals and worshiped nature spirits. A traditional legend recounts that Boniface, an eighth-century missionary, traveled to a German shrine, the sacred forest of Thor, the god of thunder. Boniface took his ax to a huge oak, the holy altar of worship. With the first blow, God felled the mammoth idol with a mighty breath of wind. The pagan barbarians were awestruck and immediately were converted. Boniface, not weak in conscience when it came to pagan things, used the wood to build a church.

Barbarian tribes conquered the Roman Empire. The western civilization that resulted, historian Bruce Shelly suggests, had a Christian character because the invaders surrendered not their arms, but their gods and spirits to a superior power of God.

As we do missions, we would do well to confront the idols and spirits of this age with the confidence of Boniface in the superior power of God.

And as we ourselves are confronted by the mighty breath of God, we will relinquish our idols and even our reliance on arms for strength.[100] (Exod 20:3; Job 4:6; Phil 4:13; 1 Thess 3:1-4; 1 John 5:4) (Confidence, God's Power, Idolatry, Missions) (CDW)

702   **Lioba.** *English Abbess and Missionary* (700–780). In the eighth
century, the gospel spread into Germany. English monks and
nuns evangelized the Germans because God compelled them to
do so. Boniface, known as the Apostle to Germany, summoned
his cousin Lioba to help him establish order among the new
converts.[101] Lioba, abbess of the English convent at Wimborne,
had a reputation for learning that included expertise in classical
philosophy, theology, canon law, and scripture. Bishops, nobles,
princes, even Charlemagne, asked for advice from her.[102]
        In 748, she and the nuns and monks accompanying her,
crossed the English Channel to answer the plea of her cousin
Boniface. She became Abbess of Bischofsheim and established
convents throughout that region of Germany. Everywhere she
went, order came from chaos. Her irenic spirit and wise counsel
calmed riotous crowds, and her soft words turned aside anger.
        With all her intelligence and power, Lioba remained a
woman committed to her relationship with God. She lived a life
of holiness before the pagans of Germany and other Christians.
She believed she had been personally chosen by God to do the
missionary task assigned her. She lived in God's presence
moment by moment, and her devotion was so intense that she
stayed in constant prayer.[103] Her communication with God
formed the most important thing in her life. The power she
wielded among bishops and princes meant nothing when
compared to the task God had set before her—to live for the
Lord among pagans and to bring those people into the kingdom
of God. Her prayer-witness was so strong that she was allowed
to pray at Boniface's monastery at Fulda, the only woman ever
allowed to do so.[104] (Ps 24:1-6; Isa 45:22-23; Jer 1:4-8; Matt
28:18-20; Acts 1:8; Rom 10:14-15) (Courage, Devotion,
Holiness, Missions, Order, Prayer) (RB)

Tenth Century

901   **William of Aquitaine.** *Monastic Reformer* (10th cent.).
Monasteries were the center of religious life in the Middle Ages.
Monks were required to take three vows of renunciation: poverty,

chastity, and obedience, in order to be totally committed to God. Like any institution, however, monasteries needed reform when commitment slackened. One of the great reform efforts was the creation of a new monastery at Cluny in Burgundy. The pious duke William of Aquitaine consulted the strictest monk he knew, Bertho of Baume. The monk said the best site for the new monastery was the land that housed William's favorite hunting lodge. The duke refused the idea of driving out his dogs until Bertho convinced him that God would reward him for monks, but not for dogs.[105]

We might think William's hesitancy over his dogs a bit trivial. But how easy is our commitment to Christian growth and personal obedience detoured by our trivial excuses? (Luke 9:57-62; 11:28) (Christian Maturity, Commitment, Excuses) (CDW)

Eleventh Century

1001   **Henry III**. *King of Bavaria* (d. 1056). During the eleventh century, Henry III was King of Bavaria. Having grown weary of his duties, he journeyed to the local monastery and presented himself to the prior. He had determined that he wanted to live the rest of his life in the monastery as a contemplative. The prior inquired, "Your majesty, do you understand that this is about obedience? Whatever I tell you under authority, you must do." Henry III answered, "Yes father, I understand." "Then, your majesty, in obedience to me, go back to your home and serve in the place God has put you." And Henry III returned to the throne and governed with skill and efficiency. Obedience is serving faithfully where we are called.[106] (John 21:21-22; Eph 4:1) (Call, Obedience) (JAW)

1002   **Muretus**. There is a traditional story about Muretus, a poor, peripatetic scholar of the Middle Ages. In Italy, he became ill and was sent to a hospital for the indigent. While the doctors were discussing his case in Latin, not imagining that he might be able to understand them, they suggested that such a worthless creature might be an object for medical experiments. Muretus looked up at them and said, "Call no man worthless for whom Christ died." (John 3:16; 15:12-15) (Death of Christ, Image of God, Self-Esteem) (JAW)

1003 **Papal Decline.** The medieval papacy was fraught with problems that cried out for reform. Lay investiture was the practice of church officers being appointed by secular rulers to their parishes. Simony, named after Simon Magnus who attempted to buy the power of the Holy Spirit, was the practice of selling church offices. It was common for persons to hold more than one church position because they had paid the price. In 1033, the effectiveness of the papacy reached its nadir when Benedict IX was named pope at the age of nine, despite the obvious violation of the church's canon law. He sold the papacy to the highest bidder when he got tired of the job.

A final problem with the church leadership was the infamous immorality of the clergy. In a period now called the Pornacracy (882–964), the papacy was controlled by Theodora and her two daughters, all harlots. They sold their bodies for positions, titles, and land. One daughter, Marozia, bedded down with Sergius III, and a son was born who later became John XI. Marozia's grandson became John XII, about whom historian William Cannon remarks, "As Octavian, in a drunken orgy he had made a toast to the Devil, and as John, he continued to live a devil's life."[107]

Several valiant efforts were made to reform the medieval church. Ultimately, it took the process called the Protestant Reformation. The medieval papacy teaches us above the seductions of power and of the flesh. Immorality must be resisted. Spirituality cannot be bought or sold. It must be experienced. Repentance must be genuine. The church must ever be reforming itself. (Acts 8:9-24; 1 Cor 6:12-20; 1 Pet 5:2-3) (Immorality, Leadership, Spirituality) (CDW)

Twelfth Century

1101 **Bernard of Clairvaux.** *Abbott, Cistercian Monasticism* (1090– 1153). The most famous and influential monk of the twelfth century, Bernard of Clairvaux, often preached on the subject of love. In fact, he did a series of 86 sermons on the Song of Songs! Bernard perceived that there were four steps to a mature Christian understanding of life. Life begins, he said, with "the love of self for self's sake." This is that infantile stage of narrow self-concern. But then one recognizes that outside resources are necessary, and so there develops "the love of God for self's sake." Here God is viewed essentially as a means to an end, and one desires God to give this and to bless that. But if someone deals with God even on this basis, there is the possibility of thethird step, "the love of God for God's sake." God is praised simply for being God. Still, beyond this stage, which may seem to be the summit of Christian maturity, Bernard adds a fourth and climactic step, "the love of self for God's sake"—to love who I am for the sake of God's kingdom.[108]

This maturity of perspective is something of what Paul was getting at when he said that we have the treasure in earthen vessels. We are only human. But that's good. That's what God created us and redeemed us to be, and we can affirm our humanity. For God uses ordinary human beings like us to bear the divine image, do the kingdom's work, incarnate love, and reveal the very face of Jesus Christ—for God's sake. (2 Cor. 4:7) (Christian Maturity, Human Nature. Image of God, Love, Self-Esteem) (JAW)

Thirteenth Century

1201 **Thomas Aquinas.** *Premier Medieval Theologian* (ca. 1225–1274). In the thirteenth century, Thomas Aquinas had an audience with Pope Innocent II. The Pope, who was counting a large sum of money, boasted of the rich treasures of the Roman church and declared, "See, Thomas, the church can no longer say, 'Silver and gold have I none.' " To that Aquinas responded, "True, holy father, but neither can she now say, 'Arise and walk.' "[109] (Acts 3:1-10) (Discipleship, Wealth) (JAW)

1202A **Francis of Assisi.** *Founder of Franciscans* (1181/2–1226). In an age of materialism, we all need to remember the example of St.

Francis of Assisi. Spurning the wealth of his father and the medieval church, Francis cared for the lepers and the outcasts. He fell in love with Lady Poverty, his symbolic bride of apostolic faith and personal holiness. Francis' search for his love, according to one tradition, led him to a mountaintop, where, like Moses on Mt. Sinai, he received a revelation from God.

Lady Poverty told Francis that she had been with Adam in paradise, but after the Fall she had become a homeless sojourner. Jesus made her his elect one and her believers increased. The monks called her their Lady until the deadly sin of avarice resulted in their separation. Upon hearing the story, Francis pledged his loyalty to Lady Poverty, and she left the mountaintop with him as his Bride.[110]

Jesus said, "Blessed are you poor, for yours is the kingdom of God." (Luke 4:16-21; 6:20) (Materialism, Spiritual Poverty) (CDW)

1202B Writers on Christian spirituality have always emphasized the need for solitude and silence. Silence is not simply the absence of speech, but it is the art of listening. In silent solitude we can see and hear. "Be still and know that I am God," says the Psalmist.

Two of the great figures of the Middle Ages were St. Dominic and St. Francis of Assisi. In our modern era, television and microphones would be in place to capture the words exchanged by such important figures when they met. On a reported visit by St. Dominic to St. Francis, the two spiritual giants met yet never said a word to each other.

Richard J. Foster, noted contemporary writer on spirituality says, "Only when we learn to be silent are we able to speak the word that is needed when it is needed."[111] (1 Kgs 19:12; Ps 46:10; Jas 3:1-12) (Silence, Spirituality) (CDW)

1202C A woman once came to St. Francis of Assisi and confessed that she had spread slanderous remarks against people in her community. She asked the great spiritual leader how she could undo the damage. Francis told her to pluck feathers from a goose and then lay one feather on the doorstep of each household against which she had wronged. When the woman completed the task, she returned to Francis. He told her to go back and gather up the feathers, and then the project would be complete. The woman returned later in tears. She cried, "The wind came and scattered the feathers. I can never recover them all." St. Francis gently admonished, "Do you realize now what you have done, my daughter? Only God can forgive such sin." (Matt 6:12; 9:6; 18:21-35; Luke 23:34) (Forgiveness, Sin) (CDW)

1202D One day Francis of Assisi told his company of fellow monks that they would go down into the village and preach. They left the cloister of the monastery and wound their way through the streets of the town and finally returned to the monastery where they had started. The boldest of the young monks spoke up, "But you told us we were going out to preach. When shall we begin to preach?"

Francis looked at all of them and responded:

> My brothers, we have been preaching all the time we were walking. We have been preaching in the streets and in the marketplace and in the shop and in the rain. We have been observed. Our behavior was marked. And so we delivered a morning sermon for Christ. My sons, it is of no use that we walk anywhere to preach unless we preach as we walk."[112]

(Matt 5:14-16; Col 3:17) (Christian Lifestyle, Ministry, Works) (JAW)

1203 **Kublai Khan.** *Leader of Mongul Empire* (1216–1294). At the Southern Baptist Convention meeting in 1990, Keith Parks, the president of the Southern Baptist Foreign Mission Board, told of a time when the door was open for the advance of the gospel but Christians failed to respond.

> In 1258, the fate of Islam hung by a thread, and only Egypt was strong. The great Mongul empire, led by Kublai Khan, stretched from the Black Sea to the Pacific Ocean. In 1266, Kublai Khan sent word by Marco Polo for the Christian church in Rome to send one hundred men to teach Christianity to his court."

It could have been a turning point in the history of the religions of the world, according to Parks. "But the Christians were so busy fighting among themselves that it was twenty-eight years before one, not one hundred, reached the great court. Already retired, the great Kublai Khan said, 'It is too late. I have grown too old in my idolatry.' "[113]

Parks challenged:

> All over this world sixty-six percent of the people do not even claim to be Christian, and twenty-six percent of the world has not even had a chance to hear the gospel. . . . Do you want to send a message to the villages of Africa, the cities of Asia? Or shall we simply send the message, "There's no one to come?"

(Matt 28:18-20; Acts 1:8; Rom 10:14-15; 1 Pet 2:9) (Evangelism, Missions) (JAW)

Fourteenth Century

1301 **Brigit of Sweden.** *Swedish Saint, Founder of Brigittenes* (ca. 1303-1373). Born into one of the most powerful and wealthy families in fourteenth-century Sweden, Brigit grew up among kings and the ruling elite. As a young mother and wife, Brigit became chief lady-in-waiting in the royal court of King Magnus and Queen Blanche in 1336.[114] During the time she lived at court, she wielded great influence with the young rulers. Brigit lived the life of a noblewoman until her husband's death. As a middle-aged widow with eight children, Brigit committed herself totally to the Lord's work. She gave away all she owned to the poor and took up the life of a nun.[115]

Christians often question how much they should involve themselves in the politics of the day, either secular or within the church. For Brigit, the question was quickly and emphatically answered with a "yes!" From the time she became a widow until her death, she challenged kings, popes, and bishops to live honestly before the Lord and to do that which is right before God. In secular politics, she took stands against political vice and corruption in the court of Sweden. She named names and called upon the king and other powerful individuals to do what was right.[116]

Brigit believed that each believer should work to spark a religious and moral awakening among God's people. Looking at the corruption around her, she saw no evidence of God at work in the world. Yet, Christians were supposed to be Christ in the world. Brigit worked, until her death, holding the wealthy and powerful of the church and the state accountable to God for their actions. Brigit died in Rome, trying to gain a hearing from church leaders about the need for holy living at every level of church life. She lived her life committed to God's dictum that believers should reflect the Lord in the world in everything they do and say. They must be involved in good. (Ps 15; Isa 11:1-5; Amos 5:21-24; Luke 20:20-26; John 14:25-31; Rom 13:1-7) (Citizenship, Culture, Holiness) (RB)

1302   **Catherine of Siena.** *Medieval Mystic* (1347–1380). In the fourteenth century, the Christian church was well-known for its corruption. Greed increasingly shaped church actions. The problems of the church were so widespread that voices of reform seemed helpless to bring about change. One person's concern would not make any difference. Every reasonable person knew that. It was especially futile to think that a lay person, particularly a woman, could ever make a difference in such a corrupt church.

Catherine of Siena was not a person constrained by limitations. The words, "It can't be done!" were foreign to her. Catherine was the twenty-third child of her Italian parents. From the age of seven, she had spiritual insight beyond her years. At age twelve, she chose celibacy over marriage. Her father gave her a 9x15 room with a plank as a bed and a log as a pillow. For three years, she lived in complete silence and solitude in order that she could become an instrument of the Holy Spirit. Her time was spent primarily in prayer. When her silence was broken, men and women sought her sacred place to listen to her spiritual wisdom. Her words were taken down by secretaries; sometimes three were necessary. Her writings are considered spiritual classics. Leaving her room, she began to minister to the sick, the needy, those in prison, and those facing execution. During the Black Death plague, she and her helpers tended to the sick untiringly.

When the urgency of the Black Death passed, Catherine focused her energy on reforming the church. What could one woman do about the vast problems of the church? In the minds of most, it was an impossible task imbedded in centuries of power. Catherine set out to reform the church regardless of the power she faced. Courageously she criticized the church for taking the offerings of the poor to use for luxuries. She pointed out the moral decline in the monasteries. Catherine spent hours every day praying for the reform of the church. Sometimes, using all three secretaries, she wrote to the powerful, kings, queens, citizens, nobles, and even to the pope himself.

Over fifty years earlier, the French had succeeded in having the papacy moved to Avignon. It was unthinkable to many Christians that the pope would be headquartered anywhere but Rome, but no one seemed to be powerful enough to get the papacy back in Rome. Catherine prodded and encouraged the pope, prevented the approaching war, and was sent to France to negotiate for the Italians. Remaining in Avignon several months, the uneducated woman of no social or political status, persuaded the pope to return to Rome.

Everyone in the fourteenth century knew that uneducated people with no status had absolutely no clout, especially if they were women. Everyone knew that, except Catherine![117] (Matt 19:26; 1 Cor 1:18-28; 2 Cor 13:4; Phil 4:13; Jas 5:16-18) (Limitations, Power, Prayer) (CDB)

1303 **Meister Eckhart.** *German Dominican Mystic* (ca. 1260–1327). As all mystics, Meister Eckhart, the most influential German mystic of the medieval period, emphasized the goal of direct experience or union with God. In a sermon focusing on the love of God, Eckhart commented on the words of the angel to the virgin Mary, "Hail, full of grace", and asked: "What help is it to me that Mary is full of grace, if I am not also full of grace? And what help is it to me that the Father gives birth to his Son unless I too give birth to him?"[118] Yes, what good is it? What good is it that Mary trusted God if I don't trust God? What good is it that Mary did God's will if I don't do God's will? Does it really matter for me that Christ was born then if Christ is not born now in my life and in my time? (Luke 2:1-20) (Christmas, Trust) (JAW)

1304 **Julian of Norwich.** *English Mystic* (ca. 1342–after 1413). Julian of Norwich has become one of the most celebrated English mystics of the medieval period. Almost nothing is known of her life except that she lived a contemplative life in a small cell in the wall of St. Julian's church at Norwich. Her fame was the result of a series of visions she recorded in *Revelations of Divine Love.*[119]

For Julian, the passion is understood as love, as the supreme manifestation of the love of God. This central focus unified all of her life and thought. She believed the cross was the standard by which all love is measured. As there is growth in the understanding of the cross of Christ, more and more dimensions of love can be seen.[120] About the passion of Christ, she wrote at the close of her work:

> You would know our Lord's meaning in this thing? Know it well. Love was his meaning. Who showed it to you? Love. What did he show You? Love. Why did he show you? For love. Hold on to this and you will know and understand love more and more. But you will not know or learn anything else—ever!
> So it was that I learned that love was our Lord's meaning. And I saw for certain, both here and elsewhere, that before ever he made us, God loved us; and that his love has never slackened, nor ever shall. In this love all his works have been done, and in this love he had made everything serve us; and in this love our life is everlasting.[121]

(Gal 6:14; Phil 3:7-11; 1 John 4:10-12) (Cross, God's Love) (DML)

Fifteenth Century

1401 **Thomas à Kempis.** *Ascetical Writer* (ca. 1830–1471). Christianity for self's sake, "imagining that godliness is a means of gain" (1 Tim 6:5), is always with us. The little fifteenth-century Christian classic by Thomas à Kempis, *The Imitation of Christ*, laments that "Jesus has now many lovers of his heavenly kingdom, but few bearers of his cross. . . . He [Jesus] finds many companions of his table, but few in his fasting." This Medieval Christian asked piercing questions that still discriminate among true and false believers today:

> Are not all those to be called mercenary who are ever seeking consolations? Do they not show themselves to be rather lovers of themselves than of Christ, who are always thinking of their own profit and advantage? . . . Yet none is richer than that man, none more powerful, none more free; for he knows how to leave himself and all things, and to set himself in the lowest place.[122]

(Matt 20:25-28; 1 Tim 6:5) (False Ministry, Service, Wealth) (WLA)

1402 **Savanorola.** *Italian Reformer* (1452–1498). Savanorola was one of the reformers of the church to precede the efforts of the Protestant Reformation. He was a prophet of purity, attempting to implement reform in Florence, Italy. His reform efforts are famous for the "bonfire of vanities," a cleansing of the material possessions that he thought led to immorality.

On one occasion, Savanorola saw an elderly woman worshiping at a statue of the Virgin Mary. He was impressed with the woman's daily trek to the statue. Such virtue would enhance the city's reform. A fellow priest, however, warned Savanorola that things are not always as they appear to be. The reality of the situation was that the woman, in her younger beautiful days, had been the model for the artist's sculpture of Mary. Consequently, she had worshiped at the statue ever since.

A bonfire of the vanities must first take place in the heart. External virtue was a source of pride that Jesus constantly saw in the most religious of persons. (Prov 16:18; Eccl 1:2; Luke 18:9-14; 1 John 2:16) (Hypocrisy, Pride) (CDW)

Sixteenth Century

1501   **Anabaptists and the Bible.** The authority of the Word of God
was central to the radical reformation of the Anabaptists. Their
beliefs in believer's baptism, a regenerate church membership,
and pacifism were based on following the practices of the New
Testament. Many of those who heard the preached message were
poor farmers, unskilled workers, and displaced persons. Often
they were completely or almost illiterate. Yet, once converted,
they began to "hide the Word in their hearts." When hailed
before the civil authorities, these unlearned believers would
frequently confound their judges by their ability to quote and
reason from the scriptures.

   The Belgian Anabaptist, Jacob de Roore, was once questioned by the Franciscan inquisitor, Friar Cornelis, about his
equation of the church of Rome with the whore of Babylon in
the Book of Revelation. Cornelis asked:

> What do you understand about St. John's Apocalypse? At what
> university did you study? At the loom, I suppose, for I understand
> that you were nothing but a poor weaver and chandler before you
> went around preaching and rebaptizing out here in the Gruthuysbosch.
> I have attended the university of Louvain and studied divinity so
> long, and yet I do not understand anything at all about St. John's
> Apocalypse; that is a fact."

Jacob replied:

> That's why Christ thanked his heavenly Father, that he had revealed
> and made it known to babes and hidden it from the wise of this
> world, as it is written, Matthew 11:25."

Exasperated, Cornelis sarcastically responded:

> Exactly; God had revealed it to the weavers at the loom, to the
> cobblers on their bench, and to the bellows-menders, lantern-tinkers,
> scissors-grinders, broom-makers, thatchers, and all sorts of riff-raff,
> and poor, filthy, and lousy beggars. And to us ecclesiastics who have
> studied from our youth night and day, he has concealed it. Just see

how we are tormented. You Anabaptists are certainly fine fellows to understand the holy scriptures; for before you are rebaptized, you can't tell A from B, but as soon as you are baptized, you can read and write. If the devil and his mother have not a hand in this, I do not understand anything about you people."[123]

We might not agree with Jacob de Roore's reading of Revelation but our dependence on the Word of God for the living of our lives is still exasperating to the world. (Matt 11:25; 1 Cor 1:26-31) (Bible, Wisdom) (TG)

1502 **Anabaptists and the Lord's Supper.** While it is generally recognized that the Anabaptists introduced and practiced for the first time in the Reformation era, believers' baptism, however, it is also conceded that they made no original or creative contribution to the understanding and practice of the Lord's Supper. But this is certainly not the case. While Luther took the element of sacrifice out of the Roman Catholic mass (transubstantiation) and introduced in theory, at least, the idea that the Lord's Supper should be observed with both bread and wine, it was Ulrich Zwingli who emphasized the non-sacramental nature of the observance. Zwingli's emphasis was upon the Lord's Supper as a "thanksgiving memorial of the one sacrifice of Christ on the Cross." In this Zwingli went further than either Luther or Calvin. Although the Anabaptists were indebted both to Andreas Karlstadt, Martin Luther's colleague, and Zwingli for certain insights regarding the Lord's Supper, they went further than any of the Magisterial Reformers in restoring what they considered a more biblical understanding and practice. They agreed with Zwingli that the Lord's Supper was indeed a memorial of the death of Christ to be observed with bread and wine. But they insisted that only believers, baptized in obedience to the command of Christ, should be participants. The Lord's Supper for them became the means of expressing their communion with Christ and with one another in *agape* love. This was a new element. For Zwingli, the Lord's Supper was to be observed in parish churches regardless of how mixed the membership. But with the Anabaptists, the Supper became a sign of disciplined discipleship and an expression of love one to another. As the

Lord's Supper became a *koinonia* (communion) of committed disciples who were declaring their love for the crucified and risen Lord, it also became a sign of the love that the brethren shared with one another in Christ. Thus the concept of the Lord's Supper as a communion of the committed became an essential feature of Anabaptist celebration of the death and living presence of the crucified one.

In light of the profound meaning that the Lord's Supper had for the Anabaptists, how shallow and superficial the observance of this ordinance appears in the theology and practice of many churches today.[124] (Matt 26:1-30; 1 Cor 11:20-34) (Lord's Supper) (WRE)

1503 Anabaptists and the Münster Rebellion. (1534–1535). That which gave Anabaptism its soiled reputation and which has stubbornly refused to be dislodged whenever the term is used, even today, was the Münster kingdom.

A group of simple but earnest people was led by men of questionable motives to converge upon the Westphalian city of Münster in North Germany under the impression that they were preparing for the second advent of Christ. Of course, as is well known, the city of saints soon turned out to be the city of sinners under siege by the armies of both Protestants and Catholics. With the fall of the new Jerusalem, tragedy compounded by tragedy became the legacy of these simple but well meaning people. This was not Anabaptism as envisioned by the Swiss Brethren in 1525 nor should it be properly considered representative of Anabaptism, but rather an aberration of the movement. While every movement has its lunatic fringe, there is more here than fanaticism gone wild, and much of it is instructive for those of us who long to be Christians according to the teachings of Christ.

The first misstep that led to Münster among the Anabaptists was a reversal of Anabaptist hermeneutics that had always made the New Testament or the New Covenant normative for understanding the Old. Coupled with this New Testament emphasis was a christological understanding of the New Testament. Christ was central and the key to interpreting the whole of scripture for the early Anabaptists. But for Melchior

Hofmann, it was the Old Testament that took precedence over the New. In addition, Hofmann put a great deal of faith in dreams and visions and accepted uncritically his own interpretations of Old Testament prophecies. The combination of this kind of hermeneutic and faith in dreams and visions, unchecked by the New Testament, led to an expectation of the early fulfillment of prophecies found in the book of Daniel.

This combination of Old Testament prophecies, as interpreted by Hofmann and reinforced by his visions and dreams, caused him to proclaim Strasbourg as the New Jerusalem. He returned to Strasbourg as Enoch to await the return of Christ who would set up his millennial kingdom within weeks. Others seized upon his prophecies but disagreed regarding the place of the Lord's return. Munster, under the leadership of Bernard Rothmann, had moved from Catholicism in a number of intermediate steps to an acceptance of the principal of Anabaptist teachings. It was at this juncture that the two Jans appeared. Jan Matthys felt himself to be a new born Gideon, and Jan of Leyden, an actor in a roving theatrical guild prominent in the Netherlands, became the most forceful personality of a group that began to proclaim boldly Münster as the "New Jerusalem." After the deaths of Jan Matthys and a group of defenders who, like Thomas Muntzer before them, had mistakenly felt themselves invincible because they were on the Lord's side, the actor Jan of Leyden seized the opportunity to play out his greatest role—that of King David. Fortified by dreams and visions and new revelations to suit every occasion, he became the King of the New Jerusalem and like David, claimed the privilege of a multiplicity of wives. In cases of insubordination, death was the penalty.

The lessons from Münster were apparently lost on the Fifth Monarchy men of England who in 1661 followed virtually the same foolhardy path fortified by their own interpretations of Daniel's prophecies. Baptists were not the only ones who fell into this millennial trap, but they were the principal actors in this drama of Münster revisited. Today there is a proliferation of false prophets who are attempting to con their followers into the acceptance of their interpretations of the prophecies regarding the last days. In the process, many simple and well-meaning people have lost their fortunes to those who are not above using religion for ill-gotten gains.

At least Münster, demonstrates that *ignorance is not bliss but positively dangerous*. To presume to know when one does not is dishonest. Both integrity and humility are not only appropriate for the would-be disciple of Christ, they are imperative. These virtues, coupled with a knowledge of history, could help the contemporary Christian distinguish actors from kings and false prophets from true people of God.[125] (Matt 24:36; Mark 13:32-37; 1 Thess 4:13-18; 2 Thess 2:1-12) (Humility, Integrity, Millennialism, Second Coming) (WRE)

1504　　**John Calvin.** *Protestant Reformer of Geneva* (1509–1564). John Calvin was called to work as a reformer in the church of Geneva in 1536. From the beginning, there were those who held him in suspicion. He is first mentioned in the registers of the city council as *ille gallus*, "that Frenchman!" Conflicts between Calvin and his fellow minister Guillaume Farel increased until they were both expelled from the city in April of 1538. Calvin reestablished himself in the city of Strasbourg, where he served happily as the pastor of a French refugee church and as a teacher in the newly established academy there.

In Calvin's absence, however, things in Geneva had gone from bad to worse. In 1541, the Genevans implored Calvin to return to their church. He was most reluctant to do so, preferring his happy situation in Strasbourg to that dangerous "gulf and whirlpool" he had left three years before.

Still, Calvin was persuaded that it was God's will for him to return to Geneva and take up again the work of reformation that had been interrupted by his forced exile three years before. He reentered Geneva on 13 September 1541. The remainder of his career as reformer was symbolized by the first official act he undertook upon his return. On the first Sunday back in Geneva, Calvin entered the pulpit of St. Pierre. The great gothic cathedral was crammed with curious Genevans who expected to hear an exultant Calvin lambast his opponents, those who had driven him from the city. Everyone expected him to deliver a burning "I-told-you-so" sermon to the whole assembly.

In a letter to Farel, Calvin told what he did: "After a preface, I took up the exposition where I had stopped—by which I indicated that I had interrupted my office of preaching for the time rather than that I had given it up entirely." Nothing could have been less dramatic or more effective. Calvin merely picked up where he had left off three years before, at the very chapter and verse of whatever book of the Bible (we don't know which one, nor does it matter) from which he had been preaching. In this way, Calvin signaled that he intended his life and his theology to be not a devise of his own making but a responsible witness to the Word of God.[126] (Matt 26:39; Acts 18:21; 1 Pet 5:2-3) (Leadership, Will of God) (TG)

1505 **Thomas Cranmer**. *Archbishop of Canterbury* (1489–1556). His life in jeopardy, Thomas Cranmer, Archbishop of Canterbury and architect of the Book of Common Prayer of the Anglican tradition, signed a recantation of his support of Protestantism. He was brought to St. Mary's Church, Oxford, to disavow publicly his former errors and to submit to the authority of Queen Mary I and the Pope. There he declared: "Now I come to that which troubles my conscience more than anything that I ever did or said in my whole life, and that is that through fear of death I signed with my hand what I do not believe in my heart. When I come to the fire, this hand shall be the first to burn." Cranmer kept his promise. When he was burned at the stake, he resolutely held his right hand in the flames.[127] (1 Pet 3:11-17) (Conscience, Martyrdom, Perseverance) (JAW)

1506 **Balthasar Hubmaier**. *Anabaptist Apostle of Religious Freedom* (ca. 1485–1528). Balthasar Hubmaier was the most highly educated Anabaptist theologian of the sixteenth century. He had received his Doctor of Theology degree at the hands of Johannes Eck, arguably the most brilliant and gifted Roman Catholic theologian of the age. Hubmaier arose to the position of vice-rector of the University of Ingolstadt, where he also lectured in theology. As the cathedral preacher in Regensburg, Germany, he led in an anti-Jewish campaign that ended with the expulsion of the Jews from the city. Before his tenure was completed, he had erected a chapel dedicated to the "Beautiful Virgin Maria" on the site of the razzed synagogue. But all of this was to change with his conversion in 1522.

Hubmaier wrote to friends in Regensburg in 1524 that "within two years had Christ for the first time come into my heart to thrive." Shortly afterwards, he began to champion the cause of reform in the city of Waldshut, just across the border from Switzerland in South Germany. A few months later, he was baptized and in turn baptized 300 members of his church upon their personal professions of faith. Thus he and his congregation became identified with the Anabaptist movement.

However, before the formal introduction of believers' baptism into the life of his church, Hubmaier enunciated principles and concepts that were later more fully developed in the Anabaptist period of his life. One of these, religious liberty, the incipient Anabaptist movement in Zurich, was also in the process of developing. However, it was Hubmaier who first clearly saw that the nature of the Christian faith, the gospel, and the concept of believers' church demanded the separation of church and state in order that religious freedom might become a reality. During his exile in the Swiss city of Schaffhausen, he enunciated this principle in petitions that he addressed to the city council, while taking refuge in the Benedictine Monastery of that city in 1524. In the same two month period during his residence in the monastery, he drew up an abstract of principles that set forth his convictions in a treatise entitled *Heretics and Those who Burn Them*. In this, the earliest plea for complete religious liberty in the Reformation era, Hubmaier set forth enduring principles that in his mind demanded freedom, even for the atheist, of whom Hubmaier said, "Who seeks nothing other than to live in his unbelief." In short, he decriminalized heresy, however defined. He closed this unique and courageous plea with his motto, "Truth is undying." (*Die Warheit ist untodtlich*)

Subsequently Hubmaier, who as a priest had led the Regensburg faithful to expel the Jews from the city, was to write in his *On the Christian Ban* (1527) that even though members have been excluded from the church for sin, this does not mean that one should withhold from them what he calls works of necessity "which involved food, shelter, and drink." These also should be shared with "Jews and Pagans." He continues: "Yes, in fact I should show friendship towards Jews and heathen." It is evident that Christ had wrought a transformation in the life of the former cathedral preacher of Regensburg.

Hubmaier's life as an Anabaptist preacher was not without its costs. Imprisoned, tortured, and in his weakness compelled to compromise, he wrote later in the *Short Apology*, "faith is a work of God and not of the heretics' tower in which one sees neither sun nor moon, and lives on nothing but water and bread." Later, in prison once again—this time in Austria under the authority of Archduke Ferdinand—Hubmaier was tortured and finally burned at the stake in Vienna on 10 March 1528. His courageous wife, Elizabeth Hugline Hubmaier, was drowned in the Danube River three days later with a millstone tied around her neck.

Those of us who take religious freedom for granted should never forget the price that has been paid by Hubmaier and other early exponents of a free and uncoerced faith. We are in their debt. The least we can do is to treat them fairly by attempting to understand the faith for which they died.[128] (Acts 5:27-32; Gal 5:1) (Independence Day, Religious Liberty) (WRE)

1507A **Hugh Latimer.** *Bishop of Worcester, England* (1485–1555). One day, with Henry VIII in the audience, the bishop of Worcester, Hugh Latimer, preached a sermon to which the king took offense. Latimer was commanded by the king to make an apology when he preached the following Sunday. The bishop addressed himself as he began his sermon. "Hugh Latimer, dost thou know before whom thou art this day to speak? To the high and mighty monarch, the king's most excellent majesty who can take away thy life if thou offendest." But then Latimer reminded himself and his hearers that God was also listening. Would he guard his words carefully to escape the king's displeasure or would be deliver the message faithfully in the sight of God? Latimer preached the same sermon he had the week before, this time with more resolve and passion.[129] (Acts 4:18-20; 5:27-32) (Church and State, Faithfulness, Obedience) (JAW)

1507B After a sham trial at Oxford during the reign of Queen Mary, known as "Bloody Mary" for her persecution of Protestants, Hugh Latimer, the bishop of Worcester, and Nicholas Ridley, the bishop of London, were condemned to be burned at the stake as heretics. As the flames were lighted, Latimer looked to his partner in martyrdom and said, "Be of good comfort, Master Ridley, and play the man; we shall this day light such a candle, by God's grace, in England as I trust shall never be put out."[130] (Matt 5:14-16; John 1:5; Eph 5:8-9) (Martyrdom, Persecution, Self-Sacrifice) (JAW)

1508A Martin Luther. *Protestant Reformer of Germany* (1483–1546). Martin Luther was struggling in his decision whether to continue in law school as his father desired or to become a monk in order to quell the religious upheaval that plagued his soul. When he was knocked down in a thunderstorm by a bolt of lightening cracking in the sky, the decision was made. It would be the life of a monk.

Luther struggled in the monastery to meet the demands of a holy and wrathful God. He thought the best method was to observe diligently all the basic components of the monastic life. Initially, this approach brought much contentment, for Luther's religious nature thrived on the life of meditation and devotion. There was prayer seven times a day, contemplation, manual labor, and study. All looked well until he was confronted with another thunderstorm of the spirit: his first mass.

It should have been a time of great significance, for in this act, Catholics believed, Luther did what was unique above all others. By the words of institution, he performed the miracle that transformed bread and wine into the very body and blood of Jesus Christ. Luther's father, still displeased with him for leaving law school, was present. As the service began, all went well until he reached the words, "We offer unto thee the only true God." Suddenly, Martin was struck by God's majesty and wrath. How could he, sinful man, address a holy God? With trembling hand and terrified heart, he completed the service only to face his father who delivered the final blow. The father denounced Martin and the monastery for his son's failure to honor his father and mother. Luther asserted in self-defense: "But Father, I was called of God in the thunderstorm!" To which his father replied in words that haunt many a minister: "God grant that your call was not an apparition of the devil!" In this experience, the security of the monastery was destroyed and the inner struggle intensified.

Luther tried other methods of achieving spiritual security: asceticism, pilgrimages to holy places, reliance on the church, and the excess merit of other believers (treasury of the saints), but none of them brought peace. Security came when he quit depending on himself or others and trusted solely in the amazing grace of God. We are made righteous in God's eyes by trusting faith in his grace.

Whether it be our salvation or our ministerial call, security comes only when we trust in grace.[131] (Mark 1:16-20; Rom 1:1, 17; 10:11-17; Eph 2:8-10; 4:1-4) (Faith, Grace, Security) (BJL)

1508B   In April, 1521, Martin Luther was called for trial at a congress of the Holy Roman Empire, called a diet, which was meeting in the German city of Worms. There, in the presence of the princes of Germany and Holy Roman Emperor Charles, Luther was questioned by his examiner, Johann Eck, an official of the Archbishop of Trier: "I ask you, Martin—answer candidly and without horns—do you or do you not repudiate your books and the errors that they contain?" Luther replied in an inimitable way: "Since then Your Majesty and your lordships desire a simple reply, I will answer without horns and without teeth. Unless I am convicted by scripture and plain reason—I do not accept the authority of popes and councils, for they have contradicted each other—my conscience is captive to the Word of God. I cannot and I will not recant anything, for to go against conscience is neither right nor safe. God help me. Amen." The earliest printed version of Luther's statement added the words, "Here I stand, I cannot do otherwise"—words that may indeed be genuine, though not recorded at that moment of high drama.[132] (Mark 13:9-13; Acts 4:18-20; 5:27-32) (Bible, Conscience, Obedience) (JAW)

1508C While setting at table Martin Luther recalled the following incident from his early life:

> When I was twenty years old, I had not yet seen a Bible. I thought that there were no Gospels and Epistles except those that were written in the Sunday postils. Finally, I found a Bible in the library and forthwith I took it with me into the monastery. I began to read, to reread, and to read it over again, to the great astonishment of Dr. Staupitz.

The story of Luther's "discovery of the Bible" was retold with considerable embellishment by Luther's early biographers. For example, one version notes that the Bible was chained so as to prevent its examination. In fact, we know that before the invention of bookcases Bibles and other books were frequently chained to reading desks in order to make them more, not less, accessible. Yet there is a kernel of truth in the anecdote. As a movement, the Reformation was about books as well as *the Book*. The invention of the printing press, together with Luther's German Bible, did in a sense "unchain" the scriptures by making them available not only to scholars and monks but also to ploughboys in the fields and milkmaids at their pails.[133] (1 Pet 2:9) (Bible) (TG)

1508D Martin Luther is known as the initiator of the Protestant Reformation. But Luther took no credit for this major event in history. Luther asserted, "I have done nothing. I have let the Word act." What Luther did do, what he was called to do, was to listen to the Word. "The nature of the Word is to be heard," he remarked. He also said: "If you were to ask a Christian what his task is and by what he is worthy of the name Christian, there could be no other response than hearing the Word of God, that is faith. Ears are the only organs of the Christian."[134] (Ps 135:17; Matt 7:24-27; John 5:24; 10:3; Rev 3:20) (Faith, Hearing the Word) (TG)

1508E Martin Luther often used the word *Anfechtung,* to describe the acute spiritual conflicts that afflicted his conscience in his tortured quest to find a gracious God. The word is often weakly translated "temptation," but really means dread, despair, a sense of foreboding doom, assault, anxiety. So desperate was Luther's condition that he wanted to creep into a mouse hole. The "whole wide world" had become too narrow for him, but there was no exit.

The experience of the *Anfechtungen* did not dissipate after his conversion. It troubled him throughout his whole life and affected how he approached theology. In a famous statement Luther confessed:

> I did not learn my theology all at once, but I had to search deeper for it, where my temptations *[Anfechtungen]* took me. . . . Not understanding, reading, or speculation, but living, nay rather dying and being damned make a theologian.

Luther teaches us that living the Christian life is a life-long process of struggle, conflict, and temptation. While faith brings with it a confident assurance, we must ever be on guard against a carnal security. Christians must daily expect to be incessantly attacked.[135] (Matt 6:13; Luke 4:1-13) (Faith, Pilgrimage, Temptation) (TG)

1508F   Martin Luther once remarked that his insight into the gracious character of God had come to him while he was *auff diser cloaca,* literally, "on the toilet." While some scholars have interpreted this saying in terms of Luther's acute suffering from constipation, we know that the expression "in cloaca" was a common metaphor in medieval spiritual writings. It referred to a state of utter helplessness and dependence upon God. Where else are we more vulnerable, more easily embarrassed, and in Luther's mind, more open to demonic attacks, than when we are—*in cloaca*? Yet is it precisely in a state of such vulnerability—when we are reduced to humility, when like beggars we can only cast ourselves on the mercy of another—that the yearning for grace is answered in the assurance of God's inescapable nearness. One of the lowest points of Luther's life was when his beloved daughter Magdalena, barely fourteen years of age, was stricken with the plague. Brokenhearted he knelt beside her bed and begged God to release her from the pain. When she had died and the carpenters were nailing down the lid of her coffin, Luther screamed out, "Hammer away! On doomsday she'll rise again."[136] (Isa 55:6; 65:24) (Dependence upon God, God's Nearness) (TG)

1508G After his death, Martin Luther's friends found the following words scrawled on a piece of paper lying on the desk beside his bed:

> Nobody can understand Vergil . . . unless he has first been a shepherd or a farmer for five years. Nobody understands Cicero . . . unless he has been engaged in public affairs of some consequence for twenty years. Let nobody suppose that he has tasted the Holy Scriptures sufficiently unless he has ruled over the churches with the prophets for a hundred years. . . . Lay not your hand on this divine Aeneid, but bow before it, adore its every trace. We are beggars. That is true.

Luther's whole approach to the Christian life is summed up in these last words. The posture of the human vis á vis God is one of utter receptivity. We are beggars—needy, vulnerable, totally bereft of resources with which to save ourselves. For Luther, the good news of the gospel was that in Jesus Christ God had become a beggar too. God identified with us in our neediness.[137] (Matt 5:3; 2 Cor 8:9; Phil 2:5-11) (Responding to God, Salvation) (TG)

1508H When Martin Luther learned that the first Protestants were being called Lutherans, he protested:

> What is Luther? The teaching is not mine. Nor was I crucified for anyone. . . . How did I, poor stinking bag of maggots that I am, come to the point where people call the children of Christ by my evil name?

Luther criticized preachers for falling prey to the temptation of vainglory. "May God protect us against the preachers who please all people and enjoy a good testimony from everybody," cried Luther. Faithful preachers should teach only the Word of God and seek only his honor and praise. "Likewise, the hearers should also say: 'I do not believe in my pastor, but he tells me of another Lord whose name is Christ; him he shows me.' "[138] (Matt 20:25-28; 1 Tim 4:12; 1 Pet 5:2-3) (Ministry, Pride) (TG)

1508I What do we really expect from prayer? Too often we want to reaffirm our own notions and divorce God from the process altogether. We engage God in prayer as if he were a celestial vending-machine. It becomes nothing more than spiritual consumerism! But genuine prayer lends a pliable soul to the sculpting and tender hand of God. Martin Luther once observed that prayer is:

> . . . As when an artist comes upon some material that is fit and suitable to be formed into a work of art. The fitness of the material is, as it were, an unfelt prayer for the form that the artist understands and fulfills as he gets ready to make what in its suitableness it longs for. So also God comes upon our feelings and thinking and sees what we pray for, what we are fit for, and what we long for. And then he grants the prayer and he proceeds to shape us into the form his art has planned.[139]

(Rom 8:26) (Prayer) (DMW)

1508J Luther never took a penny from his many books and many of his students boarded with him, along with six children born to him by his wife Catherine, and four adopted children. These along with the servants sometimes totalled as many as twenty-five living in Luther's household. Since his ministerial income was not sufficient to support a marriage, he had economic problems. In 1526, he learned woodworking so that if necessary he might support his family. But, he was committed to the study of the Word of God and trusted that the Lord would provide. However, he did take care of the garden, and Katie his wife looked after the orchard, the fish pond, and the barnyard. She also harvested fruit and fish and slaughtered pigs to provide food for the table. Thus, at least in Luther's case, Katie was the immediate means by which the Lord provided. All of us do well to remember that God often provides for others through our own sense of responsibility.[140] (1 Tim 5:8) (Providence, Responsibility) (EEJ)

1508K In October, 1529, several prominent Protestant reformers met at the Marburg Colloquy in an effort to unify the reform movement. Fourteen points of doctrinal agreement were reached, but reconciliation of the groups failed over the meaning of the Lord's Supper. Prior to the meeting, Martin Luther and the Swiss reformer, Ulrich Zwingli, had been involved in an escalating war of words about the meaning of the Supper. All participants expressed the hope for agreement, but the discussion opened ominously when Luther drew a circle with chalk upon the table and wrote within it the words, "This is my body," insisting on the real corporeal presence of Christ in the elements. Zwingli actually demonstrated some movement in his belief that the elements were merely a memorial to the idea that Christ was spiritually present in the sacrament. Still, Zwingli rejected Luther's view since flesh and spirit were incompatible.

At the end, with tears in his eyes, Zwingli approached Luther and offered his hand—not the hand of capitulation or compromise, but the hand of community. But Luther declined the overture of Zwingli's outstretched hand and declared, "I am astonished that you wish to consider me your brother," and then the Germans announced to the Swiss: "You do not belong to the communion of the Christian Church. We cannot acknowledge you as brethren." The Lord's Supper is supposed to be a symbol of our unity, but Christians have often divided over it. The church is supposed to be a place of fellowship, but Christians have often withdrawn their hand from each other.[141] (Ps 133; John 17:20-26; Gal 2:11-14; Eph 2:11-22) (Fellowship, Lord's Supper, Unity) (JAW)

1508L Once Martin Luther was threatened by a representative of the pope. Luther was reminded of the power of the papacy and warned that the day would come when his supporters would desert him. "Where will you be then?," the emissary asked Luther. Luther replied, "Then, as now, in the hands of Almighty God." (Deut 31:1-8; Acts 7:59; Rom 8:31-39; Heb 13:5-6) (God's Presence) (JAW)

1508M When he was asked what he would do today if he knew that he was going to die tomorrow, Martin Luther replied, "I would plant a tree." Only a mature perspective on the accountability of our lives to a future generation would enable someone drawing the final breaths of life to plant a tree that another would sit under. (Gen 49:1, 28; Deut 31:1-8; Acts 20:17-38; 1 Tim 1:18; 6:11-21) (Accountability, Faithfulness, Future) (JAW)

1508N Martin Luther, besieged by threats and enemies, was under excommunication by the Catholic church. Utter discouragement clouded his life. His friends were unable to dispel his depression. His wife, Catherine, determined to work her therapy.

One day when Luther came home, he found her dressed in the cloak of mourning, weeping as if in grief. When Luther called out to know who had died, Catherine replied, "God is dead, and I can't bear it, for all his work is overthrown."

Luther was shocked at hearing what he deemed to be blasphemy. "Well," Catherine answered, "you have been going around acting as if God is dead, as if God is no longer here to keep us; and so I thought I ought to put on mourning to keep you company in your great bereavement."[142]

In that exchange between Luther and his wife, the healing of hope began for him. (Rom 8:9-11; Heb 1:3-7; 1 John 4:4-5) (Hope, God's Presence, Providence) (JAW)

1508O We think of Martin Luther as the great reformer who was ready to confront any issue and anyone. But what is sometimes not understood about him was his genuine concern on a very personal level for people. The monastery in which he lived in Wittenburg became his home after he broke with the Catholic Church. Many a person who was homeless lived there for awhile. They were welcome into Luther's home.

The last trip that Luther took before he died was a trip that he took for the purpose of trying to bring two estranged friends together. It so happened that on this journey of mercy, which would appear to the world to be a small problem, while resting at Eisleben, where he was born, he died. On his lips at death were the words of John 3:16.

Jesus is the outstanding example of this manner of living. As scripture says, "He was wounded for our transgressions, he was bruised for our iniquities and by his stripes we are healed." (Isa. 53:5). The wounds of Christ are able to heal our wounds. As the famous folk song says, "There is a balm in Gilead that makes the wounded whole."

As we seek to imitate Christ, on a much smaller scale, we too can be a balm to others. While not seeking a martyr's complex, we can use our difficult times to help others face similar difficulties. Isn't it true that in love's service, only wounded soldiers will do? (Isa 53:5; Phil 2:5; 1 Pet 2:21-25) (Compassion, Healing, Imitation of Christ, Suffering) (PSA)

1509   **Felix Manz**. *Anabaptist; First Protestant Martyr* (1498–1527). It was a sad day, indeed, when Protestants resorted to the tactics of the medieval church and put to death one of their own. This is not to deny that there were extenuating circumstances, for Zwingli was caught up in a polemical battle with the Anabaptists for the minds and hearts of the people of the Canton of Zurich. They had become a thorn in the flesh. Felix Manz, Conrad Grebel, and George Blaurock were young, impulsive men of conviction and determination to share their new found faith. They were oblivious to the protocol that older heads and more formal relationships dictate. Nevertheless, while they differed on matters of faith and order in the church, they were not guilty of heresy. In fact, most of their theological concepts were the result of their study under Zwingli's tutelage. But in their desire for Reformation "without tarrying for any" they pressured Zwingli for action, even against the judgment of the city council. There was a parting of the ways. It was Zwingli who forsook his earlier theological insights gleaned from an intensive study of the New Testament. When these young men went on to press for the baptism of believers only and for a church composed only of those who had committed their lives to Christ in faith, they were legally censured by the city council under the prodding of Zwingli. Later, the death penalty was invoked against any who would re-baptize. And Felix Manz became the first victim of Protestant intolerance.

One other Anabaptist preacher had been put to death prior to Manz's execution. His name was Eberli Bolt. But it was the Roman Catholic Canton of Schwyz under whose auspices Bolt and a priest friend were burned at the stake. Since Grebel, the foremost leader among the Swiss Anabaptists, died the previous summer, Felix Manz became the target of Zwingli's wrath. Once he was apprehended by the cantonal authorities, he was placed in the Wellemburg Prison (the *Wasserturm)* in Zurich. Finally, on 5 January 1527, he was taken from the prison and sentenced to death at the Council Hall. A part of the verdict read:

> Because he confessed having said that he wanted to gather those who wanted to accept Christ and follow him, and unite himself to them through baptism, . . . so that he and his followers separated themselves from the Christian church and were about to raise up and prepare a sect of their own.

Directions were then given, instructing that Manz should be delivered to the executioner,

> who shall tie his hands, put him into a boat, take him to the lower hut, there strip his bound hands down over his knees, place a stick between his knees and arms, and thus push him into the water and let him perish in the water; thereby he shall have atoned to the law and justice. . . . His property shall also be confiscated by my lords.

The sentence was carried out on a Saturday afternoon at three o'clock. Zwingli and the city council hoped to make an example of Manz that would suppress the growing Anabaptist movement. As his arms and legs were being bound, according to the sentence, he sang out with a loud voice, "*In manus tuas domine spiritum meum.*" (Into thy hands O Lord, I commit my spirit.)

Sometime before Manz had written:

> Love to God through Christ, shall alone avail and subsist; but boasting, reviling, and threatening shall fail. Charity alone is pleasing to God; he that cannot show charity, has no part with God. The unadulterated love of Christ puts to flight the enemy.

He closed this statement with the resolution to "remain faithful to Christ."

In the death of Felix Manz, we see the diabolically tragic results of a state-church in the service of which good people can resort to unholy deeds in the name of Christ. It was this misunderstanding of the roles of the state in the life of the church that led the city council to put other Anabaptists to death before Zwingli himself died at the hands of the Roman Catholic cantons on the battlefield of Kappel. In resorting to the sword of steel to advance the cause of Christ, Zwingli became a victim of that sword in the hands of his Catholic opponents who also thought they were advancing the cause of Christ. Thus, in the martyrdom of Felix Manz we see a remarkable Christian witness that shines even the brighter against the backdrop of those who would use the sword of steel to advance the cause of Christ in terms of their own misunderstanding.[143] (Mark 13:9-13; Luke 21:12-19; Acts 5:27-32) (Church and State, Faithfulness, Martyrdom, Persecution) (WRE)

1510 **Michael Sattler**. *Anabaptist Reformer* (ca. 1490–1527). Michael was doomed. His death sentence was read. For his accusers, death was not enough. He must also experience the agony of torture: take him to the square and cut out his tongue (few things are more annoying that trying to kill a heretic who keeps proclaiming his faith!). Tie him to a wagon, then use red hot iron tongs to rip pieces from his body—twice! As the wagon takes him to the place of execution, rip off five more pieces of his body. After he is dead, burn his body into a fine powder.

What in the world had Michael done to stir up such hostility in his enemies? He had radical beliefs that many thought were dangerous. Michael Sattler believed that his loyalty to God should exceed his loyalty to the state. He believed that baptism and the Lord's Supper were symbolic acts, not sacraments. Michael believed in believer's baptism, not infant baptism. He even refused to take an oath to the state. And to top it all, he taught that Christians should not fight in wars. Clearly this man was extremely dangerous to a government of Austria and its state church who demanded ultimate authority in all matters. In 1527, the Austrian officials simply could not have people going around thinking they could decide these matters for themselves! They must kill him for his heresy and make sure the public knew what happened to those who dared to practice unapproved religions.

Since only a piece of Michael's tongue was cut out, he was still able to pray audibly for those who ripped his flesh or hurled taunting words at him. At the execution site, Michael was tied to a ladder and pushed into the fire. When the flames burned the ropes on his wrists, he lifted two forefingers. The raised fingers were the signal he had promised other Anabaptists if the martyr's death was bearable.

After Michael's death the authorities tried repeatedly to get Michael's wife to renounce her faith. She refused. Eight days later, she was given the "third baptism" or drowned. Mr. and Mrs. Sattler were indeed guilty—of living their beliefs even if their witness meant torture and death.[144] (Matt 5:33-37; 10:32-33, 38-39) (Church and State, Loyalty, Martyrdom, Witness) (CDB)

1511A **Menno Simons**. *Founder of Mennonite Anabaptism* (1496–1561). Menno Simons was ordained to the Catholic priesthood in March, 1524, when he was twenty-eight years old. He was appointed a parish priest and performed the perfunctory duties well, receiving a promotion after seven years. At the same time, he spent much time in frivolous activities, such as drinking and playing cards. He claimed never to have read the Bible until two years after his ordination as a priest, although, of course, he would have had some acquaintance with it through the Roman liturgy. He later confessed that even after he had begun to read the Bible, "I wanted that knowledge through the lusts of my youth in an impure, sensual, unprofitable life, and sought nothing but gain, ease, favor of men, splendor, name and fame, as all generally do who sail that ship." Apparently he was something of a born leader even though he was, as he put it, "a lord and a prince in Babylon." "Everyone sought me and desired me. The world loved me and I it. . . . I was pre-eminent among men, even aged men. Everyone revered me. When I spoke they were silent. When I beckoned they came. When I waved them away, they went. What I desired, they did." Later Menno came to realize, with the writer of Ecclesiastes, that all such allurements are really "vanity." When he became a Christian, Menno lost his erstwhile friends. "Heretofore I was honored; now debased. . . . Once I was a friend, now I pass for an enemy."[145] (Gen 11:1-10; Eccl 1:2; Luke 18:9-14) (Pride) (TG)

1511B From his ordination in 1537 until he died in 1561, Menno Simons exerted remarkable influence on the Anabaptists of the Netherlands and Northern Germany. During most of these years, he lived the life of a hunted heretic, preaching by night to secret conventicles of brothers and sisters, baptizing new believers in country streams and out of the way lakes, establishing churches, and ordaining pastors form Amsterdam to Cologne to Danzig.

In 1542, Emperor Charles V published an edict against Menno and offered one hundred gold guilders for the Anabaptist leader's arrest. Menno referred to himself as a "homeless man." But he did not have only himself to think about. His wife Gertrude and their three children suffered the same fate. In 1544, he lamented that he "could not find in all the countries a cabin or hut in which my poor wife and our little children could be put up in safety for a year or even half a year." His wife and two of the children preceded Menno in death. It is certain that he lived his last years as a cripple. From the beginning of his career, Menno knew that there was no way for the true Christian to avoid the cross. "If the Head had to suffer such torture, anguish, misery, and pain, how shall his servants, children, and members expect peace and freedom as to their flesh?"[146] (Mark 8:34-38; Luke 9:57-62; 2 Cor 1:5; Phil 3:10; Col 1:24) (Cross, Self-Sacrifice) (TG)

1511C For Menno Simons, following rather than faith was the great word of the Christian life. Or perhaps more accurately, faith that did not issue in following was ipso facto barren and false. The desire literally to imitate Christ was reflected in the practice of adult believer's baptism, the ordinance of footwashing, the refusal to swear an oath or to bear arms, and the willingness to embrace suffering and martyrdom. In 1553, Menno received a letter from the wife of Leonard Bouwen, who had recently been ordained an elder in the church. She begged Menno to use his influence to dissuade her husband from undertaking this work as she feared for his life because of the severe persecution of the Anabaptists. In his reply, Menno refused her request, though he admitted that "the sorrow and sadness of your flesh pierces my heart as often as I think of it." He reminded her that her husband—and she too—had committed themselves to the cross by their baptism. Since both life and death were in the hands of the Lord, she should strengthen and not weaken her husband. "In short," he advised, "prove yourself to do to your neighbor what Christ has proved to be to you, for by this only sure and immutable rule must all Christian action be measured and judged."[147] (Matt 11:28-30; Mark 8:34-38; 1 Pet 2:21; 1 John 2:6) (Cross, Imitation of Christ) (TG)

1511D The new ethic of love and nonresistance was perhaps the single most distinguishing mark of the evangelical Anabaptists of the Reformation. Other Protestant reformers were not opposed to war. Even Erasmus, the Catholic reformer who abhorred war and worked for peace, was willing to allow for a crusade against the Turks. Menno Simons repudiated all resort to physical coercion on the part of true Christians: "Christ is our fortress; patience our weapon of defense; the Word of God our sword; and our victory a courageous, firm, unfeigned faith in Jesus Christ. And iron and metal spears and swords we leave to those who, alas, regard human blood and swine's blood about alike."[148] (Hos 2:18; Zech 9:10; Matt 5:9) (Peace, War) (TG)

1512A Ulrich Zwingli. *Protestant Reformer* (1484–1531). Ulrich Zwingli was the great Protestant reformer in Zurich, Switzerland. In 1519, he began his ministry in the Cathedral Church and declared that he would not limit himself to certain prescribed biblical passages selected by the church hierarchy for worship reading, but he would preach the Gospel of Matthew verse by verse from the beginning to the end using the Greek text. Such an announcement would bring little excitement today for persons who often follow this method in Sunday School and perhaps would be received reluctantly by sermon listeners who fear rambling messages. But Thomas Platter was ecstatic that the whole Word of God was finally being preached in the original languages. In his zeal to know the ancient languages, he studied after work at night with sand in his mouth so the gritting against his teeth might keep him awake. Hearing the complete gospel story preached was such a joy that Platter said he felt as if he were being pulled by the hair on his head. In an age of religious consumerism, Platter's spiritual discipline speaks to us.[149] (Ps 46:10; 2 Tim 2:15) (Bible, Spirituality) (CDW)

1512B The Bible stood at the center of the Zwinglian Reformation. Ulrich Zwingli initiated a radical new pattern of preaching that he began when he entered the pulpit of the Zurich Great Minster on New Year's Day 1519. He abandoned the traditional lectionary in favor of a chapter by chapter exposition of the scripture. He not only was preaching from the Bible, but also was allowing the Bible to speak directly to him and his congregation. Gradually, the great cathedral began to fill with those eager to hear the Word of God. Zwingli confessed surprise at the number who came "hurrying" to his expositions. The proclamation of Holy Scripture was the single most important precipitant of reform in the city of Zurich. Zwingli was confident that within a few years all of Switzerland would embrace the gospel, followed by Germany, France, Italy, and Spain. For "the Word of God will easily blow all the dust away." To those who opposed his preaching, Zwingli warned: "Do not put yourself at odds with the Word of God. For truly, it will persist as surely as the Rhine follows its course. One can perhaps dam it up for a while, but it is impossible to stop it."[150] (Jer 23:29; Eph 6:17; Heb 4:12; 1 Pet 1:23) (Preaching, Word of God) (TG)

Seventeenth Century

1601 **Baptists of England.** *"The Dangers of Reaching Your Goal."* Have you ever noticed how dangerous it is to reach your goals, especially if you do not replace them with new goals? Have you ever seen a church that worked and sacrificed for a new building, and once they moved into the new building, things began to slide and coast? The same is true with individuals. You work vigorously to attain something; you get it; then you grow apathetic.

Baptists began in England in 1612. For the first seventy-five years of their existence, they were for the most part a harassed group. Viewed by the authorities of both church and state as a sectarian fringe movement, they were denied some of the basic religious and civil freedoms that members of the Establishment enjoyed. Baptists, therefore, preached and argued and went to jail for their freedoms. It was "freedom" that they wanted more than anything else. If they had the same freedoms others possessed, they would grow and prosper. So they thought.

In 1689, William and Mary came to the throne of England. One of their first acts was to issue the Act of Toleration. This Act gave to dissenting churches, such as Baptists, the freedom they had so longed for. Now that Baptists had the very thing they had worked for from the beginning of their existence, guess what happened? They began to *DECLINE!*

Why? Sure, it was the Age of Reason and all churches in England experienced decline. But maybe Baptists' fight for freedom had exhausted them. Maybe now that they had what they thought they most needed, they were without a new goal. What happened? Hypercalvinism got a death grip on the Calvinistic Baptists. And Unitarianism almost killed the General Baptists. Both groups of Baptists slid downward after they reached their long-fought-for freedom.[151]

Careful! You may get precisely what you are reaching for. Your church may reach its institutional goals. Then what? Apathy? Indifference? Or do you keep growing in some other direction? You get a new goal, or you die on the vine. Is this something of what George Bernard Shaw meant when he said: "There are two tragedies in life. One is to lose your heart's desire. The other is to gain it." (Exod 15:22-24; 16:2-35; Matt 26:40-45; Mark 14:37-41; Phil 3:12-14) (Apathy, Goals) (WBS)

1602A John Bunyan. *English Baptist Leader* (1628–1688). When the Baptist John Bunyan was imprisoned for preaching in the village square, an officer named Cobb attempted to persuade Bunyan to give up his public meetings. Cobb appealed to him to obey the government as the apostle Paul had instructed. "Yes," Bunyan replied, "but Paul was put in prison. There is more than one way to obey. We can obey by doing everything we are told, and we can obey by refusing and suffering what is done to us."[152] (Acts 5:27-32) (Obedience, Persecution) (JAW)

1602B There is a kind of self-centeredness that is evil, but there is another kind that is legitimate. Perhaps that is why Shakespeare said, "To thine own self be true, and it follows that as night follows day, thou canst not be false to any man." Similarly, John Bunyan in his apology for writing the devotional classic, *Pilgrim's Progress*, explained that he wrote this work not to show the world what he could do, or to please his neighbor. Rather he wrote, "I did it my own self to gratify."[153] He wrote about his own spiritual pilgrimage, but millions have found in his writing a mirror of their own journey. (Lev 19:18; Mark 12:33) (Self-Centeredness, Spiritual Pilgrimmage) (EEJ)

1603 **Henry Dunster**. *Colonial Baptist Dissenter; First President of Harvard* (1609–1659). Henry Dunster was prominent, influential, and successful. An excellent preacher and biblical scholar, he left England for the Massachusetts Bay Colony in 1640. Upon his arrival, he was quickly elected the President of Harvard, established in 1638 as the first college in America. Dunster successfully made Harvard into a school of excellence. Patterned after his alma mater, Cambridge University in England, Dunster's reputation even led some English families to send their sons across the seas to attend Harvard.

Seemingly, Dunster had it all. But in 1651, Dunster took a step of faith that would cause him to lose his reputation and popularity with the Puritan culture. He decided privately that the Baptist position of believer's baptism was a practice found in the New Testament and thus binding on all Christians. The Congregational church of the colony, of which Dunster was an outstanding member, followed the traditional Puritan practice of infant baptism. Dunster was in a quandary. How important was this matter of faith? If he publically advocated believer's baptism, he would lose his position at Harvard and he would become a social outcast. Should he move to Rhode Island, the cesspool of radical dissenters, or should he keep quiet like many Baptists in the Massachusetts Bay Colony were doing and continue in his influential good work?

As Dunster was deciding what to do, he learned of the arrest of the Baptist leader John Clarke and the infamous beating of Baptist dissenter Obadiah Holmes in the public square of Boston. Realizing the willingness of these men to be persecuted for what they believed, Dunster knew he must do the same. In 1653, he refused to have his newborn son baptized, openly declaring a belief in believer's baptism. Dunster "counted everything as loss" in favor of honesty, integrity, and the call to follow in the footsteps of Christ.

Dunster had to resign the presidency at Harvard despite his excellent work. Temporarily, he lived with Thomas Goold, a friend who had yet to proclaim in public his Baptist beliefs. Dunster's courageous suffering led Goold to "go public" and organize the First Baptist Church of Boston. Until his death in 1659, Dunster served as a pastor true to his convictions.[154] (Matt 5:14-16; Acts 4:18-20; Phil 2:7; 3:7-11) (Convictions, Discipleship, Courage, Integrity) (CDW)

1604 **Mary Dyer.** *Quaker Evangelist, Martyr* (ca. 1605–1660). Mary and William Dyer migrated to the American colonies from England. Settling in Rhode Island, William became attorney-general of the colony, and Mary thought seriously about her religious commitment.[155] In the mid-1650s, Mary went to England. While there, she became a Quaker. She traveled as a Quaker evangelist for five years in England, and then felt God calling her back to the colonies. Quakers were not welcomed in Boston, and when her ship docked, officials arrested Mary and her traveling companion Ann Burdon.[156] They held the women incommunicado and finally banished them to Rhode Island.

Mary's commitment to God and to caring for the children of God would cause her death. In 1659, Mary learned that Boston officials held two Quakers in prison. She traveled to the city to visit them and was imprisoned. The Massachusetts General Court had earlier passed a law banishing Quakers on pain of death, and now, Mary and the other two were banished under threat of execution. Within a month, Mary returned to Boston with William Robinson and Marmaduke Stevenson to protest the injustice of the anti-Quaker law.[157] Imprisoned again and sentenced to death, Mary and the two men marched to the gallows, mounted the steps, and had the ropes placed around their necks. Then, they received a reprieve and banishment, again upon pain of death. Mary would not tolerate this injustice, and in the Spring of 1660 returned. This time she was arrested and hanged.[158]

Mary Dyer refused to give up on an external principle, the right of each person to be a priest before the Lord. Today a statue of Mary Dyer stands on the grounds of the Boston State House, a symbol of freedom of conscience, of a woman willing to die for a godly principle.[159] (2 Sam 12:1-7a; Ps 34:19-22; 97:10-12; Matt 25:14-30; 2 Cor 1:3-11; 11:16-30) (Commitment, Courage, Martyrdom, Missions, Perseverance) (RB)

1605   George Fox. *Founder of Quakers* (1624–1691). At age nineteen, George Fox, the founder of the Quakers (Society of Friends), experienced a time of spiritual upheaval. He was depressed and suffered frequent attacks of blindness. The advise of the clergy was of no help, however. One told him to take tobacco and sing Psalms as a remedy for his state of mind. Another tried to bleed him with leeches, and a third flew into a rage when Fox, on the way to be counseled, accidentally stepped on the reverend's carefully cultivated flower garden. Abandoning the clergy's advise, Fox fasted, sought solitude, and mourned his sinfulness. He discovered that the truth of God was to be found in the heart as he experienced a flood of light in his inner being.

Fox began to preach in order to share his belief in the "inner light" or "Christ within." This inner light was present in every individual—pagan or Christian, Protestant or Catholic. It had but to be awakened as one recognized and accepted its presence.

The belief in the light within made a difference in the way early Quakers responded to persons. The extreme Calvinists of the seventeenth-century suggested that no one possessed even a trace of God's grace and light. God bestowed his grace only on a few, the elect, whom he had chosen in his sovereignty. All others remained totally depraved, incapable of acts of saving goodness. They had no ray of light within and were blinded forever by satanic darkness.

Instead of beginning with darkness and evil, Fox began with light and God. The incarnation, the enfleshing of the Christ of God, had brought light to all persons. "As in Adam all die, in Christ are all made alive," Paul had proclaimed. In some, the light shined forth as awakened by the Spirit; in others, it lay dormant, waiting to be awakened. Evil was serious and deadly, and Fox attacked it mercilessly, but it was not more powerful than good.

If Fox is right and all carry the light of God within, recognized or not, then it should make a difference in the way we treat all persons. You and I categorize others too easily. We often demand some social, moral, or theological conformity before we can love people. Jesus and George Fox loved persons as they were and trusted God to bring the light. And, if every individual carries something of God's light within, then each can be touched by God's love. Hope can come to the most hopeless of persons.[160] (John 1:9, 14; Rom 8:24-25; 2 Cor 5:16-21; Eph 1:18) (Hope, Light of God) (BJL)

1606   Dorothy Hazzard. *Early English Baptist Leader* (d. 1674). "When women preach and cobblers pray, the fiends in hell make holiday." In seventeenth-century England, this little rhyme described the views of upper class Anglicans and Presbyterians who were scandalized by the presence of "she-preachers" among the new sect called Baptists. The respected Presbyterian clergyman Thomas Edwards described the growth of Baptists in England as a type of spiritual gangrene, especially since they allowed women to preach.

The role of women in ministry was controversial among the first Baptists. John Smyth, the founder of the first Baptist church in 1609, favored women deacons but not women preachers. Many women did preach, however, especially among the General Baptists.

One of the most influential women preachers was Dorothy Hazzard. She was the leader of a group of dissenters from the state Church of England. For several years, she maintained a rented house just outside the boundaries of the Anglican parish and would go there on Sundays to avoid the required church attendance for parishioners. During the week, Hazzard used the house as a home for dissenter women so they could give birth outside the parish and escape the required infant baptism. Hazzard dissented to the practices of the state church in many ways, including the refusal to close her grocery store on Christmas Day since this was a pagan holiday that had defiled the church.

Hazzard was the founder of an important early Baptist church in England, the Broadmead Baptist Church of Bristol. The group of dissenters in Bristol would meet in Hazzard's home for Bible study and worship. Occasionally, the group would travel to other localities to hear ministers preach who had reputations for godliness and reform. It was a bold act to leave the parish minister to hear someone else, but Hazzard was especially bold since the minister was her husband. The dissenters would take sermon notes on their visits and would later repeat the sermons for those who had stayed home in Bristol.

In 1640, a Baptist preacher, John Canne, came to Bristol. Hazzard heard of his reputation and went to hear him preach. She insisted that he stay in her home. The civil authorities made him quit preaching in Bristol, but he preached outside of the town. Hazzard and her fellow dissenters went to listen to him. Consequently, Hazzard led the group to accept believer's baptism, and they organized the Broadmead Baptist Church. She was a pillar of the church for thirty-four years. She taught, preached, led Bible studies, and won many to Christ and the Baptist way, including one state minister, through personal evangelism. Hazzard was admired by all in the church at Bristol. The men were so impressed with her ministerial gifts that they described her as "like a he-goat before the flock."[161]

Scandalous behavior to the church, Dorothy Hazzard was a leader willing to dissent from the expected in order to be faithful to God. (1 Sam 2:25; Acts 16:15; 1 Cor 4:2; 1 Pet 5:2-3) (Dissent, Faithfulness, Leadership, Women in Ministry) (CDW)

1607A Thomas Helwys. *Minister of First English Baptist Church* (1550–1616). Religious toleration is one thing; religious liberty another. Religious toleration tolerates views assumed to be false as long as they do not overstep the tolerator's bounds; religious liberty believes every person has an equal right to freedom. Baptists have championed religious liberty. As Thomas Helwys, founder of the first Baptist church on English soil put it in 1612: "Let them be heretikes, Turks, Jewe, or whatsoever, it apperteynes not to the earthly power to punish them in the least measure." Religious toleration, self-righteousness, and religious persecution are an unholy trinity to be confronted with the biblical and Baptist view of religious liberty, Christian humility, and loving service for our enemies. Roger Williams, founder of America's first Baptist church, remarking on the career of the Apostle Paul, reminded those who oppose freedom of conscience that "these who appear soul-killers today, by the grace of Christ may prove, as Paul, soul-savers tomorrow."[162] (Acts 5:27-32; Gal 5:1) (Independence Day, Religious Liberty) (WLA)

1607B *"Just How Big Should A Church Be?"* In 1611, Thomas Helwys published a remarkable little confession of faith in Amsterdam. The next year, he and a small church of perhaps ten others returned to England to face persecution and plant the General Baptist denomination in England. Called "A Declaration of Faith of English People," Article Sixteen speaks of the size of the church:

> That the members off everie Church or Congregacion ought to knowe one another, that so they may performe all the duties of love one towards another both to soule and bodie (Mat 18.15. 1 Thes 5.14. 1 Cor 12.25). And especiallie the Elders ought to know the whole flock, whereoff the HOLIE GHOST hath made them overseers (Acts 20.28; 1 Pet 5.2,3). And therefore a Church ought not to consist off such a multitude as cannot have particuler knowledg one of another.[163]

Listen up church growth experts! Listen up laity who think that the test of your minister's leadership is his ability "to grow" a church! Listen up pastors who have sacrificed size for community. Listen up!

A church should be small enough for members to "knowe one another." A church should not be so large that the ministers cannot know "the whole flock." "A church ought not to consist of such a multitude as cannot have particuler knowledg one of another."

Why? You ask "Why?" So that they can love one another! So they can take care of one another! So they can tend to needs both of "soule and bodie."

When Lyndon Johnson announced that he was leaving Washington and returning to his ranch in Texas to live, some asked in disbelief, "Why? Why are you leaving the excitement of Washington to return out there?" "Because," Johnson said, "Out there they ask about you when you are sick and they cry when you die." He wanted to be cared for. So do you. And so do I. We all long for a community of compassion.

A local Baptist church is designed to worship God and care for people. Size has something to do with communion and community. (Matt 18:15; Acts 20:28; 1 Cor 12:25; 1 Thess 5:14; Heb 10:25; 1 Pet 5:2-3) (Compassion, Church, Fellowship) (WBS)

1608 **Obadiah Holmes.** *Baptist Leader of Colonial New England* (1606–1682). Although not as well known as the saga of Roger Williams, one of the most compelling stories in the fight for religious liberty in the American colonies was the persecution of the Baptist minister Obadiah Holmes. Holmes, a minister in Boston; John Clarke, pastor and founder of Newport Church, the second Baptist church in the colonies; and John Randall, a layman; paid a ministerial visit to an elderly, almost blind man named William Witter, a resident of Lynn, Massachusetts, and probably a member of Clarke's church. Clarke preached at Witter's home, an illegal activity, and the three men were arrested and convicted in Boston.

Clarke and Randall escaped bodily harm. An unknown benefactor paid Clarke's fine, and Randall was released after posting his own bail. Holmes received a larger fine for being so outspoken and then refused an anonymous donor's offer to pay. After spending several weeks in jail, Holmes was whipped in the Boston Commons thirty times across his bare back. Before the whipping, Holmes said he would not dull the effects of the punishment by any strong drink but would rely on the strength of the Holy Spirit. While being whipped, Holmes preached to the crowd, and when the beating was finished, he told the civil authorities, "You have struck me as with roses." Holmes' injuries were so severe that he could not leave Boston for several weeks. The only way he could rest was to be crouched on his elbows and knees. The roses left their imprints on Holmes' back for the rest of his life.[164]

The fight for religious liberty was often costly discipleship. Jesus, said, "Blessed are those who are persecuted for righteousness sake, for theirs is the kingdom of Heaven." (Zech 4:6, Matt 5:10; Acts 5:17-42) (Discipleship, Persecution, Religious Liberty) (CDW)

1609   Anne Hutchinson. *Puritan Dissenter of Massachusetts* (1591–1643). Some folks take their faith seriously enough to protect it when it is being misused. Anne Hutchinson was one of those people. Anne grew up in the home of a minister in the Church of England. When her father disagreed with the church, he said so, even though it meant he was put in prison. Naturally, Anne grew up believing that faith was something a person took seriously regardless of the consequences.

As a young woman with a successful husband and many children, Anne left the Church of England. She continued to search for truth and studied the King James Version of the Bible, which was published in 1611 shortly before she married. As she examined various Christian teachings, Anne was particularly influenced by the idea that a believer ought to be more concerned about obeying the Spirit than a set of rules. Obeying the law did not prove you were good, she concluded.

Seeking the religious tolerance she could not find in England, Anne with her husband William and children, sailed to America where she bore her fifteenth child. Settling in Boston across the street from Governor John Winthrop, Anne opened her home to women who wanted to discuss biblical matters. The religious leaders were not happy with Anne's activities. Her protests against the legalism of the church were considered very dangerous doctrine. The disturbed ministers paid a visit to Anne but were unable to stop her activities. They condemned her as a mere woman who believed in the guidance of the Spirit. Fearing she would lead others to defy the Puritan laws, Anne was tried in 1637. Her neighbor, Governor Winthrop announced her sentence: she would be banished from the colony because she was an unfit woman.

After her imprisonment, Anne and her family continued to be harassed for their beliefs. William and Anne moved their large family to Rhode Island. Although Rhode Island provided legal safety, the harassment from Boston continued to reach Anne. To place more distance between her family and her enemies, Anne and William made plans to move to New York. William died before the move. A year after she and the children moved, Indians entered her home, killing her and the six children still at home.

A religious misfit in England, a religious threat in the Massachusetts Bay Colony, a religious teacher in her community, and an example of Christian integrity, Anne Hutchinson modeled a serious faith regardless of the cost. As she said, "The Lord judgeth not as man judgeth. Better to be cast out of the church than to deny Christ."[165] (Job 27:1-15; Matt 23:23; Mark 8:34-38; Rom 1:17) (Commitment, Faith, Holy Spirit, Integrity, Legalism) (CDB)

1610   **Elias Keach**. *Colonial Baptist Minister* (1667–1701). One of the early Baptist churches in America, still in existence today, was the Pennepak Church near Philadelphia. Elias Keach, who founded the church in 1688, was the son of a prominent English Baptist minister, Benjamin Keach. When Elias came to America in 1687, he was not a Christian and had a reputation for being wild. For whatever reason, he decided to fake being a preacher like his father. Dressing up as a minister, he accepted an invitation to preach at a Baptist meeting. But playing church backfired, or more correctly, the power of the gospel changed the game plan. Keach was converted hearing his own sermon! Overwhelmed by the seriousness of sin in faking the sermon, he stopped preaching and began to tremble. The congregation thought he had become sick, but he admitted his hypocrisy and asked for the church's forgiveness.[166]

Søren Kierkegaard, the famous nineteenth-century Danish philosopher, said we play Sunday Christianity. We live lives of worldliness on weekdays and then go to church on Sunday, never admitting that our church attendance is for show rather than sacrificial worship.

It's time we stopped playing church and repented of our hypocrisy. The good news is that the power of the gospel can change the game plan and put us on the right track. (Jer 7:1-5; Luke 11:37-41; Rom 1:16) (Hypocrisy, Power of Gospel, Self-Deception) (CDW)

1611A William Penn. *Quaker Founder of Pennsylvania* (1644–1718). William Penn, the son of an admiral, customarily wore a sword as an emblem of the martial family tradition of which he was a part. As he came under the sway of Quaker teachings, including the conviction of nonviolence, Penn began to doubt whether it was appropriate for him to wear that weapon, even as an ornament. He sought the counsel of George Fox, the founder of the Quakers. Fox told him, "Wear thy sword as long as thou canst." A few weeks later, Fox encountered Penn, now without his sword. Fox asked with a smile, "Where is thy sword?" Penn responded, "I wore it as long as I could."[167] (Matt 5:9; 26:51-52; Rom 12:18; Eph 2:14; Col 3:15) (Conscience, Integrity, Peace) (JAW)

1611B The notorious treatment of Native Americans at the hands of white settlers is a blot on the pages of American history. Unfortunately, many Christians were numbered among those who took part in the brutal oppression of indigenous peoples who had occupied the country for thousands of years. This was not the case, however, with the Quakers. Because of the Quaker belief in equality, Indians were treated with respect and were not cheated by the Friends. In Pennsylvania, the Quaker founder, William Penn, made sure a jury was composed equally of white and native men when an Indian came to trial. Perhaps Penn's greatest accomplishment was his dealings with the Native Americans and land rights. He never forgot who rightfully owned the territory. When purchasing the area that would become Pennsylvania, Penn paid both the British monarchy and the Indians. When the king questioned his actions, Penn replied:

> I did this to gain thy good will, not that I thought thou hadst any right to their lands. I will bring the rights of the proper owners, even of the Indians themselves, by doing this. I shall imitate God in His justice and mercy, and hope, thereby, to insure His blessing on my colony, if I should ever live to plant one in North America.[168]

Penn signed a treaty with the Indians in June 1683, a treaty that unlike many others was upheld. (Ps 106:2; Amos 5:21-24; Mic 6:8) (Justice) (TF)

1612   **Pilgrim Fathers**. (17th cent.). In the early years of James I, a small band of earnest Christians gathered themselves into Separatist congregations along the Trent River Valley in the North of England. The new king vowed to enforce religious uniformity throughout his realm. When told about these religious dissenters, he said, "I will make them conform or else harry them out of the land." In 1608, these Separatists fled from their native land across the English Channel to Holland where they found refuge and toleration.

John Robinson was the pastor of one of these Separatist groups. They settled in the city of Leydon and carried on their worship in a peaceful manner for the next twelve years. This humble group of believers merged onto the terrain of world history in 1620 when a segment of their congregation left Holland for what one of their number, William Bradford, called "those vast unpeopled countries of America." Bradford, in telling their history, gave them the name by which they have been known ever since: "But they know they were pilgrims and looked not much on these things, but lifted up their eyes to heaven, their dearest country, and quieted their spirits."

Their pastor, John Robinson, remained behind to shepherd that part of the flock that could not go to America. In a tearful "Farewell Address," he gave the following charge that the pilgrim fathers long remembered and that became the guiding principle of their church life in the new world.

> We are now, here long, to part asunder; and the Lord knoweth whether ever he should live to see our faces again. But whether the Lord had appointed it or not; he charged us, before God and His blessed angels, to follow him no further than he followed Christ; and if God should reveal anything to us by any other instrument of His, to be as ready to receive it, as ever we were to receive any truth by his ministry, for his was confident the Lord had more truth in light yet to break forth out of His Holy Word.[169]

(Ps 119:105; Heb 11:13-16) (Spiritual Pilgrimage, Word of God) (TG)

1613 **Seventeenth-Century Martyrs.** In Wigtown, Scotland, there is a monument to two seventeenth-century martyrs, both named Margaret. One woman was in her sixties, the other sixteen. On a beautiful day in May 1685, the two of them were dragged through the streets of town to the sea, where they were interrogated about their faith. Neither would renounce Protestantism and submit to the authority of the king.

The villagers tied the older woman to a stake on the beach and let the sea begin to engulf her as the tide came in. Still, she refused to recant. Then the villagers took the young woman by the hair and asked her, "What do you see, girl, as you watch yonder woman?" She answered, "I see Jesus struggling there."

As the water buried the older woman, they affixed the younger Margaret to a stake. She, too, refused to recant her faith. The sea became her grave as she sang psalms of praise.[170] (Mark 8:34-38; Acts 7:54-60; 9:4-5; Rom 12:1-2; 1 Pet 2:21; 4:12-19) (Imitation of Christ, Persecution) (JAW)

1614A Roger Williams. *Founder of Rhode Island, Religious Liberty Advocate* (1603–1683). Roger Williams is known for his many significant contributions to American history. He founded the first Baptist Church in America in Providence, Rhode Island. He was a pioneer in establishing friendly relations with the Indians, dealing with them with respect and dignity uncharacteristic of most colonial Americans. Perhaps he is most famous for founding the colony of Rhode Island on the principles of democracy and complete religious liberty for believers and non-believers.

Williams was banished from the Massachusetts Bay Colony because he was a threat to the religious establishment of the Puritans. They criticized Williams for several of his views:

1) The native Americans were the legitimate owners of the land of the colony. The colonists were stealing the land when they acquired it by patent from the king of England. Williams retorted that the land was not the king's to give away.

2) The government should not require a "wicked person" to swear or pray. Williams objected to a type of pledge of allegiance that the colony considered primarily an oath of political loyalty because it was a form of government required prayer and worship should not be coerced.

3) He told fellow settlers that they should not hear ministers of the parish assemblies of England or from anyone who did not withdraw from that church.

4) The power of the civil authorities "extends only to the Bodies and Goods, and outward State of men." Williams believed that the Ten Commandments had two major parts. The "first table", the laws regulating a person's relationship with God, could not be governed by the state. Civil authorities could only enforce the "second table" which dealt with relationships between persons.

Liberty of conscience was sacred to Williams. The church and the state had to be separate when it came to conscience. The state cannot tell us what to believe or not to believe about God. It should not tell us when to pray or how to pray. Whenever the state forced its brand of religious belief on its people down through church history, persecution was the result.[171] (Matt 6:24; 22:21; Acts 4:19-20; Rom 13:1-7; Gal 5:1, 13; Jas 4:12; 1 Pet 2:10-17) (Civil Religion, Conscience, Religious Liberty) (CDW)

1614B In order to be genuine, religious faith has to be voluntary. Conversion cannot be coerced. Religious conformity is artificial religious experience and is a form of persecution. Roger Williams expressed these ideas in very vivid imagery. Speaking to his Puritan opponents, he said demanding that men believe was "like requiring an unwilling Spouse . . . to enter into a forced bed." Williams added that even the Indians, people the Puritans considered to be heathen, abhorred such a practice. On another occasion, Williams begged the English Parliament to avoid the religious persecution of conformity to one type of worship. This coercion of the conscience was "spiritual rape."[172] (1 Pet 3:11-17; 4:12-19) (Conformity, Conscience, Faith) (CDW)

1614C Roger Williams has been one of America's clearest spokesperson's for the separation of church and State. According to Williams, wherever there is a national church, it is inherently a political church. Edwin Gaustad, Williams' biographer, noted that Williams believed liberty of conscience was impossible in a state church since "people in power are seldom willing to 'hear any other music but what is Known to please them.' " Williams criticized the colonial Puritans for suggesting that America was the New Israel and therefore the settlers should conform to the legislators religious dictums. The Israel of the Old Testament was no longer a pattern for nations to reproduce. God now dealt with people individually. Down through the ages of the church's history, churches supported by the state have consistently spilled oceans and oceans of the blood of dissenters whose non conformity was based on conscience. The church has used the sword of the state but, Williams argued, the only appropriate sword in faith matters is the sword of the Spirit and its methods of persuasion and love. When will the church wake up, Williams bemoaned, to the fact that "the sword may make a whole nation hypocrites, but it cannot bring one single soul in genuine conversion to Christ."[173] (Matt 26:52; Phil 3:20; Heb 4:12; 1 Pet

3:11-17; 4:12-19) (America-New Israel, Conscience, Religious Liberty, Sword) (CDW)

1614D Baptists have always insisted on the principle of the right of private interpretation of scripture because of their belief in the competency of the soul and the liberty of one's conscience before God. In his most famous book, *The Bloudy Tenet of Persecution, for Cause of Conscience*, Roger Williams said that it was tragically ironic that the English Parliament went to great lengths to make Bibles accessible to "the poorest English houses" and to urge the "simplest man or woman" to study the scriptures for themselves. Why worry about whether the people read their Bibles when they must believe the official interpretations of the state church? Why ask them to search for biblical truth when conformity of the soul rather than the competency of the soul is being practiced?[174]

The words of Williams are still needed today. Whether it be conformity to a national church or a national religious organization or an authoritarian leader of any type, liberty of conscience cannot be sacrificed at the altar of coercion. Neither can the Bible. (Exod 19:4-6; Eph 2:18; 1 Pet 2:9; Rev 1:4-6) (Conformity, Soul Competency) (CDW)

1614E Often Christians debate the morality of war in terms of whether the conflict is just or unjust. Roger Williams was not a pacifist, but he said that no war is holy or of God's blessed design. Wars were human conflicts and not fought on behalf of Christ. To believe that God blessed war as a "divine right of government" was to see God as a God of wrath rather than of love. The pain of war would continue, Williams concluded, because people and nations are like Esau and Jacob grabbing after "greater Dishes and Bowls of Porridge."[175] (Gen 25:29-34; Isa 2:4; Matt 5:9; Rom 12:16-21; Jas 4:1-2) (Peace, War) (CDW)

Eighteenth Century

1701A **William Carey**. *English Baptist Missionary, Father of Modern Missions* (1761–1834). William Carey, attending the Ministers Fraternal of the Northampton (England) Association in 1787, proposed a topic for discussion: "Whether the command given the apostles to teach all nations was not binding on all succeeding ministers to the end of the world." John Ryland, Sr. responded, "Sit down, young man. You are an enthusiast! When God pleases to convert the heathen, He will do it without consulting you or me."

At the association meeting at Nottingham five years later, Carey preached a sermon from Isaiah 54:2 with the theme, "Expect great things from God; attempt great things for God." People were moved by the sermon, but it appeared that the presiding officer, Andrew Fuller, would dismiss the assembly with no specific action being taken. Carey tugged at Fuller's coat and implored, "Oh, sir, is nothing to be done? Is nothing again to be done?"

The plea was a turning point. The association adopted a resolution, "Resolved, that a plan be prepared against the next Ministers meeting in Kettering, for forming a Baptist society for propagating the gospel among the Heathen." The Baptist missionary movement was born.[176] (Matt 28:19-20; Acts 1:8; Rom 10:14-15; 1 Pet 2:9) (Missions, Persistence) (JAW)

1701B Adoniram and Ann Judson visited William Carey in India in 1812. As they walked in Carey's beautiful garden, the Judsons related to Carey how his life had inspired them to commit their lives to be Baptist missionaries. They inquired about the three attempts to murder Carey. The governmental restriction on his mission work, and the calamitous fire that had destroyed his printing house, type, plates, paper, and nearly all of his manuscripts and translations.

Ann Judson asked Carey, "But how could you get so much courage and faith to rebuild all this immediately?" Carey answered, "It was through the grace of God. As to courage, let me show you the path to my strength." Carey led the Judsons along a path in his walled garden to a quiet bower. "Here now you see my sanctuary of prayer and meditations," he said. "Without this I could not carry on through all the hindrances and hardships. I come here at five o'clock in the morning to pray aloud, talking to God and listening to him amid these flowers that he created in all their beauty. I leave the garden about six o'clock for my breakfast and to begin my work for the day. After supper, I come again for prayer and meditation with my Bible in my hand."[177] (Phil 4:6; Col 4:2; 1 Thess 5:17) (Prayer) (JAW)

1702A Jonathan Edwards. *Colonial Congregational Minister of Great Awakening* (1703–1758). Head or heart? How do we experience Christ? Some opt for a total "head" religion. The Christian experience is always palatable to reason, and feeling is evidence of psychological depravation. Others emphasize the heart and equate religious experience with foot-stomping, shouting, or any type of emotionalism. The head versus the heart issue has consistently erupted in the history of revivalism.

Jonathan Edwards, one of the prominent leaders of the First Great Awakening in the 1730s, was not thrilled with the emotional antics of shouting evangelism. But "head" religion alone never led a person to realize he/she was a sinner in need of a divine work of grace. Conversion involved the whole person, head and heart. Consequently, Edwards concluded, "There are false affections, and there are true. A man's having much affection, doesn't prove that he has any true religion; but if he has no true affection, it proves that he has no true religion."[178]

Modern believers have continued to wrestle with the relationship of the head and the heart, intellectual integrity and experiential warmth. The prominent modern biblical interpreter, Ernst Käsemann remarkably gives a response quite similar to Edwards. He wrote:

> The Holy Spirit is rarely comfortable and never without surprises. Indeed, it often brings disrepute with it. No matter what danger enthusiasm may have brought to the church, the final defeat of enthusiasm has always signalized the sleeping church, even the

busiest one. Enthusiasm is indispensable when the priesthood of all believers is to be awakened and the community represented and enlivened by the laity. There is no Christian freedom without a dose of enthusiasm.[179]

(Ps 9:1; 119:2, 10; Jer 31:33; Matt 22:37) (Conversion, Emotionalism, Intellect, Revivalism) (CDW)

1702B When he was eighteen years old, Jonathan Edwards recorded in his journal: "Resolved that all men should live to the glory of God. Resolved, secondly, that whether or not anyone else does, I will."[180] (Josh 24:14-15; 1 Cor 10:31) (Service) (JAW)

1703 **Andrew Fuller.** *Leader of English Particular Baptists* (1754–1815). In the middle of the eighteenth century, the theology of hyper-Calvinism stifled the growth of the Particular Baptists of England. Hyper-Calvinists emphasized the doctrine of double predestination, that is, God in his sovereign power selected before the foundation of the world some persons for heaven and others for hell. There was no human choice of responding to the initiative of God's grace; rather, the destiny of all persons was predetermined solely by the "pleasure" of God. As a result of this theology, ministers focused their efforts on preaching correct doctrine and often refused to offer invitations for persons to believe in the gospel since belief was impossible for those predestined to hell. Such a gospel was deadly to the growth of churches.

Amidst the stagnation caused by hyper-Calvinism, some Particular Baptist ministers led a revival, asserting that in the New Testament it was the duty of Christians to preach the gospel to all people and it was the duty of all who heard the message to repent and believe. While not rejecting their Calvinistic belief in the election of sinners by God, these ministers ceased the practice of simply preaching "correct doctrine" to professing Christians and began to preach salvation to all who would hear.

The theologian of this "evangelical Calvinism" was Andrew Fuller whose influential book, *The Gospel Worthy of All Acceptation* (1785) signaled the end of the dominance of hyper-Calvinism among Particular Baptists. Fuller's attitude toward hyper-Calvinism sheds light about rigid theologies in today's church. He warned fellow preachers that they might preach correct doctrine yet "be aside from the doctrine of the cross." Arguments over the doctrines of predestination and free grace were so intense that being orthodox was more important than the gospel message. According to Fuller, the hyper-Calvinists "almost made the *definition* of faith the very *object* of faith."[181]

The dangers of theological controversies obviously repeat themselves. (Rom 8:1, 29; Eph 1:5; 1 Pet 2:6) (Evangelism, Faith, Orthodoxy, Predestination, Theological Controversy) (CDW)

1704   Richard Furman. *Leader of Colonial Baptists* (1755–1825). Richard Furman was the most prominent and influential Baptist of the South at the end of the eighteenth and the beginning of the nineteenth centuries. He was pastor of the First Baptist Church of Charleston, South Carolina, and served as the first President of the Triennial Convention, the first national body of Baptists in America.

Furman was appreciated by American civil leaders for his outspoken support of the colonies' cause in the Revolutionary War. The British military leader Cornwallis even commented that he "feared the prayers of that godly youth more than the armies of Sumter and Marion."

During a trip to Washington, Furman was asked to preach before Congress. The President, Cabinet members, legislators, and foreign officials were in attendance because of Furman's reputation for eloquence. Furman preached on the passage, "And now why tarriest thou? Arise and be baptized." At the climax of the sermon he paused, stared at the audience of dignitaries, and repeated the words of his text. Some of the audience did not tarry but arose from their seats.[182]

If the gospel is worth telling, it is worth telling to the rich and the poor, the common folk and the dignitaries. If it is worth following, it is worth following now. (Acts 22:16) (Evangelism, Procrastination) (CDW)

1705   **John Gano.** *Colonial Baptist Minister* (1727–1804). One of the prominent Baptists of the colonial era was John Gano. Working through the Philadelphia Baptist Association, he was influential in spreading Baptist work in the Southern colonies. Thomas R. McKibbens, Jr., a scholar of Baptist preaching, says that Gano "spoke his mind at every age." On one occasion, a worldly ferryman asked Gano what was the "best and shortest way to heaven." Gano responded sarcastically, "Christ is the best way," but the shortest way that he could think of was to "place himself in the front of some army, in an engagement." In another instance, Gano was just as blunt to a Revolutionary soldier whom he heard cursing. Upon telling the soldier to pray to God about his sin, the soldier begged Gano's pardon. His response? "Oh, I cannot pardon you, carry your case to God."

Richard Furman, Gano's colleague, described him this way: "he believed, and therefore spake." Not bad advise for those of us who believe the gospel.[183] (Luke 23:34; Acts 4:20; 1 Cor 9:16; Eph 1:7; Col 1:14; Heb 9:22) (Forgiveness, Witnessing) (CDW)

1706   **John Leland.** *Colonial Baptist Religious Liberty Advocate of Virginia* (1754–1841). Baptists have been historically an anti-creedal people. They have preferred to stick with the Bible rather than to lock their souls and minds into a humanly written document. No one in Baptist life has made a better case against creedalism than did John Leland, valiant Baptist egalitarian who lived in the eighteenth century. Saucy and spirited, Leland had a way with the language. Here is his sauciness and spiritedness as it relates to creedalism.

> Confessions of faith often check any further pursuit after truth, confine the mind into a particular way of reasoning, and give rise to frequent separations. To plead for their utility, because they have been common, is as good sense, as to plead for a state establishment of religion, for the same reason; and both are as bad reasoning, as to plead for sin, because it is everywhere. It is sometimes said that hereticks are always averse to confessions of faith. I wish I could say as much of tyrants. But after all, if a confession of faith, upon the whole, may be advantageous, the greatest care should be taken not to *sacralize*, or make a petty Bible of it.

Baptists have been "liberals" in that they would not have the human spirit chained to creed, clergy, Caesars, or conventions. If you define "Baptist" any other way, you re-define it.

Hear Leland again. To make creeds the standard for belief and practice rather than the Bible leads to all kinds of trouble. It stifles the search for truth. It restricts the minds God gave us. It leads to division. "Sure," said Leland, "Creeds have been popular in Christian history." "But," he counters, "So have other forms of restrictions such as Established Churches." Tyrants are the ones who clamor for creeds; they want to tell you what to believe. "So *BEWARE*," says Leland, "Someone will turn a creed into a 'petty Bible'."[184] (2 Tim 3:16-17; Heb 4:12) (Creedalism) (WBS)

1707 **Quakers**. In American history, some of the most ardent advocates for peace have been the Quakers. They have been misunderstood and ridiculed for their mystical emphasis on having the light of Christ within one's inner being that brings the peace of God. There was once a Quaker who was going to be hanged by his neighbors because they misunderstood his ways. When the lynch mob had ridden out to the tree where the hanging was to occur, they discovered that none of them had brought a rope. The Quaker, standing bound in his own wagon, looked to the floorboard and said, "You will have to use my rope."[185]

Peace in your inner being brings a sense of comfort with loyalty to God that no insult or earthly power can destroy. Christian peace is the way of strength, not human power and arms, but the strength of Christ who loved and shared selflessly, even unto death on a cross. (Matt 5:9; John 1:9; Eph 2:14) (Peace) (CDW)

1708A **John Wesley**. *Founder of Methodism* (1703–1791). The son of an Anglican minister, John Wesley grew up in a very religious home. At age seventeen, John went to Oxford University and while there joined a group formed by his brother Charles for serious religious devotion. Their practice of constant attendance at worship, regular hours of private prayer, visitation of the sick, and strict moral code earned them such names of ridicule as the "Holy Club," the "Godly Club," or the "Bible Moths." Their methodical system of organization and study produced the name Methodist, a name later applied to Wesley's followers. Through the influence of the Holy Club, Wesley decided to become an Anglican priest, receiving ordination in 1725.

In 1735 Wesley had the opportunity to serve as missionary to the new colony of Georgia. He went as pastor to the settlers and missionary to the Indians, writing in his journal that his chief motive for going was to save his own soul. The trip over was characterized by violent storms, during which Wesley made a significant observation. The English passengers were terrified during each storm, but a group of German pietists (Moravians) on board were undaunted, singing hymns in the midst of the tumult. Wesley questioned one: "Were you afraid?" "I thank God, no," was the reply. "But were your women and children afraid?" "No, our women and children are not afraid to die." John Wesley knew that he could make no such confession. In Georgia, he met another pietist, August Spangenberg, who asked, "Do you know Jesus Christ?" Wesley responded, "I know he is savior of the world." Spangenberg continued, "True, but do you know he has saved you?" Wesley: "I hope he has died to save me." "Do you know it for yourself?," Spangenberg enquired. "I do," Wesley replied, confessing later that his answer was little more than vain words. Wesley realized that while he had strong religious convictions, he had no inner assurance of salvation.

Wesley's experience in Georgia was a disaster. Neither the colonists nor the Indians were responsive to his ministry. Back in England, he wrote: "I went to America to convert the Indian; but oh! who shall convert me?" Wesley's assurance finally came with his famous Aldersgate Experience on 24 May 1738. Attending a service on Aldersgate Street in London, he heard the speaker describe "the change which God works in the heart through faith in Christ." At that moment, Wesley wrote, "I felt my heart strangely warmed. I felt I did trust Christ, Christ alone for my salvation, and an assurance was given me that he had taken away my sins, even mine and saved me from the law of sin and death."[186]

The story is the same for us all. We can't save ourselves, no matter how hard we try. For it is by grace that we are saved.

God is the one who takes away our sin. (Rom 1:17; 2 Cor 5:16-21; Gal 5:1-6; Eph 2:8-10) (Assurance, Conversion, Legalism, Salvation) (BJL)

1708B John Wesley's itinerant style of ministry would long characterize the circuit riders of Methodism. For nearly fifty years, Wesley traveled four to five thousand miles a year, most of it on horseback. He preached over forty thousand sermons, always following his life's motto: "The world is my parish."

Wesley believed that Christ died for all persons, not for some select minority as the Calvinists suggested or for some economic and social elite as the Anglicans implied. Consequently, he introduced a new method for proclaiming the change that God works in the heart. He moved out or was thrown out of the sedate and aristocratic Anglican churches of his day and "consented to be more vile," proclaiming the gospel in highways and hedges. "Field preaching," it was called, standing in English meadows and markets, on hillsides and in city squares with a gospel to and for the disenfranchised whom the "decent people" had written off as incapable of moral transformation or spiritual experience. Many from the poor and working classes believed and were changed and Wesley scandalized Anglicans by recruiting his first lay preachers from the lower classes.

The method of open-air preaching and the call for dramatic conversion has been elaborated upon by most revivalists since Wesley. He emphasized the evangelistic heart religion of New Testament Christianity. The question that confronts our churches today is whether we have much of the method but less of the message. We contrive spontaneity and institutionalize informality, creating an evangelism with much style but often little substance. The grace gets a little cheaper, the cost of discipleship a little less costly, and the promises of material success a little bolder. Instead of growth, change, or struggle with new truths and old sins, we get a gospel of transaction. Pray a prayer, sign a card; no muss, no fuss. No need to grow, just get your doctrines straight. No need to question, we have all the answers. Wesley would have said to his day that it is possible to be an Anglican bishop without being religious and to our day that it is possible to be a Baptist evangelist without being evangelical.[187] (Luke 14:15-23; 2 Cor 5:16-21) (Evangelism, Preaching, Salvation) (BJL)

1708C John Wesley, the founder of Methodism, was asked what was the most distinctive thing about a Methodist. He gave a rather surprising answer. A Methodist was not to be distinguished by any special action, custom or opinion. A belief in the Scriptures as the inspired Word of God, the only sufficient rule for Christian faith and practice, and a love of God with all of one's heart, soul, mind, and strength were the true marks of a Methodist. Weren't these simply the common fundamental principles of Christianity? Of course, Wesley remarked. Wesley wanted to be distinguished by his life from a non-believing world and those not living according to the gospel. But with anyone, regardless of the denomination, who was attempting to follow Jesus, he would gladly be identified.

Wesley's perspective has rarely been heeded. Subsequent church history reveals a trail of interdenominational rivalries and intradenominational conflicts. As we struggle with unity in the body of Christ, holding fast to theological labels, Wesley's admonitions are worth hearing: "Dost thou love and serve God? It is enough. I give thee the right hand of fellowship."[188] (Matt 22:34-40; Mark 12:28-34; Eph 2:11-22; 4:1-6) (Cooperation, Diversity, Ecumenism, Unity) (CDW)

1708D Once a lady remarked to John Wesley, "God does not need your education." He answered her, "God can also do without your ignorance." (Mark 12:28-30; 2 Tim 2:15) (Education, Intellect) (JAW)

1709A George Whitefield. *British Revivalist of Great Awakening* (1715–1770). When George Whitefield, the outstanding evangelist of the Great Awakening, came to Philadelphia, he championed the cause of the orphan's home he was planning to build, and did build, down in Georgia. Benjamin Franklin did some printing for him, heard him preach, and respected him highly as a man of integrity. Franklin did not agree with the plan to build an orphanage in Georgia, however, which was on the edge of the colonies. He thought it should be built in Pennsylvania, which was more central. Thus when he went to hear Whitefield preach, he made plans not to give any money for the orphanage project. When Whitefield began to make his appeal for money, however, Franklin was so moved by the evangelist's sincerity, that he decided to make a token contribution. But as Whitefield pressed the matter, Franklin decided to give a little more, and when the appeal was finished, he gave all he had. Moreover, Franklin reported that a friend who had heard of Whitefield's effectiveness in persuading people to give money, deliberately left his money at home when he went to hear Whitefield preach, but when the appeal was made, the man tried to borrow money from his friends to be able to give. This story is a powerful witness to how effective the appearance of sincerity can be. Franklin testifies that in Whitefield's case the reality matched the appearance.[189] (2 Cor 9:7; Eph 4:15) (Giving, Integrity, Motivation, Sincerity) (EEJ)

1709B David Hume, the Scottish philosopher, was confronted as he was observed going to hear George Whitefield preach. "I thought you do not believe in the gospel," came the challenge. Hume responded, "I don't, but he does."[190] The gospel of abundant life engenders passion not passivity. (Rom 12:11; 2 Tim 4:1-5; Rev 3:15-16) (Commitment, Zeal) (JAW)

1709C George Whitefield was asked why he continually preached on the text "Ye must be born again." He replied, "Because you must be born again!"[191] (John 3:3) (Conversion) (JAW)

1710A **John Woolman.** *Quaker Abolitionist* (1720–1772). John Woolman, an early abolitionist and Quaker preacher, campaigned against injustice throughout his life. As a member of the Society of Friends, he believed in the absolute equality of genders and races before God. Appalled at the brutality and oppression he saw in slavery, Woolman traveled extensively throughout the country, but particularly in the South, speaking in Quaker meetings and directly confronting slaveholders in their homes. In his business dealings, he refused to write contracts or wills that involved the buying or selling of slaves. Once in a conversation with a man who was trying to justify the practice of slavery, Woolman said, "I believe he who is a refuge for the oppressed will, in his own time, plead their cause, and happy will it be for such as walk in uprightness before him."[192] Largely because of the actions and example of John Woolman, there were no Quaker slaveholders in America sixty years before the Emancipation Proclamation. (Isa 58:6) (Equality, Race, Social Gospel) (TF)

1710B John Woolman reported in his journal that his employer, who owned a black female slave, had him write out the bill of sale while the purchaser waited. Woolman did, but was so conscience-stricken that he confessed before his master and his friend that slave holding was wrong. The Quaker activist at times followed the trade of a tailor, and the wearing of clothes made from cloth produced by slave labor caused him to have such a heavy heart that he eventually protested against the holding of slaves at every annual meeting of the Society of Friends. Through his influence, more than anyone else, the Quakers freed themselves of slave holding long before the Civil War.[193] (1 Thess 5:22) (Evil, Moral Power, Race, Social Gospel) (EEJ)

Nineteenth Century

1801A **African-American Slavery** (19th cent.). A scene in the recent movie "Glory" suggests what the Christian calling to self sacrifice involves. On the night before their attack on an all but impregnable Confederate fort, the first black regiment of Union soldiers in the Civil War contemplated their likely deaths in the next morning's battle. In testimony meeting, one of their leaders finally rose to express his thoughts, saying, "If tomorrow is that great gettin' up morning, then let's let our loved ones know that we went down standing up." The task of being the church may never make us popular or successful. But that task will always place upon us—as individuals and as a church—the calling to make ourselves into an army of the meek, willing to "go down standing up" for God's rule in the world. (Matt 5:5; Mark 10:41-45) (Martyrdom, Meekness, Self-Sacrifice) (AMM)

1801B It means very little to say "God forgives you, " to one mired in the death and despair of guilt, if they cannot feel that forgiveness embodied in real human beings, in a supportive community of forgiven forgivers. In Toni Morrison's novel, *Beloved*, there is a character named Baby Suggs. At one point in the story, this slave-woman preacher called her fellow slaves to worship in a secret place of acceptance in the woods—away from the unforgiving eyes of their owners. Then she advised them:

> In this here place, we flesh;. . . Yonder they do not love your flesh. . . .*You* got to love it. This is flesh I'm talking about here. Flesh that needs to be loved. Feet that need to rest and to dance; backs that need support.

Baby Suggs understood that for flesh-and-bloodied human beings, yonder, out there in the culture, they don't love your flesh; so in the church, "in this here place," we "got to love it." Forgive it. Accept it. Baby Suggs understood that church is the human context where persons experience God's forgiveness and acceptance. (Matt 18:21-35; John 8:1-11) (Acceptance, Forgiveness, Love) (AMM)

1801C The heart of worship among the African American slaves was a ritual dance known as the ring shout. Used at all sacred times, but especially in connection with revivals and funerals, the shout involved call and response singing while rhythmically moving in a counterclockwise direction, in opposition to the movement of the sun. In its African theological background, each rising and setting of the sun painfully reminded the slaves of their new world. The sacred dance, moving counterclockwise against the sun symbolized the slaves' spiritual resistance to their slavish existence. Perhaps Christians can learn something from this African American understanding. From revival meetings to celebrations of the Mass, all worship brings together believers to participate in ritual acts designed to reinforce their Christian identity and remind them that they are a people called to resist conformity to the values of the culture around them.[194] (Rom 12:1-2; 1 Cor 12:12-13; Gal 3:28) (Conformity, Culture, Equality, Worship) (AMM)

1802   **Clara Barton**. *Founder of American Red Cross* (1821–1912). Clara Barton, one of the great humanitarians of the nineteenth century, was widely recognized for her service as a nurse during the Civil War. She provided direct aid to soldiers on the battle lines and became known as the "angel of the battlefield." She continued her life of service after the war and, in 1881, founded the American Association of the Red Cross.

While working for the Red Cross, Barton was once reminded of a wrong committed against her some years before. "Don't you remember?," inquired a friend. "No," replied Miss Barton emphatically, "I distinctly remember forgetting that." It's not really forgive and forget. It's forgive and remember in a new way.[195] (Ps 25:7; Isa 43:25; Matt 6:14-15; 18:21-35; Mark 11:25; Eph 4:31-32; Col 3:13) (Forgiveness) (JAW)

1803   **Lyman Beecher**. *Congregational and Presbyterian Minister* (1775–1863). When he was twelve years old, Wendell Phillips met the popular preacher Lyman Beecher. Beecher looked at the young Phillips and declared, "Son, you belong to Christ. Live for him." Phillips, who became a prominent abolitionist in American history, later remembered, "That very day I accepted my mission."[196] (Rom 14:7-9; 1 Cor 6;19-20; Gal 2:19-20; 1 Tim 4:11-16) (Call, Obedience) (JAW)

1804A **Catherine Mumford Booth**. *Co-founder, Salvation Army* (1829–1890). Above all else, Catherine Mumford Booth was a woman committed to God and to living her life according to the Bible. Whatever issues confronted The Salvation Army, which she and her husband William founded, Catherine always went to scripture and made her decisions based on the Word of God. A major problem for The Army was their early affirmation of women ministers. Few denominations in nineteenth-century England allowed women the freedom they exercised as Salvationists.[197]

Catherine came to her position through Bible study. When engaged to William, she wrote him, in 1855, that she had "tried to deal honestly with every passage on the subject, not forgetting to pray for light to perceive and grace to submit to the truth," no matter what that truth is.[198] In the letter, Catherine outlined her understanding of what women and men are to be before God, and she focused on how Jesus related to women and what he asked of them. She did not demand that William agree with her, just that he prayerfully consider her position. She asked of him, "I want thee to feel as I do, if thou canst; but, if not, be as honest in thy opinion as I am and I will honor thee for this."[199] Her own honesty before the Lord impelled her to expect that same honesty from others. She preached her first sermon five years after their marriage, and from that time on proved a powerful spokesperson for the Lord.[200]

Her view of scripture led her to take and maintain an unpopular stance, because she believed it was right before the Lord. God blessed Catherine and William Booth's ministry. Millions of people around the world now know Christ through the ministry and witness of The Salvation Army—a church dedicated to the equality of men and women before the Lord—because of a woman's commitment to the biblical revelation. (Ps 100; Isa 6:1-8; Amos 7:14–15; Mark 1:16-20; Eph 3:1-6; 1 Tim 4:6-10) (Bible, Call, Commitment, Overcoming Barriers, Preaching) (RB)

1804B Due to Catherine Booth, The Salvation Army, which she and her husband William founded, stood for women's equality in the Church. Catherine argued that women's secondary status in society was due to lack of training and opportunity, not lack of talent. It was a crafty device of the devil, Catherine thought, when the church followed custom and prejudice and denied women the right to ministry. The church's loss was incalculable. Catherine challenged hearers of her messages when she admonished, "Jesus Christ's principles were to put woman on the same platform as men, although I am sorry to say his apostles did not always act upon it."[201]

How will we act upon the principle of equality? (Gal 3:28) (Custom, Equality, Prejudice, Women in Ministry) (CDW)

1805A William Booth. *Co-Founder, Salvation Army* (1829–1912). A Methodist minister, Samuel Logan Brengle, who had once dreamed of himself as a bishop, traveled from the United States to England to enlist in Williams Booth's Salvation Army, when that ministry was in its infancy. Brengle became the Salvation Army's first American-born commissioner, but Booth initially accepted Brengle's offer of service only hesitantly and with much reservation. Booth said to Brengle, who had been a successful and an effective pastor, "You've been your own boss too long." In order to implant some humility into Brengle, he gave him the task of cleaning the boots of the other trainees. Brengle mused, with some agitation, "Have I followed my own fancy across the Atlantic in order to black boots?" Then, as in a vision, he saw Jesus bending over the feet of rough uneducated fishermen. "Lord," Brengle whispered prayerfully, "you washed their feet; I will black their boots."[202] (Mark 9:33-37; 10:35-45; John 13:1-20; Phil 2:5-11) (Humility, Service) (JAW)

1805B Reflecting on his life and ministry, William Booth, founder of the Salvation Army, declared: "When I got the poor of London on my heart and caught a vision of what Jesus Christ, the reigning Lord, could do with those people, though I knew there were many with greater training, greater wisdom, greater intelligence, greater power than William Booth, I was determined that the living Christ would have all of William Booth that there was." No less a commitment is expected of anyone. (Mark 8:34-38; 12:28-30; Rom 14:7-9; 1 Cor 1:26-31; Gal 2:19-20; Col 3:17) (Commitment, Dedication) (JAW)

1805C William Booth, the founder of the Salvation Army, enlisted those who had been won to faith to engage in the work of winning others. What was most important to him was genuine zeal and concern for those who had not responded to the gospel. Once a fisherman who had little education was preaching on the parable of Jesus in which the servant said to his master, "Lord,

I feared thee because thou art an austere man." The fisherman thought it was an "oyster man," and he explained how oyster fishermen had to get wet and dirty and endure cuts on their hands in order to gather the oysters. So Jesus suffered to gather the lost. That night twelve people came to faith. When someone pointed out the mistake to the fisherman, he exclaimed, "Never mind! We got twelve oysters."[203] (Mark 1:17; 1 Cor 1:26-31) (Evangelism, Zeal) (JAW)

1806A John A. Broadus. *Southern Baptist Teacher, Preacher* (1827-1895). In 1859, the Southern Baptist Theological Seminary opened with four professors and twenty-six students. Three years later, the seminary was closed due to the Civil War. Early in the summer of 1865, the four faculty members—James P. Boyce, John A. Broadus, Bail Manly, Jr., and William Williams—met to consider the possibility of reopening the school. The prospect was not encouraging. The South had been decimated. The churches were struggling. The seminary had no financial resources. Many of those who would have been students were casualties of the war. But the faculty members prayerfully made a covenant together, articulated by John A. Broadus: "Gentlemen, suppose we quietly agree that the seminary may die, but we'll die first." With that determined, sacrificial commitment, the seminary lived.[204] (Gal 6:9–10; 2 Thess 3:13; Heb 12:1-2) (Perseverance, Self-Sacrifice) (JAW)

1806B When the Southern Baptist Theological Seminary was reopened after the Civil War, the young professor John A. Broadus anticipated with eagerness a class in homiletics, for which he had been preparing a series of lectures on preaching.

The chairman of the faculty, James P. Boyce, asked him, "My dear Broadus, do you realize that you will have only one student in your homiletics class and that most unfortunately, he is blind?" Broadus responded, "I am sorry to learn that he is blind, but I shall give him my best, just as if there were one hundred in the class." Broadus' lectures, delivered faithfully to this one blind student, formed the basis of the material eventually published as the book, *On the Preparation and Delivery of*

Sermons, the long-time standard text in the field of homiletics.[205] (Matt 25:14-30; Luke 12:48; 16:10) (Faithfulness, Talents) (JAW)

1807   **Phillips Brooks.** *Episcopalian Minister* (1835–1893). Phillips Brooks was one of the premier preachers of the nineteenth century. His eulogy of Abraham Lincoln on Independence Day, 1865, brought him national acclaim. The author of many books, Brooks will always be remembered for his composition of the Christmas carol, "The Little Town of Bethlehem."

Brooks' wisdom could be seen even in humor. During his recuperative days from a serious illness, Brooks saw no visitors, not even his closest friends. He made an exception, though, for the agnostic Robert Ingersoll. Aware of the opportunity granted him, Ingersoll was curious about the reason. Brooks responded, "I feel confident of seeing my friends in the next world, but this may be my last chance of seeing you."[206] (Rom 13:11-12; Rev 20:11-15) (Heaven, Hell, Salvation) (JAW)

1808   **Amy Carmichael.** *Irish Missionary to India* (ca.1869–1951). Amy Carmichael was born in Northern Ireland in the late 1860s. She grew up in a privileged family, but as a teenager had a vital experience with God that radically altered her life and outlook. She became committed to helping the poor and needy; she promised to give God her life for missionary service. She lived out her life under the vow she made to sacrificial giving of everything she possessed.

First, Amy went to Japan but found no place of service among the many missionaries in that country. In Japan she dealt with the problem of loneliness and fear. She recounted, in one of her thirty-five books, that she climbed Mt. Arima and entered a cave to find rest. As she looked out of the cave, fear and loneliness overwhelmed her. She asked God what she could do and the answer came: "None of them that trust in me shall be desolate." She went on to say that during the more than fifty years of missionary service she enjoyed, "That word has been with me ever since. It has been fulfilled to me. It will be fulfilled to you."[207] Through the years of service in Japan, Ceylon, and finally India, Amy never forgot that incident. She based her ministry on the knowledge that God would never leave her desolate.

Other missionaries often considered Amy eccentric. The Hindu practice of taking young children as temple prostitutes was a secret protected by the government. A child who had escaped from a temple told Amy what took place there. No one believed her, because no corroboration was found. After years of careful work, Amy proved that temple prostitution existed and began to help free the children.[208] Her efforts saved thousands of children over the decades.

Amy Carmichael loved God and honored her commitment to the Lord. In return, the Lord kept the promise made on Mt. Arima: None of them that trust in me shall be desolate. (Gen. 39:20-23; 1 Kgs. 19:11-18; Ps 46:1-3; Matt 28:18-20; 2 Cor 12:1-10; Heb 10:19-25) (Commitment, Fear, God's Promises, Ministry, Missions, Solitude) (RB)

1809   **Civil War.** (1861–1865). Probably the most trying time in the history of this nation came in 1861–1865, when America was engaged in a Civil War. The major contributing factor for the Civil War was the issue of the legality of slavery, a disagreement that many thought would be settled in three months of fighting, but which instead filled four years and gained notoriety for the most Americans killed in a war.

America was not only divided on the battlefields, but in its churches as well. Both the North and the South heard the voice of support from their preachers, each side relentlessly accusing the other of being responsible. Henry Ward Beecher, the influential pastor of Brooklyn's Plymouth Congregational Church said, "I charge the whole guilt of this war upon the ambitious, educated, plotting leaders of the South."[209] He also used the pulpit to raise funds to ship rifles to Union troops in Kansas. In the South, the prominent Presbyterian spokesperson, Robert Lewis Dabney, claimed that the war was "caused deliberately" by evil abolitionists who persecuted the South "with calculated malice."[210] He also stated very plainly that he would not forgive the North for its actions. Each side enlisted God in its cause and produced plenty of scriptural references to justify its views.

It is comforting to find that someone chose not to point a finger during such a stressful time in the nation's history; it becomes a blessing when this person turns out to have been the nation's leader. Abraham Lincoln endured the Civil War, not by accusing the South, but by honestly seeking God. During one of his deepest moments of decision making, Lincoln wrote in his private journal, "The will of God prevails. In great contests each party claims to act in accordance with the will of God. Both may be and one must be wrong. God cannot be for and against the same thing at the same time."[211] Lincoln did not believe God was on either side, but that God had allowed the war for purposes unknown to humanity.

The Southern Baptist Convention has been engaged in a civil war of its own. Although no blood has been shed, we have still been guilty of killing our brother. Although no guns have been used, a much more subtle weapon called the tongue has proven to be highly effective. This weapon can be fired at will, and its owner can continually load it without drawing attention to oneself, using ammunition from the Bible and from one's own mind. Perhaps most interesting—but not surprising—is that all parties have announced that God is on their side.

The issues that face the convention are by no means trivial, nor are the convictions held by its members. We must all consider, however, the exhortation in Romans 12:3, for "every man among you not to think more highly of himself than he ought to think." It is important for us to seek God in all things. But when we begin to believe that our beliefs are always the correct beliefs, then we are thinking too highly of ourselves. God cannot be divided, nor should we attempt to live in a fantasy land where God has submitted himself to our cause in order to help us to defeat people whom he has called to serve him.

Following one of the biggest battles of the Civil War, Abraham Lincoln visited the wounded Confederate soldiers. He offered his hand to them and said, "We are enemies by uncontrollable circumstances. I bear you no malice."[212] The creation must always serve the Creator, and, in so doing, the creation must display love to the entire creation, not just to those who think alike. (Rom 12:2-3; Jas 3:2-12) (Pride, Unity, Tongue) (ALC)

1810   **Russell H. Conwell.** *Protestant Evangelical Leader* (1843–1925). Russell Conwell, the founder and first president of Temple University, was a social reformer who responded to the changing needs of the city in the late nineteenth century. His message was one of uplift: people can help themselves. In his lecture, "Acres of Diamonds," given 6,000 times, he told of a rancher in California who, upon hearing that people had discovered gold in southern California, sold his ranch and went south, never to return. A Colonel Sutter, who bought his ranch, built a mill by a stream running through it. One day, his little daughter was playing in the stream and showed him some glittering sand she found. The glittering sand contained gold, and by the time Conwell wrote, thirty-eight million had been taken from a very few acres. Conwell noted that many people go great distances looking for something better, when if they had the faith and imagination to see them, great opportunities are often near at hand.[213] (Exod 4:2; Eccl 9:10) (Imagination, Opportunities, Possibilities) (EEJ)

1811   **Evangelical Feminism** (19th cent.). In his book, *Discovering an Evangelical Heritage*, Donald Dayton reveals that modern evangelical revivalism gave birth to the women's rights movement in America. John Wesley, founder of Methodism, gave his approval to some women preachers near the close of his ministry. Charles Finney, the famous revivalist of frontier religion, encouraged women to speak and pray in public and mixed meetings. Phoebe Palmer, a Methodist lay evangelist, was the major leader of the 1857–1858 Holiness revival that helped birth several evangelical denominations. She published a 421- page defense of the right of women to preach. In it, she argued that Acts 2 indicated that, because of Pentecost, daughters would prophesy. While all evangelicals did not support women's rights, Seth Cook Rees, founder of the Pilgrim Holiness Church and a co-pastor with his wife, summarized the position of evangelicals who did support women's equality when he exclaimed, "Nothing but jealousy, prejudice, bigotry, and a stinging love for bossing in men have prevented women's public recognition by the church."[214]

Dayton is right. We need to rediscover our heritage. (Acts 2:17; Gal 3:28) (Jealousy, Women in Ministry) (CDW)

1812   **Father Damian.** *Catholic Missionary* (1840–1889). Father Damian was a Belgian missionary who went to Hawaii in the nineteenth century to work with the lepers on the island of Molokai. Single-handedly, he ministered to the physical and spiritual needs of the six hundred lepers, caring for their wounds, building them houses, and burying them. One morning, while pouring hot water, he accidently spilled some on his feet. He felt no pain. Instantly, he realized that he, too, was now a leper. He ran to the church and rang the bell calling the other lepers to worship. When all had arrived, Father Damian moved to the pulpit and announced with a strange joy, "Fellow lepers, Fellow lepers." Father Damian's ministry incarnated the very love of Christ in that leper colony.[215] (John 1:14; 1 Cor 9:19-23) (Incarnation, Love, Social Gospel) (JAW)

1813A **Charles G. Finney.** *American Evangelist, Father of Modern Revivalism* (1792–1875). Charles Finney, the father of modern revivalism, grew up in the Congregational church. After completing high school, he pursued independent studies while teaching school. Finney became a lawyer, but, while practicing law, he noticed that the Bible was frequently quoted in his legal books. He purchased his first personal Bible and began to read it. He confessed that many of the biblical passages were beyond his comprehension. Consequently, Finney began to study the scriptures and to attend a Presbyterian church.

George Gale, the church's minister, was a hyper-Calvinist who emphasized God's sovereign power to dispense grace as he wished, regardless of human free will. Finney was intrigued but not persuaded by Gale. For weeks, Finney and Gale pursued an adversary relationship as they argued theology. Finney's attitude toward his preacher is revealing:

> He was, of course, regarded as highly orthodox; but I was not able to
> gain very much instruction from his preaching. . . . He seemed to take
> it for granted that his hearers were theologians, and therefore that he
> might assume all the great and fundamental doctrines of the gospel.
> But I must say that I was rather perplexed than edified by his
> preaching.

Finney concluded that the religious efforts of the advocates
of predestination were not directed toward receiving God's power
but were an attempt to excuse their inadequacies.

Through continued study, Finney decided that the Bible was
God's true word. Therefore, he would have to decide what to do
with the biblical mandate to be converted. He wrote, "This being
settled, I was brought face to face with the question whether I
would accept Christ as presented in the Gospel, or pursue a
worldly course of life." He felt the urgency of the Holy Spirit to
decide which course of life he would follow.

During the autumn of 1821, Finney focused on his personal
conversion. He turned to the Bible as his only guide, because he
was ashamed to inform the church that his life needed to be
changed; he was afraid that if they knew, they would misdirect
him. (A sad commentary on the church!)

Compelled by an inner voice, he agreed to accept Christ that
day or die in the attempt. He walked into the woods for privacy.
Through agonizing hours of prayer, Finney felt desperate as his
pride was exposed before God, and he felt divine judgment on
his overwhelming wickedness. Finney became desperately afraid
that salvation would elude him. Then he realized: "I had
intellectually believed the Bible before; but never had the truth
been in my mind that faith was a voluntary trust instead of an
intellectual state."

Finney thought he left the woods unconverted. Later in the
day, however, he experienced a vision of Christ. This was
comforting, but he was still unsure when he went to bed. During
the night, he frequently awoke to sensations of love pervading
his mind. He knew he had been saved during his sojourn in the
woods.

Finney's conversion experience tells us a great deal about
how we often approach conversion. Preachers often preach in

ways that the listeners don't understand. Sermons are unedifying and perplexing. Finney's fear of sharing his inadequacies before the church reveals that we are often insensitive or condescending to people who are feeling the need to repent or make a commitment of rededication. They fear condemnation rather than acceptance, understanding, and nurture. On the other hand, Finney's reliance on the Holy Spirit and the scriptures is refreshing. The proper response of the seeker of God is not primarily a propositional intellectual knowledge of biblical doctrine but a total dependence of voluntary trust on Jesus. Indeed, it is the Bible that tells us that faith is not belief about God but belief in God. It is the Bible that tells us that faith is not an intellectual state but is voluntary trust in the Lord. As the Psalmist said, "The word is a lamp unto my feet, a light unto my path."[216] (Ps 119:105; John 3:16; Acts 16:31; 2 Cor 1:9-10; Gal 6:1-2) (Conversion, Faith, Preaching, Predestination, Reconciliation, Trust) (DLH)

1813B When Charles Finney was converted, he believed the experience included a call to preach. The day after being converted, He uttered one of his most famous statements. To a client, whose court date was imminent, the lawyer Finney declared, "Deacon B., I have a retainer from the Lord Jesus Christ to plead his cause, and I cannot plead yours."

Every convert is not called to be a full-time vocational member of the clergy. But if a Christian has been called into the ministry, that person will feel compelled to "plead the cause of Christ."[217] (John 20:21; 2 Cor 5:20; Eph 4:1, 12; 1 Pet 3:15) (Call, Evangelism, Lay Ministry) (DLH)

1813C As the father of modern revivalism, Charles Finney is known for introducing the "new measures" into the revival service. These new methods included the 'anxious bench,' prayer circles, 'protracted meetings,' inquiry sessions, women praying in public, cottage prayer meetings, and personal instruction. The measures showed that Finney did not believe revivals depended upon the special work of God but could be produced by human efforts. God had offered salvation to all people and revivals were the means of communicating that offer. He said, "A revival is not a miracle; it consists entirely in the right exercise of the powers of nature. . . . The connection between the right use of means for a revival is as philosophically sure as between the right use of means to raise grain and a crop of wheat." Religion was to turn people's attention to higher things and Finney believed people would not act until they were excited. Finney, or another evangelist, was to be the instrument of excitement. He became increasingly concerned, however, about the life of converts after a revival had ended. Too much superficial religion, he feared, had been produced by revivals. He came to regret that the "new measures" had been fully developed prior to his developing a theology of sanctification.[218]

We have perfected Finney's "new measures" on how to conduct a revival. Our services are so mechanized, so predictable, so emotionalized that we can produce conversions like a crop of wheat. People surely are converted in revivals, but Finney came to regret the superficiality that he introduced. Are we only interested in numbers, willing to use any "new measures" we might create, or do we share Finney's concern over superficiality and sanctification? (Matt 23; Luke 18:9-14; 2 Tim 3:15) (Revivalism, Superficiality) (DLH)

1813D   Charles Finney is known for shifting the emphasis in revivalism from the irresistable grace of a sovereign God (Calvinism) to the free-will response of any person to the offer of God's grace (Arminianism). As he described the conversion process, Finney identified four agents as inducing conversion. They were: the Holy Spirit, the truth, the messenger, and the sinner. All the agents were necessary and had their own unique role to perform.

To illustrate the interrelatedness of the four agents, Finney frequently asked his hearers to imagine that they were standing on the bank of Niagara Falls. See a man headed toward the edge of the falls, "lost in deep reverie," unaware of his impending plunge to destruction. You cry out "STOP!" and the man suddenly realizes his situation and averts disaster. With horror, he leaves the scene, and you follow him. When he sees you he says "That man saved my life." According to Finney, there is a sense in which the bystander (the messenger) saved the man. But upon further questioning, the man says that the word "STOP!" (the truth) was the "word of life" to him. After even more questioning, the man decides, "Had I not turned at that instant, I should have been a dead man." Finally, after stating that it was his act (the sinner), he cries, "O the mercy of God; if God had not interposed, I should have been lost (the Holy Spirit)."[219] (Acts 2:37-40) (Conversion) (DLH)

1813E Charles Finney was not only a great revivalist, but also a professor at Oberlin College for forty years. In a lecture series on Christian experience, Finney admitted that Christian experience was always to be interpreted through external and internal dynamics. One never has a pure experience with God because religious experience always occurs through the prisms of pesonalities and nature. Knowledge of God, others, and self was not artificially shaped by precise revivalistic formulas. Instead, one's comprehension of Christianity was always altered by the world in which one lived.

What Finney expressed to the college students in a series of lectures, he rarely shared with the revivalistic public. He feared that if variety and ambiguity were acknowledged, people would question the universality of his teachings on Christian experience. Instead of being *the truth*, his teachings would become probable truths among other possible truths. Also, it is much easier to preach about oversimplified doctrines than it is to give comprehensible sermons on complex doctrines. Consequently, Finney's desire to be heard by the masses significantly shaped his explanations of Christian experience.[220]

Finney did what we all do. We play to the crowd. We don't share our knowledge because we fear that we will be rejected or misunderstood. And we all have our pride, don't we? (Matt 4:5-7; 23:5; Heb 6:1; 1 John 2:15-17) (Hypocrisy, Integrity, Popularity, Pride) (DLH)

1813F Charles Finney did not often share his thoughts about the ambiguities of Christian experience with the masses. As his ministry progressed, however, he began to emphasize the need for sanctification in his preaching. This was not altogether popular and he lamented that most Christians were "ignorant of the power of the highest and most precious truths of the gospel of salvation, in Christ Jesus." Still, Finney preached the truth of holiness because he believed it to be true, regardless of whether it was popular.[221] (Phil 4:8; 2 Tim 1:11-14; 1 John 2:15-17) (Popularity, Truth) (DLH)

1813G In addition to his emphasis on conversion, Charles Finney taught the importance of sanctification. He urged the church to strive after a higher standard of Christian life and called for the ministers to establish a definite standard for Christian living. He believed that for the minister and the church to accept any standard short of perfection was equivalent to granting an indulgence for sin. Such a concession would undermine biblical morality. He chided his opponents by urging them to explain that if the holiness standard of entire sanctification was not possible, then what was to be the Christian standard? He asked, "If Christians are not expected to be wholly conformed to the will of God in this life, how much is expected of them?" If entire sanctification (practicing love by fulfilling the moral demands of the law) was not possible, then God was guilty of trifling with converts by telling them to become perfect.[222] (Matt 5:48; 1 John 2:1-6; 3:1-10; 4:18) (Sanctification) (DLH)

1813H In his teaching on the need for sanctification, Charles Finney argued that a consecrated love for God necessarily meant a consecrated hatred for sin. The only way to attain holiness and to progress in the work of sanctification was to adopt "the principle of total abstinence of sin." Total abstinence from sin must be every man's motto, or sin will certainly sweep him away as with a flood."[223] (Ps 101:3; 119:104, 113, 163; 1 John 2:1-6; 3:1-10) (Sanctification, Sin) (DLH)

1813I Twentieth-century evangelicalism has often separated evangelism and social reform. Evangelical roots, however, reveal a close interrelationship between evangelism and social activism. Many evangelicals of the northern churches were especially active in the anti-slavery movement. Charles Finney led the way. Finney believed that slavery was a major hindrance to revivals. When the churches took "the wrong ground" on slavery they lost the power of moral suasion. Support for slavery destroyed all claims of holiness. Finney also believed that slavery was the worst blight on America's character. He lamented that a nation professed to be moral would stand, "with its proof foot on the neck of the millions of crushed and prostrate slaves! O horrible! This is a less evil ... than the dismemberment of our hypercritical union!"[224] (Eph 6:5-9; 1 Thess 3:11-13; 2 Tim 3:5) (Moral Power, Sanctification, Slavery) (DLH)

1813J   Charles Finney pursued the traditional line of privatized ethics by chiding Christians who wore the latest fashion and attended the theater. He also addressed corporate social themes such as the morality of war. Any war based on selfishness, such as the Mexican-American War, was immoral and was to be opposed by Christians. Finney lambasted the maxim "Our country right or wrong," and he believed that sympathizing with the government in the prosecution of a war unrighteously waged involved the guilt of murder.[225] (Isa 2:4; Matt 5:38-48; Jas 4:1-2) (Peace, War) (DLH)

1814   **Washington Gladden.** *Congregational Pastor; Leader of Social Gospel Movement* (1836–1918). During the last half of the nineteenth century, the typical economic attitude was that poverty was the result of the inherent laziness and worthlessness of the poor. In other words, they deserved their plight. This attitude prevailed, even when the American landscape changed from rural to urban amidst the explosion of industrialization and capitalism.

Some Christians, however, realized that biblical social teachings were not simply a personal affair, but needed to be applied to the new problems of the city. This perspective, known now as the Social Gospel Movement, advocated that philanthropy was not enough. It dealt with symptoms but not the disease—the structures of society that allowed the rich to get richer by whatever unethical means they chose while the poor got poorer.

Washington Gladden, known as the Father of the Social Gospel Movement, was pastor of the First Congregational Church in Columbus, Ohio. He was concerned that many workers in his city were not attending church. In 1886, he sent them a questionnaire to ask why, and they responded that the rich church members, dressed in their fine clothes, did not want the poorer common folk in church. One worker doubted the sincerity of the employers' faith:

> We see them [the manufacturers] so full of religion on Sunday, and then grinding the faces of the poor the other six, we are apt to think they are insincere. . . . When the capitalist prays for us one day in the week, and preys on us the other six, it can't be expected that we will have much respect for his Christianity.[226]

Gladden and other social gospelers advocated fair wages, better working hours, safer working conditions, and respect for the laborers as persons rather than property. They decried the greed and graft of Christian businessmen. They asserted that the gospel must attack conscienceless corporations.

Redeemed persons must be about redeeming the society in whch they live. Since salvation redeems the whole person, it must impact the whole life, personal and social. (Matt 25:31-45; Jas. 2:14-17) (Business, Ethics, Social Gospel) (CDW)

1815 **William B. Johnson.** *First President of Southern Baptist Convention* (1782–1862). Baptists have often been exercised over the subject of "What do Baptists believe?" W. B. Johnson, elected the first president of the Southern Baptist Convention in 1845, is a good guide for what Baptists of the South believed in the middle of the nineteenth century. Johnson published a book the next year entitled *The Gospel Developed Through The Government and Order of The Churches of Jesus Christ*. Note carefully his emphasis:

> The denomination to which I have the honor to belong, holds the true fundamental principles of the gospel of Christ. These are, the sovereignty of God in the provision and application of the plan of salvation, the supreme authority of the scriptures, the right of each individual to judge for himself in his views of truth as taught in the

scriptures, the independent, democratical, Christocratic form of church government, the profession of religion by conscious subjects only, and the other principles of scripture truth growing out of these or intimately connected with them.

Now list what Johnson called "the true fundamental principle of the gospel." They look like this:

1. God's sovereignty in salvation.
2. The supreme authority of the scriptures.
3. The right of private interpretation of scriptures.
4. Congregational church government.
5. Believer's baptism.

Here are five principles for Baptists to hold to! (John 7:16; 2 Tim 4:3; Heb 13:9) (Baptist Distinctives) (WBS)

1816   Ann Hasseltine Judson. *Baptist Missionary to Burma* (1789–1826). "I have this day publically professed myself a disciple of Christ and covenanted with him at his sacred table."[227] Ann Hasseltine Judson understood the concept of God's covenant. Raised in a privileged family in Massachusetts, the daughter and granddaughter of Congregational ministers, Ann received a classical education and grew up attending church. At the age of sixteen, she made a profession of faith that she understood to be a covenant with God. That covenant guided her life to its early end as a Baptist missionary in Burma in 1826 at the age of thirty-six.[228]

Ann was a woman who kept promises, and she did not make them lightly. Her promise to love God came first, her promise to be wife to Adoniram Judson came next; her promise to work for the kingdom of God gave her a purpose with which to face overwhelming odds. Married less than six weeks, she and her husband set sail from Boston in 1812 as Congregational missionaries to India. Knowing they would encounter the Baptist William Carey, Ann and Adoniram studied the New Testament passages relating to baptism. Both concluded, after landing in India, that they could no longer accept the Congregationalist position, and they became Baptists.[229]

American Baptists began supporting them as they moved to Burma. Ann wrote about her commitment to the covenant she had made with God as a teenager:

> We have found by experience since we left our native land, that the Lord is indeed a covenant-keeping God, and takes care of those who confide in him. I have ever considered it a singular favour that God has given me an opportunity to spend my days in a heathen land. . . . If I may be instrumental of leading some infant female to lisp the praise of God, I shall rejoice in the sacrifice of country, reputation, and friends.[230]

Ann did lead Burmese women to become Christians. And she kept her covenant with God, as the Lord did with her. (Exod 19:4-6; Deut 29:10-15; Ps 25:8-15; John 15:16-17; Acts 1:1-8; 1 Cor 15:50-58) (Covenant, Evangelism, Faithfulness, God's Character, Missions) (RB)

1817   **Elijah Lovejoy.** *Presbyterian Minister, Abolitionist* (1802–1836). In 1835, exercising his right to speak and publish literature freely, Presbyterian minister Elijah Lovejoy defended and supported the "abolitionists for they rejected the view that black men and women were mere chattel." "The only master of human beings was Almighty God," declared Lovejoy, "and slavery usurped His prerogative 'as the rightful owner of all human beings.' "

Lovejoy proclaimed his beliefs and convictions fearlessly. He had printed many newsletters in support of the abolitionist movement and had four printing presses destroyed by angry mobs. Lovejoy grew weary of the constant persecution he received and grew tired of moving from place to place in hopes that he would find safety. After arriving in Alton, Illinois, he decided he was not moving again. "I have concluded . . . to remain at Alton, and here to insist on protection in the exercise of my rights. If the civil authorities refuse to protect me, I must look to God; and if I die, I have determined to make my grave in Alton." On 7 November 1837, Lovejoy was killed in an attack by an angry mob.

Elijah Lovejoy's dedication to defending the freedom of all human beings and the freedom of the press is inspiring. His faith in God helped him to persevere, continuing to print anti-slavery newspapers even though he and has wife were harassed every day and night. His love of God resulted in a love for all people. Over one hundred and fifty years ago it was certainly not popular to be a freedom fighter, but Lovejoy believed that the Bible declared that all persons were equal.

Edward Beecher, in his narrative of Lovejoy's martyrdom, commented: "I am sure that if good men would thus come near to God, they could not long remain divided from each other." These words are not unlike those penned by the apostle Paul, "There is neither Jew nor Greek, slave nor free, male nor female, for you are all one in Christ Jesus" (Gal 3:28).[231] (Gal 3:28; 2 Tim 4:5-7) (Equality, Freedom, Perseverance) (CKP)

1818 **Millennialism.** (19th cent.). "But of that day or that hour no one knows, not even the angels in heaven, nor the Son, but only the Father" (Mark 13:32). These were Jesus' words about the end of the age; nevertheless, many Christian peoples have been obsessed with eschatological charts, timetables, and predictions of Jesus' second coming. Many religious groups in America were formed out of these types of concerns.

In 1828, after an intense study of the book of Daniel, William Miller, a Baptist preacher, decided that Christ would return "about 1843." He kept his belief secret until he told some friends three years later. Then in 1836 Miller published a book, detailing his prediction. A financial panic in 1837 created a good climate for millennial fervor, and gradually Miller began to lecture all over the country. Finally, in January 1843, Miller said the return of Jesus would take place between 21 March 1843 and 21 March 1844. Excitement heightened for 50,000 convinced believers and a million more others who were skeptically expectant. The dates passed but Miller said that there had been a minor miscalculation and he set a new date of 22 October 1844. That day obviously passed, people were disappointed, and Miller was discredited.

But wait! "The Great Disappointment" remained a challenge to some. A remnant reorganized under the leadership of Ellen White. Given to visionary experiences, White said the promised advent of the Lord had been delayed because of the failure of Christians to observe the Sabbath. Consequently, the Seventh Day Adventists were born, worshiping on the Sabbath, following the Old Testament food laws, and anticipating the imminent return of Jesus.

Other nineteenth-century groups developed along similar lines. The United Society of Believers in Christ's Second Coming, better known as the Shakers, asserted that their leader Mother Anne Lee (1736–1784) was the manifestation of Christ's second coming. The Mormons' official title is the Church of Jesus Christ of the Latter-Day Saints. Joseph Smith, the founder, believed that he was restoring the true Christian Church in the new Promised Land, the Zion of America. And then there are the Jehovah Witnesses, who have made more predictions of the end-time that any other American religious group. Charles Taze Russell, the founder, was like William Miller in his attraction to biblical prophecies. In 1875 he spoke of the "secret presence of Christ" that had begun a year earlier. Later, he predicted that Jesus would return in 1914. Joseph Rutherford succeeded Russell in 1916 and popularized the phrase "millions now living will never die." In 1975, Jehovah Witnesses predicted a new date of 1977. A year later, about 30,000 apostasized from the movement.[232]

It seems we would do well to avoid predictions, charts, and timetables. Our obsession with the fulfillment of certain biblical prophecies could use an overhaul. Jesus was clear: no one knows the time for the end of the age. Whenever it comes, we are told to watch so we will be ready. No more and no less. (Matt 24:36; Mark 13:32-37; 1 Thess 4:13-18; 2 Thess 2:1-12) (Millennialism, Second Coming) (CDW)

1819A Dwight L. Moody. *American Evangelist* (1837–1899). Dwight L. Moody was the most famous American evangelist of the last half of the nineteenth century. Historian George Marsden calls Moody a "Horatio Alger figure—the honest and industrious boy from a

New England village who went to the city to find fame and fortune."[233] Moving to Boston at the age of seventeen in 1854, Moody was first attracted to evangelical interests through the work of the YMCA, an evangelistic organization for young men living in urban areas. Moody moved to Chicago and by 1860 had given up a promising shoe business to devote himself to full-time Christian work in the YMCA and other groups. Moody's YMCA work took him to England where he conducted some evangelistic services. The response was overwhelming and a national revival ensued.

Moody was a firm believer that every Christian should share the gospel with the unsaved. During his early Christian pilgrimage, he believed that witnessing was basically the responsibility of the ministers. God taught him otherwise, Moody declared, when a teacher in the Sunday school he had organized for poor and immigrant children came to him dying with an illness and distraught. The teacher was dejected because he had not led any of the girls in his class to be converted. Moody related that he had never heard anyone talk like that before. Moody suggested to the teacher that they go visit the class members. When they shared the gospel and the need for conversion with the girls, all of them were saved. From this experience, Moody said that he was "disqualifed for business; it had become distasteful to me. I had got a taste of another world, and cared no more for making money."[234] (Matt 28:19; Acts 1:8) (Evangelism, Materialism) (CDW)

1819B The wealthy Englishman Edward Studd lost a bet with a friend and had to attend a revival service in which Dwight L. Moody preached. Studd sat on the front row and his eyes never strayed from Moody. Studd returned to the revival meeting the next night and each successive night until he made a decision to follow Christ. Studd lived just two years after his conversion, but he was remembered at his funeral as one who did more for Christ in those two years than most do in twenty. Studd had turned his mansion into a meeting place for believers. He witnessed to friends and business associates. Everyone recognized that Studd's life had been changed. His coachman said of him, "All I can say is that though there's the same skin, there's a new man inside." Paul put it this way: "So if anyone is in Christ, there is a new creation: everything old has passed away; see, everything has become new!" (2 Cor 5:17).[235] (2 Cor 5:17; Eph 4:22-24; Col 3:5-17) (Conversion, New Creation) (JAW)

1819C D. L. Moody was known for his down-home style and simple theology. Moody told of a man who approached him and said, "Mr. Moody, now that I am converted do I have to give up the world?" Moody responded, "No, sir, you don't have to give up the world. If you give a good ringing testimony for the Son of God, the world will give you up pretty quick. They won't want you."[236] (Matt 5:14-16; Eph 4:1; 1 John 2:15; 3:1; 4:4-5) (Witnessing, Worldliness) (CDW)

1820 **Lottie Moon**. *Baptist Missionary to China* (1840–1912). Lottie Moon is the most famous of Southern Baptist missionaries. Southern Baptists have named their foreign mission Christmas offering after her, and her work in China is legendary. In 1885, after twelve years of mission work in China, Lottie traveled fifty miles inland to P'ingtu, becoming the first Southern Baptist woman to begin a new mission outpost in China.

In her early days in China, Lottie maintained distinctly Western style dress, believing that to wear Chinese clothes was to pretend to understand a culture that could never be fully assimilated. She considered the Chinese to be heathens, with a fascinating but distasteful culture. Their life-style, food, and sanitary habits led her to join others in labeling them the "Great Unwashed." With time, however, she became increasingly more Chinese in her own life-style and chastised those in China and America who persisted in calling the Chinese heathens. Non-Christian peoples were to be respected. Lottie believed that missionaries must wear the Chinese dress and live in Chinese houses, rejoicing in the footsteps of him who "though he was rich, yet for our sakes he became poor." The Chinese did not have to become Western to become Christian.

As Lottie grew old in China, she struggled with periods of depression. By 1912, she was given to deep melancholia, convinced that her people in P'ingtu were starving. Determined to die with them, she stopped eating. When the missionaries finally discovered her secret, it was too late. She died on a ship bound for America.

Lottie Moon teaches us about humility. She did not point to the "heathen" Chinese and say: "Lord, I thank you that I am not like those sinners." Rather, she identified with them and became one with them. Not only Christian mission methodology, but also Christian daily living should follow Lottie's imitation of Jesus. As Paul wrote, Jesus emptied himself, humbled himself, and became of no reputation so that we might know the love of God.[237] (Luke 18:9-14; 2 Cor 8:9; Phil 2:5-11) (Humility, Missions, Spiritual Poverty) (BJL)

1821A Walter Rauschenbusch. *Social Gospel Theologian* (1861–1918). Walter Rauschenbusch was a Baptist who learned his trade as a minister in New York's poverty-stricken Hell's Kitchen. He articulated a vision of the kingdom of God's transforming power that united both individual salvation and social justice. In times, when many testify to being Christians with their mouths but show little desire to change our world into a more just and peaceful place, Rauschenbusch's vision of the kingdom is a call to the Church to repent. He wrote: "The church must either condemn the world and seek to change it, or tolerate the world and conform to it."[238] (Luke 4:16-21; Rom 12:2) (Christian Lifestyle, Justice, Kingdom of God, Social Gospel) (WLA)

1821B Living ethically in the world, especially the world of business, has never been easy for Christians. Critics are being only partly facetious when they say "business ethics" is an oxymoron. In early Christian history, St. Jerome, translator of the Latin Vulgate Bible, said, "A merchant can seldom if ever please God." The great Augustine added, "Business is in itself evil."

Modern capitalistic society is obviously a different world from the Roman empire. Being Christian in the business sector has remained a concern for devout Christians. Walter

Rauschenbusch, the leading advocate of the social gospel in America at the turn of the century, reminds us of our ever present dilemma:

> But suppose a business man would be glad indeed to pay his young women the $12 a week that they need for a decent living, but all his competitors are paying from $7 down to $5 down. Shall he love himself into bankruptcy? In a time of industrial depression, shall he employ men he does not need?[239]

Our everyday world is about the business of profit, survival ,and competition. The temptations toward greed and unethical means to achieve ends are overwhelming. Isn't our call to serve God with our money by meeting the needs of others? One thing is clear: we cannot serve God and money, for no one can serve two masters. (Matt 6:24) (Business, Ethics, Materialism) (CDW)

1822 **Amanda Smith.** *African-American Holiness Evangelist* (1837–1915). Wherever He leads, I'll go. Wherever He leads? That promise may be rather risky! For Amanda Berry Smith following God's lead meant an incredible leap from slavery to world-wide fame. Amanda, one of thirteen children, was born a slave in 1837 in Maryland. Through hard work, her father eventually purchased the freedom of most of his family. Amanda had only a few months of formal education, but her parents taught her to read at home. As a young girl, she worked as a maid and washwoman.

Two marriages, five children, and the death of one husband and all five children made life very hard for Amanda Smith. She worked long hours as a washwoman and maid to provide even a bare existence for herself and her children before they died. By 1869, she was all alone again. Her reputation as an effective speaker spread beyond her community. Invitations to give her testimony soon became invitations to preach. Amanda preached in many churches in the New York-New Jersey area, although some African Episcopal pastors opposed her preaching. Before long, she was preaching to white camp meetings. By 1870, Amanda gave up domestic work for full-time evangelism. For eight years she was a very familiar figure in the pulpits of holiness churches from Knoxville, Tennessee, to Kennebunk, Maine.

Smith's successful ministry in the eastern United States led to invitations to minister in England and then India from 1878 to 1881. So effective was Smith that the Methodist Episcopal Bishop of India said that he learned more that was "of actual value to me as a preacher of Christian truth [from Amanda] . . . than from any other one person I had ever met." The next eight years were spent in Africa working with Methodist missionaries. Over a decade after she left the United States for a three month visit to England, Amanda returned having ministered in four nations. Back home, she tried to alleviate the suffering of black orphans, opening an orphan's home in 1899. Income from her preaching funded the orphan's home until she died in 1915.

From slavery to freedom, to marital misery, to a motherhood of tragedy, to years of hard labor, to giving testimonies, to preaching, to full-time evangelism, to international evangelist, to the head of an orphanage—one step at a time, God led Amanda Smith. "Wherever" can be risky. "Wherever" took Amanda Smith a long way from home.[240] (Matt 8:19-22; Acts 1:8; 2:17; 18:26) (Call, Missions, Women in Ministry) (CDB)

1823A Sojourner Truth. *African-American Abolitionist* (1797–1883). Slavery, Lerone Bennett says, was a black man who stepped out of his African hut and ended up ten months later in Georgia with bruises on his back and a brand on his chest. Slavery was belonging to a master—having no family and no name—sold anytime, anywhere. Slavery was the eleven year-old child Isabella sold at auction for $150 as her parents, freed by the master's last will and testament, watched helplessly. Slavery was Isabella herself, a generation later, watching as her own son, Peter, was sold and taken from her. A year later, unable to stand the bondage of slavery any longer, Isabella ran away only to be captured. In the days after her capture, she turned beyond herself and her world of despair to Jesus. When freedom came to all slaves in New York state in 1827, Isabella immediately went to court, sued the man who had taken her son, and regained custody of her boy with damages. She was learning that she, too, was a person of worth.

Isabella began to tell of her faith and her slavery, working with evangelical groups and street preachers in the Bowery of New York among the poor. One day in 1843, she felt the conviction that her old slave name was taken away and that God had given her the name of Sojourner Truth. Her life would be a pilgrimage for the Truth of God. Sojourner Truth traveled throughout the eastern states, singing to draw a crowd, telling the story of slavery and Jesus. She joined the northern abolitionist movement and her message spread. On one occasion, she was accosted by a man who demanded: "Old woman, do you think your talk about slavery does any good? Do you suppose people care what you say? Why, I don't care any more for your talk than I do for the bite of a flea." "Perhaps not," she replied, "but the Lord willing, I'll keep you scratching."[241]

Sojourner Truth shows us what one person can do, overcoming mountains of prejudice and hatred, scratching for truth, equality, and social justice wherever her Christian pilgrimage took her. (Gal 3:26-4:27) (Equality, Freedom, Justice, Truth) (BJL)

1823B Sojourner Truth, the African-American abolitionist, traveled widely to share her story of personal slavery and sustaining faith in Jesus. Sometimes clergymen challenged her right to speak to men. Women were to keep silent. At one rally, confronted by many males, she shouted:

> I could work as much and eat as much as any man and bear the lash as well, and aren't I a woman? I have borne children and seen them sold into slavery, and when I cried with a mother's grief, none but Jesus heard me. And aren't I a woman? Some say woman can't have as much rights as a man cause Christ wasn't a woman. Where did Christ come from? From God and a woman. Man had nothing to do with him. If the first woman God ever made was strong enough to turn the world upside down all alone, all women together ought to be able to turn it back and get it right side up again, and now that they are asking to do it, the men better let 'em.[242]

The crowd applauded. Shouldn't we? (Gen. 1:27; Judg 4:8; Acts 2:17; Gal 3:28) (Equality, Forbearance, Women's Rights) (BJL)

1823C In the 1960s, the civil rights movement had freedom rides and protest marches. Sojourner Truth, the African-American abolitionist of the antebellum North, knew the pain of discrimination that existed after freedom from slavery. Once on a segregated railroad car, she sat in the white section with a white woman companion. The conductor grabbed her and ordered her off. The white friend protested. "Does she belong to you?" the conductor demanded. "She belongs to humanity," Sojourner's friend replied. The conductor threw them both off the train. Sojourner Truth sued the railroad for assault and battery. The conductor was fired, and Sojourner said that before the trial was over northern railroad cars looked like "salt and pepper." Sojourner Truth left no injustice unchallenged. Freedom, justice, and truth must ever be the concerns of Christian pilgrims.[243] (Gal 3:28; Jas 2:1) (Justice, Race) (BJL)

1824A **Southern Religion.** (19th cent.). Culture has the power to re-shape Christian faith. The late nineteenth-century Southerner J. B. Stinson composed new "Lost Cause" lyrics to the melody of the popular hymn, "When the Roll Is Called Up Yonder":

> On the mistless, lonely morning when the saved of Christ shall rise, / In the Father's many-mansioned home to share: / Where our Lee and Jackson call us to their homes beyond the skies, / When the roll is called up yonder, let's be there.[244]

(Josh 24:14-15; Rom 12:1-2) (Conformity, Culture) (AMM)

1824B Evidence for being "convicted" of Christian faith comes in unusual ways. On the southern frontier a preacher once encountered a woman in a remote backwoods cabin. Seeking to win her to the faith, he asked her if she had any religious convictions. She replied, "Naw. Not my ole man neither. He was tried for hog stealin' once, but he warn't convicted." A key question, however, might be whether her or our lifestyles provide evidence enough to convict us of Christian faith. (Matt 5:13-16;

Rom 12:1-2; Jas 2:14-17) (Christian Lifestyle, Convictions) (AMM)

1824C In the history of Christianity, one is struck by the irony of causes to which the churches will commit themselves. The people ostensibly committed to a gospel of peace and reconciliation have too often actively supported contradictory values. One of the first commanders of the Confederate Army was Louisiana Catholic layperson, General Pierre G. T. Beauregard. Catholics and Protestants alike enthusiastically responded to Beauregard's appeal for their congregations to contribute their church bells for recycling into ammunitions for the war effort. How often is the church guilty of using that which is designed to call persons into the healing and reconciling love of God for the diametrically opposing purpose of dividing, killing, and conquering. (Isa 2:4; Matt 5:9) (Peace, Reconciliation, War) (AMM)

1825A Charles Haddon Spurgeon. *English Baptist Evangelist* (1834-1892). Charles Haddon Spurgeon, one of the most famous Baptist pulpiteers, began his ministry as a seventeen year-old preacher in 1851. In two and a half years, the membership of his first church grew from forty to one hundred. At age nineteen, he assumed the pastorate of New Park Street Chapel, formerly one of London's leading churches. His first sermon was to eighty people in the church's 1,200-seat auditorium. His ministry was an immediate success. Within months, the auditorium was too small, and the church had to rent London's 10,000-seat auditorium. By 1861, New Park had built Metropolitan Tabernacle. For thirty-one years, attendance averaged 5,000 morning and evening.

Spurgeon's preaching focused on the cross and resurrection. The gospel was in its essence a converting force, and the desire for people to accept God's love through faith in Christ was the passion of his life. Spurgeon believed in the power of the preached Word. Reflecting on his conversion, he said, "The revealed Word awakened me, but it was the preached Word that saved me; and I must ever attach peculiar value to the hearing of the truth, for by it I received the joy and peace in which my soul delights."[245] (Rom 10:14–15; Phlm 18) (Preaching) (CDW)

1825B Basically a Calvinist in theology, Charles Spurgeon often said, "I fear I am not a very good Calvinist because I pray that the Lord will save all of the elect and then elect some more." Commenting on Romans 9 and 10, Spurgeon said Paul's use of "whosoever" in 10:13 sounded like the free will of John Wesley. But the Apostle talked like John Calvin in 9:11 with his emphasis on election. Spurgeon concluded, "The fact is that the whole system of truth is neither here nor there. Be it ours to know what is scriptural in all systems, and accept it."[246] Good advise for all Christians tied to a system of theology rather than to the Word of God! (Rom 9:11; 10:13) (Bible, Election, Free Will, Salvation) (CDW)

1825C C. H. Spurgeon was primarily an evangelist. Yet, his evangelistic ministry was not narrow-minded. The gospel message was to the whole person. Spurgeon was regarded as a political liberal and social activist. He supported striking workers of a young English labor movement. He began orphanages for abandoned children and homes for the elderly and the poor. He worked to give education to those who could not afford the private school education that the rich received. The Englishman was not afraid to confront slavery, the sin of American society:

> They call it a "peculiar institution," until they forget in what peculiarity it consists. It is, indeed, a peculiar institution, just as the Devil is a peculiar angel, and hell is a peculiarly hot place.

Americans who published Spurgeon's sermons began editing out his remarks about slavery so sermon sales would not suffer. Spurgeon has been called a prophet for boldly preaching the whole gospel.[247] Will we be so bold in our preaching or will we fear the loss of sermon sales? (Luke 4:16-20; Phlm 16; 2 Tim 1:8) (Preaching, Race, Slavery, Social Gospel) (CDW)

1825D One's youth is admired and often desired by those who are older. The thoughts of teenage years bring back memories of care-free days and childish pranks; of days when one could not wait until tomorrow, but tomorrow never seemed to come; when one's immaturity explained one's actions and excused one from harsh punishment.

In those years of growing up, one's wisdom is seldom accepted. The Apostle Paul wrote to Timothy, a young preacher boy who was mature beyond his age, delivering to him a word of encouragement and challenge: "Let no one look down on your youthfulness, but rather in speech, conduct, love, faith and purity, show yourself an example of those who believe" (1 Tim 4:12).

When Charles Spurgeon, the mighty English preacher of the nineteenth century, first went to Cambridge, he joined St. Andrews Baptist Church. There he became active in Sunday School and a member of the Lay Preachers Association. One Saturday, Spurgeon and an older man were assigned to be in charge of the Sunday evening services at Taversham, a small village just four miles from school. As they walked along the country road, Spurgeon wished his friend God's blessing on his service. Dumbfounded, the older man remarked that he had never preached before nor did he have the ability to preach. He asked Spurgeon to speak, suggesting that one of the youngster's Sunday School talks would work. Spurgeon reflected to himself, "Surely I can tell a few poor cottagers of the sweetness and love of Jesus, since I feel them in my own soul." At the conclusion of Spurgeon's message, an elderly woman commented to him, "Bless your dear heart, how old are you?" Spurgeon replied, "I am under sixty." "Yes, and under sixteen," said the old lady. "Never mind my age," replied the boy preacher, "think of Jesus and His preciousness."[248]

Paul's words to Timothy were also for Spurgeon, and they are also for us today. But one must be mindful that with maturity comes responsibility. To gain the respect of a congregation or one's peers, one must be faithful in his actions. (1 Tim 4:12) (Christian Maturity, Wisdom, Youth) (GJC)

1825E After one of C. H. Spurgeon's sermons, an admirer gushed, "Oh, Mr. Spurgeon, that was wonderful!" Spurgeon responded, "Yes, madam—so the devil whispered into my ear as I came down the steps of the pulpit."[249] (1 Cor 2:1-5; 2 Cor 10:17-18; Gal 6:14; Phil 3:3-5; 1 Pet 5:5-6) (Boasting, Humility, Pride) (JAW)

1826A Elizabeth Cady Stanton. *Human Rights Activist, Feminist* (1815–1902). Elizabeth Cady Stanton, an activist for women's suffrage, was rebuked by a married clergyman for speaking in public at a woman's rights convention in Rochester. "The apostle Paul enjoined silence upon women," he declared. "Why don't you mind him? Stanton countered, "The apostle Paul also enjoined celibacy upon the clergy. Why don't *you* mind him?"[250] (1 Cor 14:33-36; Gal 3:28; 1 Tim 2:12) (Bible, Equality, Women in Ministry) (JAW)

1826B Elizabeth Cady Stanton was a leader of the human rights crusades in the late nineteenth century. She was an abolitionist and worked with Lucretia Coffin Mott and Susan Anthony for human rights. Stanton was a precursor to the twentieth-century feminist readings of the Bible. In 1895, she published the *Woman's Bible*, a series of biblical interpretations from a feminist point of view. When many, women and men, criticized her project, she held to her convictions and responded: "Come, come, my conservative friend, wipe the dew off your spectacles and see that the world is moving."[251]

Interpreting the scriptures is a delicate matter for all serious students of the Bible. Can we wipe the dew off our spectacles and hear what people different from us are saying? As the world moves on, can we dialogue and cooperate, yet still have convictions? Will the left, middle, and right, all ultimately be judged to have been intolerant and possessed by a lack of charity? Is unity in Christ possible amidst our diversity? (1 Cor 13:1-3; Eph 2:11-22; 4:1-6) (Convictions, Diversity, Unity, Tolerance) (CDW)

1827 Calvin Stowe. *Biblical Scholar; Husband of Harriet Beecher Stowe* (19th cent.). Most everybody has heard of Harriet Beecher Stowe, the author of the famous novel, *Uncle Tom's Cabin*, that took the world by storm with its denunciation of slavery in antebellum America. Not very many people know anything about Calvin Stowe, her husband. Calvin Stowe was a professor of biblical studies, having married Harriet while teaching at Lane College of Ohio. Within a year of the publication of her groundbreaking work, Harriet was invited to tour England. Calvin accompanied her. During the trip, he said he was "inexpressibly blue." According to Calvin, he was not jealous of his wife's fame and the constant demands on her time. Whatever the case, he was amazed that everyone from the Archbishop of Canterbury to Charles Dickens was anxious to greet Harriet. Calvin was more disgusted, moreover, with the kind of reaction that the British were making toward Harriet's book. It seemed to him that they loved the book primarily because it was extremely critical of something immoral being perpetuated in American society that was no longer a problem in England—slavery.

During an observance of Anti-Slavery Day, Calvin was given the opportunity to preach before a crowd of 4,000 people. In the words of many a sermon audience, Calvin quit preachin' and got to meddlin'. He told his listeners that they were proud that England had ceased the practice of slavery. Great. They were hypocrites, however, for participating in business ventures for cotton grown and picked by slaves in the southern states of America. Stowe reminded his listeners that four-fifths of southern cotton was sold to England. If the British would refuse to buy from slaveowners, slavery in America would die. Calvin bluntly asked, "Are you willing to sacrifice one penny of your profits to do away with slavery?"[252]

The crowd booed Calvin. He was an ungrateful guest. Perhaps he was just a jealous insecure husband. Wasn't he supposed to practice a religion of civility? Who was he to suggest that their business dealings was an ethical issue? (Matt 6:24; 1 Tim 6:19; Jas 1:22) (Business, Ethics, Slavery) (CDW)

1828A Billy Sunday. *Protestant Revivalist* (1862–1935). "Train up a child in the way he should go and when he is old he will not depart from it" (Prov. 22:6). I remember as a youth the training that I received from my parents. They were very concerned that I read about other Christians and their experiences. One of those

Christians became a hero to me as a youth: William Ashley Sunday, better known as the great evangelist Billy Sunday.

Billy Sunday was born into a Christian home. His father was a kind Christian gentleman, but he died of pneumonia when Billy was very young. Billy's mother tried hard to raise her boys, but due to the poverty that followed the death of their father, she had to send them to the Soldiers' Orphans' Home in Ames, Iowa. Billy was only six years-old when he left his mother, but those six early years left an impression upon his life. Sunday's parents were not always there, but it is interesting to note that he remembered their faith.

Baseball was in Billy's blood, and as a young man he signed on with the Chicago Whitestockings. On Sunday afternoons, Billy often went out with some of the other players and got drunk. Once, while in a bar, he heard from across the street sounds of a hymn that he once heard in Sunday school as a young boy. At a friend's urging, he went to the Pacific Garden Mission where he heard and accepted the gospel message.

A new Billy Sunday emerged. He later left baseball to become an evangelist. Billy and wife Nell often left their four children at home with a housekeeper while they were on the road in evangelistic meetings. Billy was a colorful evangelist who was able to attract large crowds. Millions of people heard the message of this evangelist who preached against the evils of that day and the need to be reconciled with God. Some have estimated that he led hundreds of thousands to the Lord.

Was Billy Sunday successful? He will always be one of my heroes, but he was also a man of failure. He was very much like the priest Eli in the book of 1 Samuel. Eli, no doubt, loved God very much, but his sons were a shame to him. Billy Sunday won many to Jesus, but he neglected to win his own children. Only one of his cchildren professed Christ, his daughter Helen. His boys, Paul, George, and Billy, Jr., died tragic deaths all before their fortieth birthdays. One can feel the guilt and pain that Sunday suffered over his children when he reminisced with his wife:

> It's funny; in the last twenty years I guess I've spoken to more than
> 85 million people, and had the joy of seeing hundreds of thousands

come to Christ. . . . Yet my own children, the people closest to me, have found no peace and happiness anywhere. Is it my fault Nell?

Billy's wife Nell later advised Ruth Graham that she should stay home and take care of the children while Billy Graham was on the road. Billy and Ruth Graham took their advice. Many of us would do well to take the biblical advice of training our children in righteousness. We can't leave it to the Sunday school or other church ministries. As Deuteronomy 6:7 reminds us, we are to teach the ways of God diligently to our children.[253] (Deut 6:7; 1 Sam 2:12-36; Prov 22:6; 2 Tim 1:5) (Christian Education, Evangelism, Parenthood) (ARN)

1828B Billy Sunday's popularity as the preeminent American evangelist was at its peak during the years of World War I. While he is known for his Vaudeville-type antics on the pulpit stage, Sunday also "competed with George M. Cohen and Teddy Roosevelt for the position of most extravagant patriot" in America. Although largely uninterested in the war before the United States became involved, in 1917 he declared that "Christianity and Patriotism are synonymous terms and hell and traitors are synonymous." His sermons took on a strong patriotic coloring, often ending with a jumping Sunday waving a flag and shouting, "If you turn hell upside down, you will find 'Made in Germany' stamped on the bottom."[254]

Billy Sunday fell prey to identifying loyalty to God with patriotism, a temptation easily succumbed to by many Christians, especially during periods of war and heightened patriotic feelings. Having pride in one's country is laudable, but equating God and country is not. Jesus said we should give to Caesar what is Caesar's, but he added that we must give to God what is reserved for God alone. Confusing the Bible with the flag can justify unholy war in the name of God. Civil religion can persecute dissenters and propagate political agendas in the name of God. God alone is Lord of the conscience. (Mark 12:17; Rom 13:1-7) (Civil Religion, Church and State, Independence Day) (CDW)

1828C Billy Sunday once encountered a man who was obviously drunk. The man expressed delight at seeing Sunday and said that he was one of Sunday's converts. To that, Sunday replied that the man must have been, for he certainly wasn't one of God's. (John 3:3; 2 Cor 5:17; Eph 2:8-10; 4:22-24; 1 Pet 4:3-7) (Conversion, Drunkenness) (JAW)

1829 **Emily Tubman**. *Antebellum Southern Human Rights Advocate* (1794–1885). Emily Tubman was a wealthy widow in Georgia in the 1840s. Quite some time before the Civil War, this southern lady petitioned the Georgia legislature for permission to free her slaves. In 1844, she gathered her slaves, giving each the choice of remaining with her or being free. Sixty-nine chose to be free men and women. They asked Mrs. Tubman to send them to Liberia. She responded by chartering a ship to take them to Cape Palmas, Liberia. To assist them after their arrival, she made a generous contribution to a fund providing housing and supplies for newly arrived blacks from America. (In 1943, the Republic of Liberia elected its eighteenth president, William Vaccanarat Shadrach Tubman, the grandson of two of Emily Tubman's former slaves.)

Seventy-five of Emily Tubman's slaves chose to remain in the United States. Mrs. Tubman wisely understood that freedom was not enough. The freed slaves also needed assistance during the transition from slavery to freedom. Emily Tubman gave them land and clothes and provided for them regularly until they were able to take care of themselves.

In the First Christian Church of Augusta, Georgia, tribute is paid to Emily Tubman on a marble tablet. The inscription reads: "If you seek her monument, look around."[255] (Luke 4:16-21; Phlm 15) (Compassion, Justice, Love, Oppression, Slavery) (CDB)

1830 **Mary Webb**. *Baptist Missionary of New England* (1779–1861). Mary Webb dismantled barrier after barrier in answering God's call in her life. Confined to a wheelchair and physically weakened by illness at the age of five, Mary Webb became a Christian when nine-years-old. She put off baptism until she was nineteen, because she felt she could undergo the physical awkwardness more easily as an adult than a child.[256]

Her pastor, Thomas Baldwin, believed strongly in the missionary work of William Carey and urged his church to support the missionary's Indian labors. Perhaps Mary caught the missionary fire from Baldwin. Whoever prompted her, God placed within her a burning desire to do something substantive for missions. Incapable of moving freely, Mary still managed to organize an ecumenical group of women into the first woman's missionary society in the world—the Boston Female Society for Missionary Purposes—in 1800.[257] At the age of twenty-one, Mary moved outside herself and into the world through the efforts of the women with whom she labored for God.

For fifty years, Mary Webb served as secretary/treasurer of the society. During those years, she encouraged the members to go beyond themselves in their efforts to raise money for missions. Her love of God overcame the physical restrictions of her body. Known for her "spunk" and lively wit, Mary Webb worked from where she was; she gave what she had. God multiplied that gift richly. By 1817, Mary corresponded with more than two hundred other women's missionary societies around the country.[258] With appropriate humility, Mary Webb wrote in 1812,

> It affords us much pleasure, to hear from time to time of the constitution of Female Societies in various parts of the United States, for the purpose of prayer and of aiding Missionary exertions. And the Lord, we trust, has condescended to use these Institutions as a means of extending the triumphs of the cross.[259]

(Exod 4:10-12; 2 Sam 9:1-7; Ps 23; Matt 28:18-20; Phil 4:13; Jas 2:14-17) (Commitment, Discipleship, Ecumenism, Handicaps, Humility, Missions, Overcoming Barriers) (RB)

1831   **Lucinda Williams**. (19th cent.). When Lucinda Williams moved to Dallas, Texas, from Missouri, she wanted to find a Baptist church. She asked her landlady for directions, but was surprised to find that there was no Baptist church in town. When the landlady remarked that she hoped there never would be one,

Williams said with quiet determination, "I am very sorry, Mrs. Moore, to hear you say that. I am a Baptist, and if I am to live here, I want a Baptist church here."

On 20 July 1868, Lucinda Williams, her husband, seven other women, and two other men organized a Baptist church. Three previous efforts to start a Baptist church in Dallas had failed, but this church survived because of the commitment of Lucinda Williams and her husband. The primary effort for forming the church had been Lucinda's. She also helped start its first Sunday School and led its initial woman's missionary society. In the early years, the church had no building, and its survival was in doubt. Lucinda, however, energized the women of the church to raise funds to construct their own facility. In 1873, the women raised over $600 toward the building. The money was enough to begin the project, and the women's efforts convinced the men that the women were serious about the church's survival.

Commitment, vision, and action went hand in hand for Lucinda Williams. She refused to be denied a Baptist church in which to worship. Her example embodies the breadth and character of women's ministries in the total life of the church. Her church? The First Baptist Church of Dallas, Texas.[260] (Prov 29:18; Luke 8:18; 9:57-62) (Determination, Vision, Women in Ministry) (CDW)

1832   **Brigham Young.** *Mormon Leader* (1801–1877). People are often afraid to learn from different religious groups, especially when those groups have doctrines that are deviant from traditional orthodoxy. Nevertheless, such groups, amidst their theological differences, often excel in emphasizing certain aspects of the faith that orthodox groups sometimes neglect. One example is the Mormon belief in the sanctity of work. Brigham Young, the successor to Mormon founder Joseph Smith, was committed to the importance of human labor. Outside the back door of the Brigham Young house in Salt Lake City today stands a large pile of sand. When a beggar came to the door requesting food (a common practice in Young's day), the Mormon leader always invited the stranger to have dinner. While they were waiting for the food to be prepared, Young asked the visitor to move the pile of sand down to the barn. The next time a beggar visited, Young would ask him to move the pile of sand near the barn up next to the house. Thus, the sand pile went from house to barn to house to barn. The beggars learned self-esteem as they sat down for a rewarding dinner, and Young enjoyed his commitment to the value of work.[261] (Gen 1:31; 3:17-19; John 5:10-20) (Work) (CDW)

Twentieth Century

1901A　Theodore Adams. *Southern Baptist Minister* (1898–1980). Jesus talked a lot about faith and trust. He even indicated that when times are the hardest, there is a resiliency that comes to God's people that sustains them in the gathering storms. During his tenure at First Baptist Church in Richmond, Virginia, Dr. Theodore Adams observed that God's people, undergirded by his grace, possessed tremendous coping ability. In his book, *Making the Most of What Life Brings*, Adams wrote:

> When changes in your outer circumstances cannot be altered, then you must make inner adjustments. In one tragic hour a woman of strong Christian convictions lost her loved ones, her home, and her money. Others who lacked her faith might have cursed God and longed for death. But she continued to live with a serene and calm confidence. "How did she do it?" she was asked? Her glowing reply was, "The chaos is around me, not within me."[262]

(Matt 6:34) (Anxiety, Peace, Serenity) (DMW)

1901B　Theodore F. Adams, the long-time pastor of the First Baptist Church, Richmond, Virginia, often preached about the struggles that are present in the Christian journey. Adams believed that in all circumstances, God encourages his creation to continue to struggle with the life of faith, for in their struggles they are never alone. Adams wrote:

> As you resolve to meet his challenge and to measure up to his standards, you are encouraged to know that he is your constant companion along the way. What you lack he will supply, if you

submit to him your life, both what you are and what yet you can be. He transforms your inertia into effort, your failure into achievement, your worst into your best.[263]

God's grace is always sufficient for the journey. The challenges are real but Hih presence is our accompanying strength. (2 Cor 12:9) (Grace, Providence, Strength) (DMW)

1901C In the midst of suffering, one of the most difficult challenges is the challenge of trust. We ask, "what good is coming out of this pain?" The answer, say Theodore Adams, is found in looking at life with an eternal perspective. He said:

> Life may baffle and confuse you. In bewilderment you may ask: "Why in the world do some of these things happen? Why do the good so often suffer and the evil seem to prosper?" But if you see life in terms of eternity, you realize that the crisis of the moment is only a very small part of life as God sees it. . . . God will one day balance the scales of life. If you trust God for all eternity, those things which now are unrequited will one day be cared for. Sin will be punished. Virtue will be rewarded.[264]

With kingdom hope, we must in faith believe that "God causes all things to work together for good to those who love God." (Rom 8:28) (Providence, Suffering, Trust) (DMW)

1902 **Baptists and Adolf Hitler**. (1934). Genuine Christianity takes us beyond individualistic personal piety and single-issue politics. Some Christians at the 1934 Baptist World Alliance in Berlin actually praised Adolf Hitler, stating: "Chancellor Adolf Hitler gives to the temperance movement the prestige of his personal example since he neither uses intoxicants nor smokes." Charles F. Leek, a delegate to the Alliance from Alabama figured that since Hitler was anti-communist he deserved support, writing:

> Our observation is, that while Hitlerism is doubtless not the ultimate end, for Germany directly or Europe indirectly, it is for Germany a safe step in the right direction. Nazism has at least been a bar to the universal boast of Bolshevism.[265]

True Christianity requires learning to discern the difference between the eternally significant and the presently popular in religious values, to be personally pure without neglecting the weightier matters of justice, mercy, and faith. (Matt 23:23) (Civil Religion, Hypocrisy, Piety, Social Gospel, Spirituality) (WLA)

1903A Karl Barth. *Swiss Theologian* (1886–1968). One of Karl Barth's former students visited the famous theologian and proudly reported how large crowds were coming to hear him preach. Barth is said to have responded, "Then you must not be preaching the gospel!"[266]

Effective ministry is not always counted quantitatively. The crowds left Jesus when he said they must eat the bread of life. The Rich Young Ruler did not follow Jesus because the discipleship was too costly. How do we define successful ministry? Do we preach the gospel? (Mark 10:17-22; John 6:66) (Discipleship, Ministry) (CDW)

1903B During his only visit to the United States, the eminent Swiss theologian Karl Barth lectured at Union Seminary in Richmond, Virginia. After his formal address, he engaged in some informal conversation with the students. One young man asked Barth if he could state the core of what he believed. Barth took a moment to light his pipe, and then, as the smoke drifted away, he replied, "Yes, I think I can summarize my theology in these words: 'Jesus loves me, this I know, for the Bible tells me so.' "[267] (John 3:16; Rom 5:8; 1 John 4:9) (God's Love) (JAW)

1904A Dietrich Bonhöffer. *German Theologian* (1906–1945). Dietrich Bonhöffer was imprisoned in various concentration camps in Germany during WWII because of his opposition to Nazism. Eyewitnesses to Bonhöffer's death at the Flossenburg concentration camp recalled a remarkable ending to a remarkable man's life.

On Sunday 8 April 1945, Bonhöffer held a service of worship for the prisoners and preached on the text, "with his stripes we are healed" (Isa 53:5). One prisoner later reflected, "He found just the right words to express the spirit of our imprisonment, the thoughts and the resolution it had brought us." When Bonhöffer's concluding prayer was barely finished, two civilians entered the room and said "Prisoner Bonhöffer,ome with us." The prisoners knew the language—Bonhöffer was headed for the gallows. As the prisoners exchanged farewells with their friend, Bonhöffer asked Payne Best, an English officer, to send special greetings to the bishop of Chichester, if he ever achieved freedom. Regarding his imminent death at the hands of the Nazis, Bonhöffer told Best: This is the end—but for me, it is the beginning of life."

On 9 April 1945, Bonhöffer was executed. The camp doctor saw Bonhöffer, before taking off his prison garb, kneeling on the floor praying fervently to God. At the place of execution, Bonhöffer again said a short prayer and climbed the step to the gallows brave and composed. The camp doctor reflected that in his fifty years as a doctor he had hardly ever seen a man die so serenely.[268]

In Bonhöffer's life, death was faced with bravery and confidence. Perhaps you and I could not do it so well. But it is hopeful to know that he could. (Isa 53:5; John 14:1-7; Rom 6:5-11; 2 Cor 5:1; Phil 1:21; 2 Tim 2:8-13; 4:6-8; Heb 3:6; 6:11) (Bravery, Courage, Death, Hope) (PSA)

1904B While Bonhöffer was a prisoner, his guards took a liking to him. They thought he was a man of unusual strength, composure, and bravery. He thought about this, and he realized there was a difference between what they thought about him and what he felt about himself. He wasn't so sure, though, at the end, he seemed to be. As he struggled with what we now speak of as his identity, he offered this prayer, "Whoever I am, I am thine. Amen." (Mark 14:36; Phil 1:21) (Bravery, Christian Identity) (PSA)

1904C Dietrich Bonhöffer spent Christmas in 1943 in a Nazi prison camp, but he wrote to his parents that he would not let his loneliness get him down. Rather, he thanked his parents for the wonderful memories they gave him of past Christmases and assured them that those memories made the pain of separation more bearable.

Parents do well to remember that the memories they create can either bless or curse the lives of their children, depending on the kind they are.[269] (Luke 22:19; Phil 1:3; 2 Tim 1:5) (Christmas, Gratitude, Memories) (EEJ)

1904D While in prison, Dietrich Bonhöffer wrote a wedding sermon in which he exhorted the couple with these words, "Live together in the forgiveness of your sins, for without it no human fellowship, least of all a marriage, can survive. Don't insist on your own rights, don't blame each other, don't condemn each other, don't find fault with each other, but take one another as you are, and forgive each other everyday from the bottom of your hearts." It is still good advice.[270] (Matt 6:1-15; 18:21-35; 1 Cor 13) (Forgiveness, Love, Marriage) (EEJ)

1904E In his book *Life Together*, Dietrich Bonhöffer wrote, "Let him who cannot be alone beware of community," and "Let him who is not in community beware of being alone." He also suggested that many seek fellowship because they are afraid of loneliness, but they are often disappointed, because they are not really seeking fellowship but simply desire to escape from their loneliness. Those who really learn the joy of fellowship for its own sake can handle loneliness better. Similarly, those who learn to deal with solitude creatively are better prepared to have fellowship with others.[271] (Jer 15:17; Ezek 20:1-8) (Community, Loneliness, Solitude) (EEJ)

1904F In his book, *Life Together*, Dietrich Bonhöffer reminds pastors that God did not give them the church in order that they might "become its accuser before God and man." He also reminds us that we must first accept the Christian community as God's gift. For if a pastor begins judging the church to be the ideal picture he has, and "acts as if he is the creator of the Christian community," he is inviting disaster. When he does not get his way, he often will call it a failure. Thus when his ideal picture is destroyed, "he becomes, first an accuser of his brethren, and an accuser of God, and finally the despairing accuser of himself."[272] (John 15:17; Acts 20:28; Eph 4:4-16) (Church, Ministry) (EEJ)

1904G Dietrich Bonhöffer was once asked why he meditated. His reply? "Because I'm a Christian." (Gen 24:63; Ps 1:2; 63:6; 119:148; Matt 14:13) (Meditation) (CDW)[273]

1905 **Corrie ten Boom.** *Holocaust Survivor* (1892–1983). Corrie ten Boom lived a life unknown to the world until the outbreak of World War II when her family home became "the Hiding Place" for Jews who were attempting to escape Nazi terror. As a result, she spent time in a concentration camp and lost her father and sister to the cruelties of the Nazi regime.[274]

After the Netherlands had been liberated in 1945, Corrie was told the name of the man who turned her family over to the Gestapo. This letter shares the message of God's love and the true meaning of forgiveness. The first portion reads:

> Dear Sir:
> Today I heard that most probably you were the one who betrayed me. I went through ten months of concentration camp. My father died after ten days, my sister after ten months of imprisonment.
> What you meant to be harmful, God used for my good. I have become closer to Him. A severe punishment is awaiting you. I have prayed for you that the Lord will accept you if you will turn to Him. Think about the fact that the Lord Jesus also carried your sins on the cross. If you accept that and will be His child, you will be saved forever.
> I have forgiven you everything; God will forgive you everything also, if you ask Him. He loves you, and He Himself, has sent His son to earth to forgive you your sins, that is, to bear the punishment for you and me. From your side an answer must be given. When He says: "Come to me, give your heart," then your answer must be: "Yes, Lord, I will. Make me your child."[275]

(Matt 6:14-15) (Forgiveness, Salvation) (DML)

1906 **William Marrion Branham.** *Pentecostal Faith Healer* (1909–1965). Divine healing revivalism has been on the American religious landscape for over 100 years. The contemporary emphasis on faith healing, however, dates back to a revival that erupted in 1946 in the ministry of William Marrion Branham, a "Holy Ghost Baptist preacher" from Jeffersonville, Indiana. Branham was extremely popular in the Pentecostal subculture, attracting large crowds in America and Europe while reporting thousands of healings. The revival declined temporarily in the late 1950s and Branham's ministry struggled. He turned to preaching new revelations and claimed to be the "end-time" prophet that would forerun the second coming of Jesus, just as the prophet John the Baptist had done for the first coming. Branham's sermons focused on his prophetic identity and the exact time of the second coming. Branham was hesitant to pick a date, but he strongly implied that Jesus would return for the Bride of Christ in 1977. In one of his books, Branham acknowledged that Jesus said no one knew the day or hour of the end-time. Jesus did not say, however, that we could not receive a revelation from God about the year. Branham died in 1965 but his followers still exist across the world. They consider him to be the end-time prophet and his sermons have become the Word of God for this age. His followers believe that they are the special Bride of Christ, possessing knowledge of the end-time that other Christians don't have.

People who grant excessive authority to a preacher usually follow him no matter what he says. Often the followers' devotion is so slavish that they encourage the leader to magnify his own person. It's time Christian people quit feeling important because of their association with a "famous" person. Our identity is to be found in Jesus Christ.

Leaders with excessive authority often make outlandish predictions or claim some inspired interpretation about the events surrounding the second coming of Jesus. Curiosity kills the cat and brutalizes the reading of scripture. Jesus was quite clear: "But of that day and hour no one knows, not even the angels of heaven, nor the Son, but the Father only."[276] (Matt 24:36; Mark 10:42-45; 13:32-37; 1 Thess 4:13-18; 2 Thess 2:1-12; 1 Pet 5:2-3) (Pastoral Authority, Millennialism, Second Coming) (CDW)

1907A Harry Emerson Fosdick. *Protestant Preacher, Modernist Leader* (1878–1969). One of the most powerful preachers in early twentieth century America was Harry Emerson Fosdick. While his notoriety came through his distinguished pulpit ministry at New York's Riverside Church, there was another formative experience that shaped his preaching. During his time as a student at Union Theological Seminary in New York, young Fosdick suffered an emotional collapse and spent four months in a sanitarium.

Years later, Fosdick reflected on this painful episode in his life. He wrote:

> In that experience I learned some things about religion that theological seminaries do not teach. I learned to pray, not because I had adequately argued at prayer's rationality but because I desperately needed help from a Power greater than my own. I learned that God, much more than a theological proposition, is an immediately available Resource.[277]

Indeed, what Fosdick was saying had been written by the Psalmist many centuries prior: "My help comes from the Lord." (Ps 121:2) (Prayer, Providence) (DMW)

1907B One winter evening, Harry Emerson Fosdick was awakened by a banging on his door. It was an inebriated young student who wanted Fosdick to explain to him the difference between modernism and fundamentalism. Fosdick advised the student, "Go home and sober up, and come back when you have slept it off, and I will gladly give you the answer." The young man broke into a sob: "The trouble is, doctor, when I'm sober, I won't give a damn!"[278] (Ps 133; John 17:20-26; Eph 2:11-22) (Unity) (JAW)

1907C During World War I, Harry Emerson Fosdick served as a chaplain to the troops in France. He initially supported the war effort and thought that modern war would make the world safe for democracy. He soon doubted the validity of the war and became an ardent pacifist. He maintained this stance during World War II.

At the Riverside Church of New York, 12 November 1933, Fosdick preached a pacifistic sermon for Armistice Day entitled the "Unknown Soldier." He told his hearers that he had to settle an account with the Unknown Soldier of war. Fosdick wondered whether he had ever met the soldier during his chaplaincy. Regardless, Fosdick was sure that everyone could imagine some of the soldier's basic characteristics. He had to be a boy sound of mind and body, a specimen of strength. The ancient gods required that the sacrificial animals were the best, without blemish. Fosdick commented that the "god of war" required the same unblemished soldiers for its bloody sacrifices. "Of all insane and suicidal procedures can you imagine anything madder than this," Fosdick added, "that all the nations should pick out their best, use their scientific skill to make certain that they are the best, and then in one mighty holocaust offer ten million of them on the battlefields of one war?"

The reasons for disliking war were endless, Fosdick believed. Look what it has us do to our enemies. We bomb mothers and starve children. We slaughter men and use science to make a hell on earth. Hatred is bred and lies are propagated.[279] Shall we say more? (Matt 5:9, 38-48; 26:52; Rom 12:16-21) (Peace, War) (CDW)

1908   **Billy Graham**. *Protestant Evangelist* (b.1918). We all need someone to help us keep things in proper perspective—to see things as they really are. For Billy Graham, the most famous evangelist of modern revivalism, that someone is his wife, Ruth. Graham tells a story about the time that he thought he put a dollar in an offering plate. It was a ten dollar bill, however, and the mistake was significant in the early years of the marriage when money was tight. Billy complained to Ruth about the financial blunder. Ruth responded, "In the Lord's sight you'll get credit for only an offering of one dollar—not ten—because that's all you meant to give." Biographer William J. Petersen comments, "Billy tells the story to help his listeners understand a little about giving, but it also helps one understand a little about Ruth."[280] (2 Cor 9:7; Eph 5:21-33) (Giving, Marriage) (CDW)

1909A Clarence Jordan. *Founder of Koinonia Farm* (1912–1969).
Clarence Jordan was a prophet for racial integration in the South.
In 1942, after receiving his doctorate in Greek at The Southern
Baptist Theological Seminary, he returned to his native south
Georgia and established Koinonia Farm, an experiment in
Christian interracial communal living. On one occasion, after
preaching to a Southern congregation on the spirit of brotherhood
and equality found in the New Testament, he was accosted by an
elderly woman captive to her culture: "I want you to know that
my grandfather fought in the Civil War, and I'll never believe a
word you say." Jordan replied, "Ma'am, your choice seems quite
clear. It is whether you will follow your granddaddy or Jesus
Christ."[281]

The scribes and Pharisees were judged for following the
traditions of the elders rather than God. And so are we. (Matt
23:13-28; Mark 7:1-13) (Culture, Discipleship, Hypocrisy, Race,
Tradition) (CDW)

1909B What we say we believe and how we act are often miles
apart. Clarence Jordan got straight to the point, "We'll worship
the hind legs off Jesus, but never do a thing he says."[282] (Mark
8:34-38; Luke 18:9-14) (Commitment, Hypocrisy) (CDW)

1909C One weekend a student from India studying at Florida State
University visited Koinonia Farm. He requested the Jordans to let
him visit a Protestant worship service. When they took him to a
local Baptist church, the congregation chilled the hot summer day
with their icy reception. According to Dallas Lee, author of
Cotton Patch Evidence, the congregation acted as if the Indian
student was a disguised "nigger." The church's new pastor went
to see the Jordans and complained that the Koinonians were
causing disunity in his church.

"The man was dark, but he did not look like an American
Negro," Florence Jordan replied. "We thought the people would
be delighted to meet him. He was not a Christian, but was
interested and wanted to go to church."

Some church members paid a second visit to the farm and
requested the Koinonians to leave their church alone. Jordan said

they would apologize in front of the church if they had done anything wrong. He gave a Bible to a deacon and asked him to point out what scriptural teaching had been disobeyed. The man slammed the book down and retorted, "Don't give me any of this Bible stuff." Jordan calmly responded, "I'm not giving you any Bible stuff. I'm asking you to give it to me." After adding that the man should either accept the Bible as the "holy, inspired Word of God" or leave the Baptist church, the frustrated man left.[283]

How conveniently we follow only part of the scriptures, avoiding those parts that get in the way of our sins. Jordan reminds us that being Christian is hearing and doing the whole Word of God, no matter how unpopular it may be. (2 Tim 3:16-17; Jas 1:22; 2:14) (Bible, Faith and Works, Race) (CDW)

1909D Carranza Morgan, who lives adjacent to the Koinonia Farm in Americus, Georgia, was asked what he remembered most about Clarence Jordan. He answered quickly, "He didn't have no feathers." Morgan went on to explain: "Granddad was a slave. Slaves were careful what they said. They that ran away in the night to escape slavery, they had feathers. When they left the plantation for green pastures on the other side they had feathers." But Clarence never ran away; he didn't go to green pastures. He stayed on the job right here. He never had no feathers."[284] (1 Cor 15:58; Gal 5:1; Eph 6:10-17; 2 Tim 2:1-13) (Commitment, Steadfastness) (JAW)

1909E Clarence Jordan illustrated the contemporary church's tepid and timid commitment to a life of self-sacrificial service. Jordan once startled the local pastor who had invited him to speak to his south Georgia congregation. Having given Jordan a tour of the church plant, the pastor proudly pointed out an ornate steeple decorated with a beautiful cross, noting, "That cross alone cost us $10,000." Jordan, iconoclastic curmudgeon that he was, sniffed, "Time was when Christians could get one of those for free." (Mark 8:34-38; John 15:18-21) (Commitment, Cross, Self-Sacrifice) (AMM)

1909F Being a truly spiritual Christian means being a doer of the Word as well as a hearer. Southern Baptist minister Clarence Jordan founded an interracial Christian community in south Georgia in the 1940s. Jordan sought his lawyer brother's help in the face of persecution. Having political aspirations, the brother refused. Clarence suggested that his brother should go back to the rural church where they had both walked the aisle to accept Christ and explain something. "Tell them," said Clarence, "what you really meant to say was that you *admire* Jesus, not that you want to *follow* him." (Matt 7:21; Mark 8:34-38; Jas 1:22) (Discipleship, Faith and Works) (WLA)

1910A **Martin Luther King, Jr.** *African-American Baptist Minister, Civil Rights Leader* (1929–1968). In February 1968, with the prospect of death beginning to cloud his life, Martin Luther King, Jr. went to Acapulco with Ralph Abernathy. Around three o'clock one morning, Abernathy awoke to find that King was not in his bed. Frightened, Abernathy went out into the living area of their hotel suite and discovered King standing on the balcony in his pajamas, gazing at the ocean.

Abernathy approached King: "Martin, what are you doing out here this time of night? What is bothering you?" With his eyes still fixed on the ocean and his ears attuned to the roar of the waves, King only said, "You see that rock out there?" "Oh, sure, I see it," Abernathy replied. "How long do you think it's been there?" King asked. "I don't know," Abernathy said. "I guess centuries and centuries. I guess God put it there."

"Well, what am I thinking about?" King said. Abernathy remained silent. "You can't tell what I'm thinking?" King said again. "No," replied Abernathy. King began to sing, "Rock of Ages, cleft for me: let me hide myself in thee."[285] (Ps 18; 31; 61:1-4; 62; 71; 94:22) (Confidence, Death, Providence) (JAW)

1910B During the Montgomery, Alabama, bus boycott, some African-Americans declined rides in the car pool that had been organized and "demonstrated with their feet" by walking to and from work every day. One elderly woman, known affectionately as Old Mother Pollard, was among those who walked. Martin Luther

King, Jr., told her at church one evening, "Now listen, you have been with us all along, so now you go on and start back to ridin' the bus, 'cause you are too old to keep walking."

"Oh, no," she protested, "I'm gonna walk just as long as everybody else walks. I'm gonna walk till it's over." King responded, "But aren't your feet tired?" "Yes," Old Mother Pollard said, "My feet is tired, but my soul is rested."[286] (Isa. 26:3; 40:29-31; Matt 11:28-30; Heb 4:9-11) (Peace, Rest, Serenity) (JAW)

1910C In January 1957, as reaction to the civil rights movement in Montgomery became violent, Martin Luther King, Jr., addressed a mass meeting in church. For the first time, he broke down in public. Clutching the pulpit as he began to pray, King cried, "Lord, I hope no one will have to die as a result of our struggle for freedom in Montgomery. Certainly I don't want to die. But if anyone has to die, let it be me."

The congregation intoned, "No! No!" King could not continue his prayer and stood at the pulpit, motionless. With some difficulty, some friends finally helped him to sit down. King's biographer, Stephen B. Oates, commented:

> "Unexpectedly," King wrote later, "this episode brought me great relief." After the meeting, many people assured him that we were all together until the end. But the incident was cathartic in another way too: by praying that he be killed if somebody must be, he freed himself from his guilt that *I am to blame. I have caused all this suffering.* He was ready to lead again. He felt strong again. He felt God beside him, and he did not fear to die. It was as though he had told the forces of evil in the universe: kill me if you will, but the forces of light shall never cease to struggle for righteousness.[287]

(Mark 8:34-38; John 1:5; 15:12-13; 1 Pet 2:21; 1 John 4:4-5) (God's Power, Imitation of Christ, Self-Sacrifice) (JAW)

1910D An orthodox majority exiled Roger Williams, an orthodox majority hung Quaker Mary Dyer on Boston Commons in 1662, and an orthodox majority defended slavery by the authority of the Holy Scriptures. On 17 April 1961, when a majority of Southern Baptists believed segregation to be the will of God, some dissenting professors welcomed Martin Luther King, Jr., to the pulpit of The Southern Baptist Theological Seminary. Young Turks Henlee Barnette, Wayne Ward, Willis Bennett, and Penrose St. Amant went stalking racism in the Southern Baptist Convention. Dr. Ward says that Dean St. Amant offered King a position as Professor of Preaching. Can you imagine? So great was the controversy that a majority of the seminary trustees voted to "express regret for any offense caused by the visit of Rev Martin Luther King, Jr., to the campus of the seminary." Critics said Southern Seminary lost over $250,000 in donations because of that event. Today let us say it was money well spent. The will of the majority is not always the same as the will of the living God. Heirs of the dissenting tradition, most Southern Baptists today are more supportive of status quo than dissent, more sympathetic with establishment than minorities. We are always tempted to sacrifice radical faith for a mess of establishment pottage.[288] (Gen 25:29-34; Rom 7:14-8:2) (Church and State, Conformity, Majority Religion, Race) (BJL)

1911 **Malcolm X.** *Black Muslim Leader* (1925–1965). The need to have one's human dignity affirmed cuts across all boundaries of faith or theological differences. An incident in the life of actor Ossie Davis suggests this. A devoted Christian and Baptist Sunday School teacher, Davis delivered the eulogy at the funeral of Black Muslim leader, Malcolm X. In the days that followed, he received many inquiries asking why he had seen fit to praise such a "militant Muslim troublemaker." A magazine editor's query led Davis to respond that of all who had wondered why he eulogized Malcolm, no blacks had done so. Every letter and comment he received from blacks had lauded Malcolm as a man and commended Davis for speaking at the funeral. While most persons took care to indicate their significant disagreement with some of Malcolm's views, as Davis wrote, "Every last, black, glory-hugging one of them knew that Malcolm *was a man*." Then Davis noted, "White folks do not need anybody to remind them that they are men. We do! This was his one incontrovertible benefit to his people."[289] (Gen 1:26-27; Ps 8:5-8) (Dignity) (AMM)

1912A Carlyle Marney. *Baptist Leader of South* (1916–1978). One of the most prominent and controversial Baptist leaders of the twentieth century was Carlyle Marney. He identified with the Baptist heritage but often had skirmishes with leaders who disliked his theology and his ecumenism. In an attempt to be a change agent among Baptists in the South, Marney often relied on humor, realizing that "the Baptist tradition included a 'folksiness' that often enabled Baptists to laugh at themselves." He often used the following story when speaking to Baptists:

> I once heard of a Quaker farmer in Texas who owned a particularly ill-tempered cow. One morning as he was giving the cow some feed prior to milking, he stood too close to the cow, and it bit him. Later, as he adjusted his milking stool the cow swatted him with its tail. Finally after he had finished milking, he turned away for a few seconds and the cow kicked over the milk bucket. That was the last straw. The farmer marched around and looked the cow straight in the eye. "Cow," he said, "thou tryest my patience. Thou hast hurt me and angered me. Thou knowest that the principles of my faith keep me from harming thee. What thou dost not know, however, is that I am going to sell thee to a Baptist."[290]

Laughing is fun. Being able to laugh at ourselves is healthy and can be quite revealing about what we believe and how we practice our beliefs. (Matt 5:38-42; 1 Cor 13:4; 2 Cor 6:6; Jas 5:8) (Humor, Non-violent Resistance, Patience) (CDW)

1912B Raised and educated as a Southern Baptist, Carlyle Marney developed an ecumenical ministry and gained national prominence while the pastor of Myers Park Baptist Church in Charlotte, North Carolina, from 1958 to 1967. As he skirmished with Southern Baptist leadership, he had his church dually align with the American Baptist Convention, and he became increasingly hesitant about denominational labels. After his ministry at Myers Park, Marney finished his career as the founder of the Interpreter's House, an inter-denominational ministry for broken ministers.

Earlier in his ministry, Marney wanted to help reform the Southern Baptist Convention. Gradually, he became disillusioned with what he felt was authoritarian and parochial leadership.

Marney decided, moreover, that all denominations suffer from "structural problems and cultural lag" and probably were not capable of reform. When asked why he remained a Baptist, Marney often responded:

> Everywhere I go people ask me why I remain a Baptist. Being a Baptist is like being in a dark, slimy well: it's cold, clammy, uncomfortable and filled with lots of creepy things. For years I tried to climb out, but it was hard: the walls were slippery, I was half-blind, and there were impediments everywhere. Finally, however, I got to the top. I looked around at last to see what the world was like in other denominations. After I had a good look—I just dropped back into the well.[291]

We can hear Marney saying many things. Disillusionment is painful. In life, even when things are going bad, the grass isn't always greener on the other side. More to the point, however, is Marney's disillusionment with religious organizational structures. Loyalty to any organization is usually expected from any team member, but a conformity that allows no dissent is not. That might be the model of some secular businesses, but it cannot be the way of the church. All institutions are prone to sin and often are wrapped up in sin. The social gospel, ministering to people trapped by fallen structures, reminds us of that truth. Institutional loyalty must always be subject to our loyalty to Christ. (Acts 4:18-20; Gal 5:1) (Denominationalism, Disillusionment, Institutional Loyalty) (CDW)

1913 **J. C. Massee.** *American Baptist Leader* (1871–1965). In the 1920s, the Fundamentalist-Modernist controversy engulfed the Northern Baptist Convention. Fundamentalists, led by W. B. Riley, John Roach Straton, and J. C. Massee, felt that liberalism was ruining the denomination, and they attempted to rescue educational institutions, missionary operations, and denominational agencies from liberal control. Riley and Straton were particularly militant and dominant personalities, and a rift developed between them and Massee when the latter was willing to accept an investigative report that recommended the recalling of just four missionaries for unacceptable theology. Massee feared that the fundamentalist movement, with which he had been identified, would split the denomination. He opted for the path of cooperation for the sake of missions and evangelism, his first love. Reflecting on his repudiation of the fundamentalist movement, Massee said:

> I left the fundamentalists to save my own spirit. They became so self-righteous, so critical, so unchristian, so destructive, so incapable of being fair that I had to go elsewhere for spiritual nourishment.

Massee was conservative in theology, but he saw the dangers of enforced conformity and a "my way or no way" definition of cooperation. In the 1940s, commenting on divisions that had occurred in Northern Baptist life, Massee said in traditional anti-creedal Baptist fashion: "Fellowship cannot be coerced. . . . No human being has either the right or the power to select a vocabulary in which my faith is to be expressed."[292]

Good advice for those battling coercion and conformity! Church history has indeed left us a cloud of witnesses to freedom and cooperation. (Luke 18:9-14; 1 Cor 12:14-26; Col 3:14) (Coercion, Conformity, Cooperation, Freedom, Militancy) (CDW)

1914   **Thomas Merton.** *Catholic Trappist Monk* (1915–1968). Hugh Kerr suggests that it is ironic that a Trappist monk, who took a vow of silence, became, through the medium of writing, one of the most articulate and eloquent voices of the Christian faith in the twentieth century. In 1941, Thomas Merton entered the Trappist monastery of Our Lady of Gethsemane in Kentucky and proceeded to become a leading authority on spirituality. Writing on faith, Merton reasoned that our modern age is one of paradox. Millions of people have a blind faith in everything they read in the newspaper and in every charlatan they see in the movies. Political propaganda is gobbled up at the same time we acknowledge that it is known for a lack of concern for the truth. The situation is tragically ironic, Merton concluded, that these millions, so quick to have faith in fallible humanity, say it is impossible and absurd to have faith in God.[293] (Mark 11:22-23; 2 Cor 5:7; Gal 5:5; Heb 11:1) (Faith and Reason, Modernity) (CDW)

1915 **Helen Barrett Montgomery; William Montgomery.** *American Baptist Leaders* (1861–1934, dates for HBM). How the Montgomerys loved to give! In virtually every area of living they found ways to share themselves and their money. Helen Barrett was a well-educated young women whose love for Greek would later lead her to produce the Montgomery translation of the New Testament. She married William Montgomery in 1887. William was already a successful businessman when a young man presented him with a problem. The young man had invented a self-starter for automobiles, but he had no money to finance its production. For William, the solution was easy. He provided the capital, the young men the starter.

With their investments tied up in the early production years, Helen and William had a significantly reduced income. To make it financially, they had to dismiss their domestic help, sell their grand piano, and even sell their comfortable home as they moved into smaller living quarters.

During their years of prosperity, the Montgomerys had given very generously to their church, Lake Avenue Baptist Church in Rochester, New York. Although they had significantly reduced their own lifestyle during the financially tight years, they refused to give any less than generously to their church. William explained, "Pastor, I may have to cut this. I expect I will. But you may be sure that if I cut my pledge, it will be the last thing that I cut, not the first." That generous contribution was never reduced even when they had to sell their own home!

Helen gave of her abilities in many arenas of life, serving as president of the Woman's American Baptist Foreign Mission Society for ten years, president of the Northern Baptist Convention, writing six books on missions, serving on the school board and city council of Rochester, working with Susan B. Anthony to get the University of Rochester to open its doors to women, and faithfully teaching a Sunday School class for 44 years. Ironically, William refused to buy a car, preferring to give his car money away to those who needed it. Finally, the doctor ordered him to get a car for health reasons. At their deaths in the 1930s, the Montgomerys kept on giving. Eight or more churches, schools, hospitals, missions, or other charities received monies from the Montgomery estate.

Financial distress, personal inconveniences, or reduced lifestyle were no reason for the Montgomerys to deny themselves the joy of giving![294] (Deut 10:18; Matt 19:21; 2 Cor 9:7) (Giving) (CDB)

1916A E. Y. Mullins. *Southern Baptist Theologian* (1860–1928). E. Y. Mullins, president of The Southern Baptist Theological Seminary and noted Baptist statesman, once observed that the human conscience serves as a "voice within. It is like a bell. It rings softly when the smallest sin is committed. It rings loudly when great sins are committed. Conscience cannot be escaped."[295]

Sometimes the "bell tolls" in our lives through the quiet awakening of the Spirit. In those tender moments, God whispers his affirming word to us and something leads us away from self and back to the Savior; but sometimes that word rings loudly and clearly, not only to call us back to life and faith, but to call others as well. God's ways—both in whisper and in shout—remind us to Whom we ultimately belong. We are created by him, for him. Hence, his voice remains audible even above the clamor of our souls. (1 Kgs 19:12) (Conscience) (DMW)

1916B   E. Y. Mullins once observed: "Love is self-communication. And as it is essential to God, it is necessary self-communication. To give himself, then, belongs to the very nature of God." The New Testament affirms this self-disclosing nature of God. Inherent in his Being is the capacity to lay bare his heart and indisputably to prove his love for all creation. Mullins continues this theme by asserting that God's love rolls out like a "mighty ocean" towards humanity.[296] Hence, the incarnation is the crowning jewel of God's condescending movement toward us, his self-communicating nature thrust him earthward so that the vast scope of his love would not only be heard, as with the prophets of old, but experienced as through his son, Jesus the Christ. (1 John 1:1-3) (God's Love) (DMW)

1917A Martin Niemöller. *Leader, Confessing Church of Germany* (1892–1984). Martin Niemöller, along with Karl Barth and Dietrich Bonhöffer, helped to form the Confessing Church in Germany and to draw up the Berman Declaration, the Confessing Church's theological rallying point. Pastor Niemoller was imprisoned by Adolph Hitler for his opposition to the Nazi regime, and he spent eight years in concentration camps.

Until about the fourth year of his incarceration, Niemöller had not always recognized his opportunity and responsibility to witness even in prison. Then one night, Niemöller had a dream. He saw Hitler standing before the judgment seat of God, pleading that he had never heard the gospel. Niemoller recounted: "In my dream, I heard the voice of God directed toward me inquiring, 'Were you with him one whole hour and did not tell him about my Son'?" When Niemöller awoke and reflected on his dream, he remembered that once he had spent one whole hour with Hitler and had said nothing to him about Jesus Christ. From that moment, Niemöller seized every opportunity to bear witness to his faith with his guards and any who came to his cell.[297] (Acts 1:8; 16:16-34; Rom 10:14-15) (Evangelism, Missions) (JAW)

1917B Pastor Martin Niemöller, imprisoned in one of Hitler's concentration camps, declared: "It took me a long time to learn that God is not the enemy of my enemies. He is not even the enemy of his enemies."[298] (Matt 5:38-48; Rom 5:10-11; 12:16-21; 2 Cor 5:18-20) (Enemies, Love) (JAW)

1918 Oral Roberts. *Pentecostal Healing Evangelist* (b.1918). Oral Roberts is one of the giants of twentieth-century healing revivalism. He is readily criticized for his vision of a 700-foot giant Jesus, constant demands for money to keep his ministry alive, his emphasis on faith healing, and receiving miracles through a seed-faith covenant with God.

While many Christians cast a skeptical eye toward Roberts, everyone can identify with his experience of miracle and faith as he sought to deal with the death of his daughter who was killed in a small plane that crashed in a rural area during an electrical storm. On his Sunday morning televisionprogram, the regular format was abandoned so Oral and his wife, Evelyn, could simply talk through their grief. When he first received the news of the tragedy, Roberts thought of his daughter's body lying in a corn field in the rain. Amidst the terrible pain, he remembered that God lost his only son. Yet, he and Evelyn still had other children. Identifying with God who suffered for us and with us helped the Roberts, and it can help all of us deal with our pain. Oral concluded with the true essence of a faith that produces hope: "God raised his son to life again in the resurrection. And the resurrection is the promise that my daughter shall live again too. And that's the real comfort." (Rom 8:18, 24-25; 1 Cor 15) (Death, Hope, Resurrection, Suffering) (CDW)

1919A Albert Schweitzer. *Missionary to Africa; Biblical Scholar* (1875-1965). The brilliant Albert Schweitzer, who could have been successful in various careers in comfortable places, chose instead to serve as a jungle doctor in Africa. He explained, "It struck me as incomprehensible that I should be allowed to lead such a happy life, while I saw so many people around me wrestling with care and suffering."[299] (Mark 10:41-45; Heb 13:16; 1 John 3:16–17) (Love, Missions, Self-Sacrifice, Service) (JAW)

1919B How much is enough? In a world where so many have so little, can we have too much? Albert Schweitzer's standard attire was a white pith helmet, white shirt and pants, and black tie. He had worn one hat for forty years and a tie for twenty. When he was told that some men owned dozens of neckties, Schweitzer observed, "For one neck?"[300] The stewardship of possessions is a matter of all that God has given us and not just some token or tithe we resignedly deem to be divine tribute. (Luke 12:13-21; 16:19-31; 1 Tim 6:6-10) (Materialism, Stewardship) (JAW)

1920 Fulton J. Sheen. *American Catholic Leader* (1895–1979). Edward Chinn, pastor of the All Saints Church in Philadelphia, has noted a striking point of contact in the lives of two individuals of notoriety. Near the beginning of the twentieth century in a country church in a small village in Croatia, an altar boy named Josip Broz served the priest at the Sunday Mass. The boy accidentally dropped the glass cruet of wine, shattering it into pieces. The priest struck the boy on the cheek and angrily demanded, "Leave the altar and don't come back." The boy never returned to the church. He grew to become Tito, the leader of Communist Yugoslavia after World War II. At about the same time, an altar boy named Peter John also dropped the wine cruet while serving the priest at Mass in St. Mary's Cathedral in Peoria, Illinois. The boy later recalled, "There is no atomic explosion that can equal in intensity of decibels the noise and explosive force of a wine cruet falling on the marble floor of a cathedral in the presence of a bishop. I was frightened to death." The priest, though, with an understanding smile gently whispered, "Someday you will be just what I am." That young man, who dropped his first name, "Peter," and began to use his mother's maiden name, "Fulton," became in adulthood Archbishop Fulton J. Sheen, a prolific writer and pioneer in religious broadcasting.[301]

Chinn concludes, "What a difference the words of those two celebrants at Mass made in the lives of those boys!"[302] The Apostle Paul recognized the dynamic, creative power of words: "Let no evil talk come out of your mouths, but only what is useful for building up, as there is need, so that your words may give grace to those who hear." (Prov 12:18; Eph 4:29) (Evil Speech, Tongue) (JAW)

1921 **Fred Shuttlesworth.** *African-American Civil Rights Leader* (b.1922). Baptist minister Fred L. Shuttlesworth pastored the Bethel Baptist Church in Birmingham, Alabama, during the tumultuous civil rights years of the 1950s and 1960s. In June 1956, after the Alabama Legislature outlawed the NAACP, Shuttlesworth responded with the founding of a new organization to fight for civil rights, the Alabama Christian Movement for Human Rights. Later that year, Shuttlesworth publically warned the civic leaders of Birmingham that African-American bus riders would begin seating themselves in previously white sections of buses. But on Christmas Night, 1956, the local Ku Klux Klan had other plans. Beneath the bedroom of Shuttlesworth's home, they planted sixteen sticks of dynamite, designed to disturb the "Silent Night," and snuff out the minister's courage, if not his life. The explosion demolished the entire front of the parsonage, but Shuttlesworth, who had been in the bed and unwittingly shielded from the blast by the mattress, emerged with only minor scratches. As he was getting into a car to take him to the hospital for examination, his seven year-old daughter, Carolyn, crawled up into his lap, and said, "They can't kill us, can they, Daddy?" The next day, Shuttlesworth and his followers rode the buses as promised. Perhaps they could have killed the Shuttlesworths, even as they did others in the civil rights movement. But Shuttlesworth's courage could not be overcome. And because of it, neither could his people. (Deut. 31:1-6; Ps 7:14) (Civil Rights, Courage) (AMM)

1922 Alexander Solzhenitsyn. *Russian Dissident, Author* (b.1918). One of the dark truths of human experience is the potential evil that lurks in the shadows of every human heart. Sometimes it lies just beneath the surface, eagerly waiting for its moment of actualization. At other times, it seems to be deeply imbedded in our soul and makes but a fleeting appearance. It is then that we face the brutal truth about ourselves; namely, within each of us there lies the potential for evil.

That haunting realization came to the Russian dissident Alexander Solzhenitsyn during the years of his imprisonment in a Soviet prison. He carefully noted that "good and evil passes not through the states, nor between classes . . . but right through every human heart—and even in the best of hearts, there remains . . . an unuprooted small corner of evil." The best way for us to face the truth about ourselves is to face the darkness within. Only then will the remnants in our own "small corner of evil" ever be fully exposed and given the chance of Life.[303] (Jer 17:9; Rom 3:23) (Evil, Sin) (DMW)

1923A Southern Religion. Spiritual realities are not always learned in the church. I remember that in my childhood in Texas, we went most Januarys to the Southwestern Exposition and Fat Stock Show in Fort Worth. My favorite event was the bull-riding, and with the bulls came the clowns in painted faces and baggy pants, hiding in open-ended barrels. They jumped around, fell down, and looked absolutely incapable of anything but stupid antics—until a rider flew off a cavorting bull, and then the clowns became dead serious in their efforts to protect the defenseless, sometimes hurting, rider.

Gradually, it began to dawn on me. The clowns were not just there to be funny or entertaining. The cowboys and the audience needed them desperately.

Somehow, in the mystery that is God, the world needs us. Oh, we look silly in the baggy pants of our theology, the painted faces of our practice, and the open-ended barrels of our ethics. But there we are in the center ring where some people need to be protected, where others are hurting, and where those who have fallen need the safety of a second chance. And as foolish as it sounds, that's why the vulnerable God/man on the cross could not save himself and, in doing that, save others. But now that cross is empty. The circus is over. But where in the world are the clowns?[304] (1 Cor 1:18-28; Gal 6:2) (Bearing Burdens, Cross) (BJL)

1923B A religion for *this* world. For the rural poor and, one suspects, for all believers, religion is never totally escapist. Faith becomes an inescapable part of building human meaning for this life. Psychiatrist Robert Coles noted this in his study based on a late 1930s sociological survey of Tennessee tenant farmers. In troubled times, they found solace in God: "If he had not stood by me, I would not have lived through the trouble I have had." Would the absence of a loving God affect them? One farmer replied, "Wouldn't have any encouragement then sure enough. Would just end it up sometime."[305] (Mark 11:22-23; Luke 6:20; John 14:1) (Escapism, Faith, Poverty) (AMM)

1923C Writer Anne Siddons once discussed the dangers of conformity to culture in an interview with V. S. Naipaul, who was writing a book about the South. Growing up in the farming and railroad town of Fairburn, Georgia, Siddons was a part of a culture tied to the land and agricultural horizons. "Our sort don't go to college," said her neighbors, "We are farmers." She spent her elementary and high school years, by her estimation, "trying to hide the fact that I was a bright child." Never encouraged to prize her mind or individuality, she notes, "to be a great thinker, to have a great talent and pursue it, would cut you right out of the herd." And to be "cut out of the herd," was to be "totally exposed, totally vulnerable to chaos."[306] All this suggests that to avoid "being squeezed into the world's mold" requires some internal principle of order with which to challenge the chaos of nonconformity. (Rom 8:29; 12:1-2) (Conformity, Culture) (AMM)

1923D John S. Workman, long time religion editor of the *Arkansas Gazette*, allowed himself the freedom to complain about ministers' telephone etiquette. The phone rings and a secretary's voice asked, "Dr. Workman, will you hold for Dr. Bigpreacher?" After twenty-five minutes and all sixteen stanzas of the recorded strains of "I Come to the Garden," Dr. Bigpreacher comes on the line: "Good morning, John, a beautiful day the Lord has made, isn't it?" Workman wonders, "How am I supposed to respond to that?" On another occasion comes the click-click of the call waiting feature, followed by the inevitable, "Pardon me a moment, I've got to get this other call." Workman confessed, "For us folks with sensitive psyches, it is pretty crushing to be informed so abruptly that we're being demoted to second place." Then, there is the fortunately rare pastor whose unlisted number cannot be disclosed by the secretary. Workman rightly notes that his irritation at such slights, insignificant though they may ultimately be, are symbols of more important matters. They say something about the ministers' calling, and that of those they lead, to be servants of humanity rather than Madison Avenue business tycoons.[307] (Mark 10:41-45; Eph 1:18; Phil 3:12-14) (Call, Service) (AMM)

1923E Sectarian religion is often ostracized by more mainline and majority groups. Social differences and a rigidity of faith and practice are often looked upon with disfavor or at least discomfort. Sectarian believers have always taught others a thing or two about ministry, however. In particular, they have ministered to the poorest of the poor and have ignored racial barriers.

Healing revivalists are often a maligned group for their usually unbelievable healing claims and their theology of prosperity. Nevertheless, these evangelists integrated their meetings in the 1950s when mainline groups were receivng much resistance from their members. A. A. Allen, one of the most influential healing revivalists in the South at mid-century, broke the racial barrier in southern cities like Atlanta, Little Rock, and Winston-Salem. He declared, "When hearts are hungry and God is moving, there is no time for color lines!" Historian David E. Harrell comments,

> During the 1960s, when mainstream southern churches were wrestling with troubled consciences in all-white congregations, the big tents of the healing revivalists moved through every city of the South hosting tens of thousands of blacks and whites who found on their benches a common haven from their wretched poverty.[308]

In his book *Brother to a Dragonfly*, Will Campbell told the story of a Church of God preacher in Mississippi named Horace Germany. When they met, Germany had been badly beaten. Germany had made the mistake of wanting to build a Christian school that would produce farmers that could preach the gospel. Sounded good; but he advertised that the school would have no racial barriers. When the first three students turned out to be black, one of the mainline churches in the area had a meeting to discuss the school. The church was packed with two hundred people and another five hundred gathered as close to the open windows and doors as they could. The church sent a committee to warn Germany that his family and "them imported niggers" had forty-eight hours to leave town or "we will not be responsible for what happens." Germany didn't leave, and a mob beat him into unconsciousness. He sold his unfinished school building to "one of the biggest bootleggers in the county . . . who wants to make a dance hall out of my school. And sell whiskey."

When Campbell asked Germany about selling to a person he obviously didn't approve of, the Church of God preacher said, "I told these people that if they won't let God do his work in this county, the Devil will sure move in and do his. You know, there's alot more to this race thing than segregation." His words, Campbell remarked, were a fitting epitaph to the Bay Ridge Christian College. (1 Cor 1: 26-31; Gal 3:28; Eph 2:11-22) (Equality, Race, Social Gospel) (CDW)[309]

1924A Mother Teresa. *Catholic Nun of India* (b.1910). Those of us who live in the Western world often become entrapped by our own warped sense of value and success. We have mistakenly bought into the idea that riches will buy happiness and peace of mind. The Bible, however, truthfully acknowledges that "no one can serve two masters."

Mother Teresa of India has explored the very depths of poverty in her work among the poor, and yet she asserts that in contrast to the beggars, "the rich [are] much poorer. . . . They always need something more."[310] Perhaps someday, we will learn that more is not best and that peace and contentment do not bear a price tag. (Matt 6:24) (Spiritual Poverty, Materialism) (DMW)

1924B In a recent interview with *Time* magazine, Mother Teresa spoke of her ministry to the poor and disenfranchised citizens of Calcutta. During the course of the interview, Mother Teresa was asked if she possessed extraordinary spiritual qualities that enabled her to work with those whom society has rejected. She said:

> I don't think so. I don't claim anything of the work. It is his work. I am like a little pencil in his hand. That's all. He does the thinking. He does the writing. The pencil has nothing to do with it. The pencil has only to be allowed to be used.[311]

In God's hands, what kind of pencils are we? To borrow from Jeremiah's imagery, what kind of clay are we? Are we respondent to the shaping of the Potter's hands? Ar we allowing God to do through us that task for which we were created? Mother Teresa was right. For those who are obedient to his voice, we indeed become "pencils in the hands of God." (Jer 18:6) (Humility, Obedience) (DMW)

1924C A priest asked Mother Teresa how to live out his vocation as a priest. She responded in what is wise counsel for any of us, "Spend one hour a day in adoration of your Lord and never do anything you know is wrong, and you will be all right."[312] (1 Thess 5:15-22) (Christian Lifestyle, Worship) (JAW)

1925 **Paul Tillich.** *Protestant Theologian* (1886–1965). A popular legend about the theologian Paul Tillich recounts that he had just lectured on the authority of scripture when a seminary student, gripping tightly in his hand a large, black, leather-bound Bible, approached him. The student demanded, "Do you believe this is the Word of God?" Tillich looked at the student's fingers clutching the book, and he said, "Not if you think you can grasp it. Only when the Bible grasps you."[313] (2 Tim 3:16-17; Heb 4:12-13) (Bible) (JAW)

1926 **Desmond Tutu.** *South African Bishop* (b.1931). In the late 1980s, Ted Koppel asked Bishop Desmond Tutu on "Nightline," the nightly news program, if the situation in South Africa, with its apartheid or racial segregation, was hopeless. Tutu replied, "Of course it is hopeless from a human point of view. But we believe in the resurrection, and so we are prisoners of hope."[314]

Prisoners of hope—indeed an arresting image. We do not desperately clutch at hope. In the resurrection we have been taken captive by the hope that will never release us but will liberate us from all hopelessness. (Ps 42:5; Zech 9:12; 1 Cor 15:19–22; 1 Thess 4:13–18; 1 Pet 1:3–7) (Hope, Race, Resurrection) (JAW)

Notes

[1]W. H. C. Frend, *Martyrdom and Persecution in the Early Church* (Grand Rapids: Baker Book House, 1981) 161-66.

[2]*Didache* 1-6. See J. B. Lightfoot, *The Apostolic Fathers*, edited and completed by J. R. Harmer (Grand Rapids: Baker Book House, 1976) 126.

[3]Ignatius, *Letter to The Ephesians* 10. See Lightfoot, 66.

[4]Ignatius, *To The Ephesians* 15. See Lightfoot, 67.

[5]*Barnabas* 9. See Lightfoot, 145-46.

[6]Justin Martyr, *Second Apology* 10. See Alexander Roberts and James Donaldson, eds., *Ante-Nicene Fathers: Translations of the Writings of the Fathers Down to A. D. 325*, vol. 1 (Grand Rapids: William B. Eerdmans, 1979) 191. Hereafter *ANF*.

[7]Justin Martyr, *Second Apology* 13. See Roberts, *ANF*, 1: 193.

[8]W. H. C. Frend, *The Rise of Christianity* (Philadelphia: Fortress Press, 1984) 150.

[9]*The Martyrdom of Polycarp* 10. See Lightfoot, 112.

[10]Clement of Alexandria, *The Instructor* 1.4. See Roberts, *ANF*, 4: 211.

[11]Cyprian, *Epistle* 6.5. See Roberts, *ANF*, 5: 286.

[12]Cyprian, *Treatise* 10.7. See Roberts, *ANF*, 5: 493.

[13]See E. Glenn Hinson, *The Evangelization of the Roman Empire* (Macon: Mercer University Press, 1981) 97-110, 183-92.

[14]"The Passion of Perpetua and Felicitas." See Roberts, *ANF*, 3: 699-706.

[15]Patricia Wilson-Kastner, *et al., A Lost Tradition* (New York: University Press of America, 1981) 22.

[16]Ibid., 28.

[17]Ibid., 30.

[18]"Passion of Perpetua and Felicitas," 704.

[19]Tertullian, *On Idolatry* 1. See Roberts, *ANF*, 3: 61.

[20]Roland H. Bainton, *The Church of Our Fathers* (New York: Charles Scribner's Sons, 1941) 55-56.

[21]John Chrysostom, *On the Priesthood* 1.5, 6. and *Letter to a Young Widow* 1. See Philip Schaff, ed., *The Nicene and Post-Nicene Fathers of the Christian Church*, 1st ser., vol. 9 (Grand Rapids: William B. Eerdmans, 1978) 34, 122. Hereafter *NPNF*.

[22]John Chrysostom, *Matthew, Homily 88*. See Schaff, *NPNF*, 10: 523.

[23]John Chrysostom, *Matthew, Homily 14*. See Schaff, *NPNF*, 10: 87.

[24]E. H. Flanery, *The Anguish of the Jews: Twenty-Three Centuries of Anti-Semitism* (New York: Paulist Press, 1985): 50-51.

[25]Bruce Shelley, *Church History in Plain Language* (Dallas: Word Publishing, 1982) 72.

[26]Herbert Workman, *Persecution in the Early Church* (New York: Abingdon Press, 1960) 25-26.

[27]*Sayings of the Fathers* in *Western Asceticism*, ed. Owen Chadwick, vol. 10, Library of Christian Classics (Philadelphia: Westminster Press, 1958) 62.

[28]Ibid., 69.

[29]Ibid., 114.

[30]Ibid., 72.

[31]Ibid., 6: 6.

[32]Ibid., 10: 94.

[33]Eusebius, 1.13. See Eusebius, *The Ecclesiastical History of Eusebius*, trans. Christian Cruse (Grand Rapids: Baker Book House, 1976) 43-47.

[34]F. L. Cross and E. A. Livingstone, eds., *The Oxford Dictionary of the Christian Church*, 2d ed. (New York: Oxford University Press, 1978) 1254.

[35]Tertullian, *First Apology* 50. See Roberts, *ANF*, 3: 55.

[36]See G. Warren Bowersock, *Julian the Apostate* (Cambridge: Harvard University Press, 1978).

[37]Mary L. Hammack, *et al.*, "Other Women of the Early Church: A Few of the Many," *Christian History* 7/17 (1988): 15.

[38]Ibid.

[39]*The New Schaff-Herzog Encyclopedia of Religious Knowledge*, 1977 ed., s.v. "Macrina," by F. Loops.

[40]Hammack, 15.

[41]Barbara J. MacHaffie, *Her Story* (Philadelphia: Fortress Press, 1986) 45.

[42]Bainton, *Church*, 81.

[43]For information on Monica, see Edith Deen, *Great Women of the Christian Faith* (New York: Harper and Row, 1959) and Mary L. Hammack, *A Dictionary of Women in Church History* (Chicago: Moody Press, 1984).

[44]Augustine, *Confessions* 5.

[45]Palladius, *Dialogue on the Life of St. John Chrysostom*, trans. Robert T. Meyer, *Ancient Christian Writers; The Works of the Fathers in Translation* 45 (New York: Newman Press, 1985) 114.

[46]Sozomen, *Ecclesiastical History* 8.24. See Philip Schaff and Henry Wace, eds, *NPNF*, 2d ser., 2: 414-15.

[47]Ruth A. Tucker and Walter Liefield, *Daughters of the Church* (Grand Rapids: Zondervan Publishing House, 1987) 118-19.

[48]Nancy A. Hardesty, "Paula: A Portrait of 4th-Century Piety," *Christian History* 7/17 (1988): 17-19.

[49]Ibid.

[50]*Preaching* (November-December 1988): 54.

[51]Augustine, *Confessions* 10.

[52]Augustine, *Confessions* 8.

[53]Augustine, *Confessions* 3.

[54]See Peter Brown, *Augustine of Hippo, A Biography* (Berkeley: University of California Press, 1967) 169. I have relied on this excellent book primarily, as well as the writings of Augustine and writings about him (PSA).

[55]Williston Walker, *A History of the Christian Church*, 4th ed. (New York: Charles Scribner's Sons, 1985) 201.

[56]Augustine, *Confessions* 1.1.

[57]Ibid., *Retractions* 2.32, cited by Brown, 165.

[58]Ibid., *Confessions* 10.33.33, cited by Brown, 178.

[59]Ibid., *de civ. Dei* 15, cited by Brown, 326.

[60]Ibid., Brown, 326-28.

[61]Ibid., *de civ. Dei* 14.28.7-16, cited by Brown, 327, 329. See Henry Bettenson, ed., *The Later Christian Fathers* (London: The Chaucer Press, 1977) 196. Augustine spoke of pride as a "craving for perverse elevation, the beginning of all sin."

[62]Brown, 262.

[63]Ibid., 329. I repeat this passage, cited by Brown, in Augustine *de civ. Dei*, 22.24.11, in endnote 65 deliberately because these passages focus a basic point in Augustine's philosophy of life, in which "evil" is more than compensated for by "so much good." His is not a dualistic view, in which the outcome is uncertain. Augustine's confidence in God's goodness and power pervades his outlook. In his last months he was "still active in mind and body" (Brown, 431). Despite the collapse of Roman Africa, Augustine spoke of his "unshakeable stability," his "wholehearted love of life," and his *Gift of Perseverence*, his last book (Brown, 407).

[64]Augustine, *de civ. Dei* cited by Brown, 328.

[65]Ibid., 329.

[66]Ibid., *Confessions* 10.8.15, cited by Brown, 168.

[67]Ibid., See Plotinus, *Ennead* 4.8.4.

[68]Brown, 169.

[69]Ibid.

[70]Augustine, *Confessions* 5.2.2, cited by Brown, 168.

[71]Goethe, *Faust* in R. L. Ottley, *Studies in the Confessions of St. Augustine* (London: Robert Scot, 1919) 116-17.

[72]Brown, 173.

[73]*Misg. Agostin.* 1.212, cited by Brown, 254.

[74]Brown, 254.

[75]Ibid., 173.

[76]Ibid., 257.

[77]Ibid., 173.

[78]Ibid., 251-52.

[79]Ibid., 257. See *Serm.* 37.2. Italics in the source.

[80]Ibid., 178.

[81]Ibid., 81.

[82]Augustine, *Confessions* 10.37.62. Italics mine.

[83]Brown, 178. See Augustine, *Confessions* 10.24.35.

[84]Ibid.

[85]Ibid.

[86]Brown, 169-71.

[87]Ibid., 410.

[88]I am indebted to colleague and friend, Wayne Oates, for this comment.

[89]Possidius, *Vita* 31.9.

[90]Quoted by Brown, 297-98.

[91]Leslie Weatherhead, "Turning a Corner," *City Temple Tidings* (London) January 1954, 1.

[92]Bainton, *Church*, 76-77.

[93]Ibid., 78.

[94]Ibid.

[95]Gregory I, *Pastoral Care* 3.11. See Schaff and Wace, *ANPF*, 12: 33.

[96]*The New Schaff-Herzog Encyclopedia of Religious Knowledge*, 1977 ed., s.v. "Hilda, Saint."

[97]Tucker, *Daughters*, 135.

[98]Bede, *A History of the English Church and People*, trans., Leo Shirley-Price, rev. by R. E. Latham (New York: Penguin Books, 1977) 247.

[99]Ibid., 245-47.

[100]Shelley, 170.

[101]Tucker, *Daughters*, 136.

[102]MacHaffie, 48.

[103]Tucker, *Daughters*, 136.

[104]Eleanor McLaughlin, "Women, Power and the Pursuit of Holiness in Medieval Christianity," in *Women of Spirit*, eds. Rosemary Reuther and Eleanor McLaughlin (New York: Simon and Schuster, 1979) 107.

[105]Margaret Deanesly, *A History of the Medieval Church: 590-1500* (London: Methuen & Co., LTD, 1978) 93.

[106]*Preaching* (November-December 1990): 41.

[107]William Ragsdale Cannon, *History of Christianity in the Middle Ages; From the Fall of Rome to the Fall of Constantinople* (Grand Rapids: Baker Book House, 1983) 132, 142, 184.

[108]E. Glenn Hinson, *Seekers After Mature Faith: A Historical Introduction to the Classics of Christian Devotion* (Nashville: Broadman Press, 1968) 71-72.

[109]F. F. Bruce, *The Book of Acts* (Grand Rapids: William B. Eerdmans, 1984) 84.

[110]Shelley, 222.

[111]Richard J. Foster, *Celebration of Discipline: The Path to Spiritual Growth*, rev. ed. (San Francisco: Harper and Row, 1988) 102.

[112]For biographical information on Francis, see G. K. Chesterton, *St. Francis of Assisi* (Garden City, NY: Doubleday, 1957).

[113]Morris Rossabi, *Khubilai Khan: His Life and Times* (Berkeley: University of California Press, 1988) 147-52.

[114]Barbara Obrist, "The Swedish Visionary: Saint Bridget," in *Medieval Woman Writers*, ed. Katherina M. Wilson (Athens, GA: University of Georgia Press, 1984) 227.

[115]Tucker, *Daughters*, 160.

[116]*The New Schaff-Herzog Enclyclopedia of Religious Knowledge*, 1977 ed., s.v. "Bridget, Saint, of Sweden," by Herman Lundstrom.

[117]See Igino Giordani, *Catherine of Siena: Fire and Blood* (Milwaukee: Bruce Publishing Co., 1959). See also Deen, *Great Women*, and Hammack, *Dictionary of Women*.

[118]Matthew Fox, *Breakthrough: Meister Eckhart's Creation Spirituality in New Translation* (New York: Doubleday, 1980) 93.

[119]Tucker, *Daughters*, 152.

[120]Grace M. Jantzen, *Julian of Norwich: Mystic and Theologian* (London: SPCK, 1987) 89-93.

[121]Julian of Norwich, *Revelations of Divine Love* (New York: Penguin Books, 1966) 211-12.

[122]*Imitation of Christ*, 2.11. See Thomas á Kempis, *Imitation of Christ* ed. Harold C. Gardiner (Garden City, NY: Image Books, 1955) 93.

[123]Timothy George, *Theology of the Reformers* (Nashville: Broadman Press, 1988) 273-74. As mentioned in the preface, Timothy George drew most of his illustrations, with slight variations, from the above book published by Broadman Press.

[124]Leonhard von Muralt and Walter Schmid, *Quellen zur Geschichte der Taufer in der Schweiz* (Zurich: S. Hirzel verlag, 1952).

[125]Cornelius J. Dyck and Dennis D. Martin, eds., *The Mennonite Encyclopedia*, vol. V (Scottdale, PA: Herald Press, 1990).

[126]George, 184-85.

[127]Bainton, *Church*, 162.

[128]See William R. Estep, ed., *Anabaptist Beginnings (1523–1533): A Sourcebook* (Nievwkoop: B. De Graaf, 1976) and William R. Estep, *The Anabaptist Story* (Grand Rapids: William B. Eerdmans, 1975) and H. Wayne Pipkin and John H. Yoder, *Balthasar Hubmaier: Theologian of Anabaptism*, Classics of the Radical Reformation (Scottdale, PA: Herald Press, 1989).

[129]R. Kent Hughes, *Mark*, 2 vols. (Westchester, IL: Crossway Books, 1984)1: 19-20.

[130]Bainton, *Church*, 162.

[131]Bill J. Leonard, *Word of God Across the Ages: Using Christian History in Preaching*, enlarged ed. (Greenville: Smyth & Helwys Publishing, Inc., 1991) 36.

[132]Roland Bainton, *Here I Stand: A Life of Martin Luther* (New York: Mentor Books, New American Library, 1950) 144.

[133]George, 79.

[134]Ibid., 54.

[135]Ibid., 60-61.

[136]Ibid., 105.

[137]Ibid., 104.

[138]Ibid., 53, 72.

[139]Martin Luther, *Lectures on Romans*, trans. Wilhelm Pauck (Philadelphia: Westminster Press, 1961) 243.

[140]Bainton, *Here*, 191-92.

[141]Ibid., 249.

[142]Benjamin Browne, *Illustrations for Preaching* (Nashville: Abingdon Press, 1977) 99-100.

[143]See Estep, *Anabaptist Story*. See also Harold S. Bender and C. Henry Smith, eds. *The Mennonite Encyclopedia*, vol. 3 (Scottdale, PA: Mennonite Publishing House, 1957).

[144]See Estep, *Anabaptist Story*.

[145]George, 258.

[146]Ibid., 263.

[147]Ibid., 304-305.

[148]Ibid., 305-306.

[149]Roland Bainton, *The Reformation of the Sixteenth Century* (Boston: Beacon Press, 1952) 82-84.

[150]George, 127.

[151]See A. C. Underwood, *A History of the English Baptists* (London: Kingsgate Press, 1947).

[152]Bainton, *Church*, 179.

[153]John Bunyan, *The Pilgrim's Progress*, ed. E. Glenn Hinson, vol. 1, *The Doubleday Devotional Classics* (Garden City, NY: Doubleday, 1978) 318.

[154]Thomas R. McKibbens, Jr., *The Forgotten Heritage: A Lineage of Great Baptist Preaching* (Macon: Mercer University Press, 1986) 111-15.

[155]Rosemary Reuther and Rosemary Skinner, eds., *Women and Religion in America*, vol. 2, *The Colonial and Revolutionary Periods* (San Francisco: Harper and Row, 1983) 279.

[156]Margaret Hope Bacon, *Mothers of Feminism: The Story of Quaker Women in America* (San Francisco: Harper and Row, 1986) 26.

[157]Reuther, *Women*, 279.

[158]Bacon, 26.

[159]Ibid.

[160]Leonard, 43-46.

[161]H. Leon McBeth, *Women in Baptist Life* (Nashville: Broadman Press, 1979) 27, 30, 31, 35.

[162]H. Leon McBeth, *A Sourcebook for Baptist Heritage* (Nashville: Broadman Press, 1990) 70-72.

[163]William L. Lumpkin, *Baptist Confessions of Faith* (Valley Forge: Judson Press, 1969) 121.

[164]Edwin S. Gaustad, ed., *Baptist Piety: The Last Will and Testimony of Obadiah Holmes* (Grand Rapids: Christian University Press, 1978) 22-29. See also H. Leon McBeth, *The Baptist Heritage* (Nashville: Broadman Press, 1987) 140.

[165]Selma R. Williams, *Divine Rebel: The Life of Anne Marbury Hutchinson* (New York: Holt, Rinehart & Winston, 1981).

[166]McBeth, *Baptist*, 125.

[167]Cliff Fadiman, *The Little, Brown Book of Anecdotes* (Boston: Little, Brown and Company, 1985) 216-17.

[168]Charles Holder, *The Quakers in England and America* (New York: The Neuver Company, 1913) 506.

[169]Timothy George, *John Robinson and the English Separatist Tradition* (Macon: Mercer University Press, 1982) 90-92.

[170]*The Baptist Program* (October 1987): 23.

[171]Edwin S. Gaustad, *Liberty of Conscience: Roger Williams in America* (Grand Rapids: William B. Eerdmans, 1991) 24-44.

[172]Ibid., 31, 66.

[173]Ibid., 65, 67, 79-80.

[174]Ibid., 71.

[175]Ibid., 127, 168.

[176]McBeth, *Baptist*, 183-85.

[177]Browne, 75.

[178]Hugh T. Kerr, *Readings in Christian Thought*, 2d ed. (Philadelphia: Fortress Press, 1990) 201.

[179]Ernst Käsemann, *Jesus Means Freedom*, trans. Frank Clarke (Philadelphia: Fortress Press, 1972) 54.

[180]Donald E. Demeray, *Pulpit Greats: Whats Makes Them Great* (Chicago: Moody Press, 1973) 55.

[181]McKibbens, 44-50.

[182]Ibid., 159.

[183]Ibid., 135-37.

[184]See John Leland, *The Writings of John Leland*, ed. L. F. Greene (New York: Arno Press, 1969; rpt. of 1845 ed.).

[185]John Killenger, "What Can You Do for the Peace of the World," sermon delivered 29 May 1983, First Presbyterian Church, Lynchburg, Virginia.

[186]Leonard, 51-53.

[187]Ibid., 53-56.

[188]Kerr, 192-93.

[189]Benjamin Franklin, *The Autobiography of Benjamin Franklin: A Genetic Text*, eds. J. A. Leon Lemay and M. Zall (Knoxville: University of Tennessee Press, 1981) 105.

[190]Hughes, xii.

[191]For information on Whitefield, see Harry S. Stout, *The Divine Dramatist: George Whitefield and the Rise of Modern Evangelicalism* (Grand Rapids: William B. Eerdmans, 1991).

[192]John Woolman, *The Journal of John Woolman and A Plea for the Poor* (Secaucus, NJ: The Citadel Press,) 56.

[193]Ibid.

[194]Sterling Stuckey, *Slave Culture: Nationalist Theory and the Foundations of Black America* (New York: Oxford University Press, 1987) 40.

[195]Fadiman, 42. See also Daniel G. Reid, ed., *Dictionary of Christianity in America* (Grand Rapids: Intervarsity Press, 1990), s.v. "Barton, Clarissa," by K. E. Güenther.

[196]See Barbara Cross, ed., *The Autobiography of Lyman Beecher*, 2 vols. (Harvard: Harvard University Press, 1961).

[197]Nancy A. Hardesty, *Women Called to Witness* (Nashville: Abingdon Press, 1984) 66.

[198]Catherine Mumford, "Letter to William Booth, 1855" in *Women in the Salvation Army*, comp. John D. Waldron (Oakville, Ontario: The Salvation Army, 1983) 35.

[199]Ibid., 40.

[200]Flora Larsson, *My Best Men Are Women* (London: Hodder and Stroughton, 1974) 13.

[201]Donald Dayton, *Discovering An Evangelical Heritage* (Peabody, MS: Hendrickson Publishers, 1976) 94-95.

[202]Richard Collier, *The General Next to God* (Glasgow: Collins, 1965) 72.

[203]Bainton, *Church*, 196.

[204]McBeth, *Baptist*, 446.

[205]McKibbens, 190.

[206]Ruth Tucker, *Guardians of The Great Commission* (Grand Rapids: Academie Books, 1988) 130-31.

[207]Frank Houghton, *Amy Carmichael of Dohnavur* (London: Society for the Propagation of Christian Knowledge, 1954) 62.

[208]Tucker, *Guardians,* 132.

[209]Mark Noll, "The Puzzling Faith of Abraham Lincoln," *Christian History* 11/33 (no. 1): 11.

[210]Mark Galli, "Firebrands and Visionaries," *Christian History* 11/33 (no. 1): 18.

[211]Noll, 12.

[212]Ibid.

[213]Russell Conwell, *Acres of Diamonds* (Westwood, NJ: Fleming H. Revell Company, 1960) 17.

[214]Dayton, 85-98.

[215]Delos Miles, *Master Principles of Evangelism* (Nashville: Broadman Press, 1982) 25.

[216]D. Leslie Hollon, "Love As Holiness: An Examination of Charles G. Finney's Theology of Sanctification, 1830–1860," (Unpublished Ph.D. dissertation, Southern Baptist Theological Seminary, 1985) 21-23.

[217]Ibid., 27.

[218]Ibid., 119.

[219]Ibid., 116, n. 113.

[220]Ibid., 123-24.

[221]Ibid., 154.

[222]Ibid., 142-43.

[223]Ibid., 180.

[224]Ibid., 195.

[225]Ibid., 205. For a biography of Finney, see Kenneth J. Hardaman, *Charles Grand-ison Finney, 1972–1875: Revivalist and Reformer* (Grand Rapids: Baker Book House, 1990).

[226]George C. Bedell, Leo Sandon Jr. and Charles T. Wellborn, *Religion in America,* 2d ed. (New York: MacMillan, 1982) 338. For information on Gladden, see Jacob Henry Dorn, *Washington Gladden: Prophet of the Social Gospel* (Cleveland: Ohio University Press, 1967).

[227]Cecil B. Hartley, *The Three Mrs. Judsons,* rev. ed. (Philadelphia: John E. Potter & Company, 1863) 27.

[228]*Encyclopedia of Southern Baptists,* 1958 ed., s.v. "Judson, Ann Hasseltine," by E. C. Routh.

[229]Ibid.

[230]Nancy Judson, "Letter to Mrs. Carleton," *Massachusetts Baptist Missionary Magazine* 3 (May 1813): 295-96.

[231]Edwin S. Gaustad, *A Religious History of America* (San Francisco: Harper Collins Publishers, 1990) 166-67.

[232]See Catherine Albanese, *America: Religion and Religions* 2d. ed. (Belmont, CA: Wadsworth Publishing Co., 1992) 225-34, 240-43, 432.

[233]George Marsden, *Fundamentalism and American Culture: The Shaping of Twentieth Century Evangelicalism, 1870–1905* (New York: Oxford University Press, 1980) 83.

[234]D. L. Moody, *Anecdotes, Incidents and Illustrations* (Chicago: The Bible Institute Colportage Association, 1898) 26-27.

[235]J. C. Pollock, *Moody* (New York: MacMillan, 1963) 162.

[236]Moody, 83.

[237]Leonard, 81-84.

[238]Walter Rauschenbusch, *Christianity and the Social Crisis* (New York: Macmillan, 1907) 342.

[239]Bedell, 342.

[240]See Amanda Smith, *An Autobiography: The Story of the Lord's Dealings with Mrs. Amanda Smith* (Noblesville, IN: Newby Book Room, 1972). See also Nancy Hardesty, *Great Women of Faith* (Grand Rapids: Baker Book House, 1980).

[241]Leonard, 68, 70-71.

[242]Ibid., 70.

[243]Ibid., 71-72.

[244]Charles R. Wilson, *Baptized in Blood: The Religion of the Lost Cause, 1865-1920* (Athens, GA: The University of Georgia Press, 1980) 26-27.

[245]William R. Estep, "The Making of a Prophet: An Introduction to Charles Haddon Spurgeon," *Baptist History and Heritage* 19 (October 1984): 7.

[246]Ibid., 6.

[247]Ibid., 12.

[248]Ernest W. Bacon, *Spurgeon, Heir of the Puritans* (Grand Rapids: Baker Book House, 1967) 28-29.

[249]Fadiman, 519.

[250]Ibid., 521.

[251]Kerr, 241.

[252]William J. Petersen, *Martin Luther Had a Wife, Harriet Beecher Stowe Had a Husband* (Wheaton, ILL: Tyndale House Publishers, 1983) 132-33.

[253]Lee Thomas, *Billy I* (Van Nuys, CA: Son-Rise Books, 1974) 110-11. See also Lyle W. Dorsett, *Billy Sunday and the Redemption of Urban America* (Grand Rapids: William B. Eerdmans, 1991).

[254]Marsden, 142.

[255]See Deen, *Great Women*, and also Hammack, *Dictionary of Women*.

[256]McBeth, *Women*, 77.

[257]Tucker, *Guardians*, 64.

[258]Ibid., 65.

[259]Mary Webb, "Addressing the Female Society," *Massachusetts Baptist Missionary Magazine* 2 (May 1812): 156.

[260]McBeth, *Women*, 101-102.

[261]For information on Young, see Klaus J. Hansen, *Mormonism and the American Experience* (Chicago: University of Chicago Press, 1981).

[262]Theodore F. Adams, *Making the Most of What Life Brings* (New York: Harper and Brothers, 1957) 85.

[263]Ibid., 98-99.

[264]Ibid., 120.

[265]*Alabama Baptist*, XCIX, 36 (6 September 1934).

[266]Clark Pinnock and Delvin Brown, *Theological Crossfire: An Evangelical/Liberal Debate* (Grand Rapids: Zondervan Publishing House, 1990) 33.

[267]John Claypool, *The Light Within You* (Waco: Word Books, 1983) 216.

[268]Dietrich Bonhöffer, *Life Together*, trans. John W. Doberstain (San Francisco: Harper and Row, 1954) 13. See also Dietrich Bonhöffer, *Letters and Papers from Prison* (New York: MacMillan, 1953) 225.

[269]Bonhöffer, *Letters*, 55-58.

[270]Ibid., 31-32.

[271]Bonhöffer, *Life*, 67.

[272]Ibid., 18-19.

[273]Foster, 19.

[274]Tucker, *Daughters*, 395.

[275]Carole C. Carlson, *Corrie ten Boom: Her Life, Her Faith* (Old Tappan, NJ: Fleming H. Revell Company, 1983) 127.

[276]See C. Douglas Weaver, *The Healer-Prophet, William Marrion Branham: A Study of the Prophetic in American Pentecostalism* (Macon: Mercer University Press, 1987).

[277]Harry Emerson Fosdick, *The Living of These Days* (New York: Harper and Brothers, 1956) 75.

[278]Fadiman, 214-15.

[279]Harry Emerson Fosdick, "Unknown Soldier," in *Baptist Life and Thought: A Source Book*, ed. William H. Brackney (Valley Forge: Judson Press, 1983) 373-76.

[280]Petersen, 159.

[281]Dallas Lee, ed., *The Substance of Faith and Other Cotton Patch Sermons By Clarence Jordan* (New York: Association Press, 1972) 7.

[282]*Peacework*, November-December 1989/January-February 1990, 24.

[283]Dallas Lee, *Cotton Patch Evidence: The Story of Clarence Jordan and the Koinonia Farm Experiment (1942-1971)* (Americus, GA: Koinonia Partners, Inc., 1971) 75-76.

[284]*Koinonia Newsletter*, November 1989, 2.

[285]Stephen B. Oates, *Let the Trumpet Sound: The Life of Martin Luther King, Jr.* (New York: Mentor Books, New American Library, 1982) 447-48.

[286]Ibid., 73.

[287]Ibid., 107.

[288]Leonard, 99.

[289]Alex Haley, *Autobiography of Malcolm X* (New York: Grove Press, 1965) 521, 524.

[290]John J. Carey, *Carlyle Marney: A Pilgrim's Progress* (Macon: Mercer University Press, 1980) 36.

[291]Ibid., 138.

[292]C. Allyn Russell, *Voices of American Fundamentalism* (Philadelphia; Westminster Press, 1976) 128, 130.

[293]Kerr, 378.

[294]Helen Barrett Montgomery, *Helen Barrett Montgomery: From Campus to World Citizenship* (New York: Fleming H. Revell Co., 1940). See also Deen, *Great Women* and Hammack, *Dictionary of Women*.

[295]Edgar Young Mullins, *Faith in the Modern World* (Nashville: Sunday School Board, 1930) 14.

[296]Ibid., 48.

[297]Miles, 41-42.

[298]J. Wallace Hamilton, *Who Goes There?* (Old Tappan, NJ: Fleming H. Revell Co., 1958) 127-28.

[299]Albert Schweitzer, *Out of My Life and Thought* (New York: Mentor Books, 1953) 69-70.

[300]Fadiman, 493.

[301]Fulton J. Sheen, *Treasure in Clay: The Autobiography of Fulton J. Sheen* (Garden City, NY: Doubleday, 1980) 10, 12.

[302]Edward Chinn, "Words Can Bless or Burn," *Preaching* (January-February 1991): 61.

[303]Jim Forest, *Religion in the New Russia: The Impact of Perestroika on the Varieties of Religious Life in the Soviet Union* (New York: Crossroads, 1990) xiii.

[304]Leonard, 17-18.

[305]Robert Coles, "God and the Rural Poor," *Psychology Today* 5 (January 1972): 31-41.

[306]V. S. Naipaul, *A Turn in the South* (New York: Vintage Books, 1989) 39-42.

[307]John S. Workman, *Fireflies in a Fruit Jar: On Religion, Politics and Other Wonders by A Southern Preacher-Turned Journalist* (Little Rock: August House, 1988) 80-81.

[308]David E. Harrell, Jr., "The South: Seedbed of Sectarianism," in *Varieties of Southern Evangelicalism*, ed. David E. Harrell, Jr. (Macon: Mercer University Press, 1981) 53-54.

[309]Will D. Campbell, *Brother to a Dragonfly* (New York: The Seabury Press, 1977) 156-59.

[310]"A Pencil in the Hand of God," *Time*, 4 December 1989, 11.

[311]Ibid.

[312]H. Stephen Shoemaker, *The Jekyll and Hyde Syndrome* (Nashville: Broadman Press, 1987) 114-15.

[313]Thomas G. Long, "Where's the Treasure?" in *Shepherds and Bathrobes* (Lima, OH: C. S. S. Publishing Co., 1987) 34. See F. Forrester Church, ed., *The Essential Tillich: An Anthology of the Writings of Paul Tillich* (New York: MacMillan, 1987).

[314]For the thought of Tutu, see Desmond Tutu, *Hope and Suffering: Sermons and Speeches*, ed. John Webster (William B. Eerdmans, 1984).

Article Index

Scripture Index

1:18—1605, 1923D
2:8-10—1508A, 1708A, 1828C
2:11-22—201, 1508K, 1708C,
    1826B, 1907B, 1923E
2:14—1611A, 1707
2:18—1614D
3:1-6—1804A
4:1-4—1508A
4:1-6—1708C, 1826B
4:1—1001, 1813B, 1819C
4:4-16—1904F
4:12—1813B
4:15—1709A
4:22-24—304B, 1819B, 1828C
4:29—401G, 1920
4:31-32—1802
5:8-9—1507B
5:22-33—201, 1908
6:5-9—1813I
6:10-17—1909D
6:17—1512B
6:18—202A

Philippians
1:3—1904C
1:21—1904A, 1904B
2:5-11—1508G, 1805A, 1820
2:5—304B, 1508O
2:7—1603
3:3-5—1825E
3:7-11—1304, 1603
3:10—1511B
3:12-14—1601, 1923D
3:20—1614C
4:6—311A, 1701B
4:8—104B, 1813F
4:13—701, 1302, 1830

Colossians
1:14—1705
1:24—1511B
3:5-17—1819B

3:13—1802
3:14—1913
3:15—1611A
3:17—1202D, 1805B
4:2—1701B

1 Thessalonians
3:1-4—701
3:11-13—1813I
4:13-18—1503, 1818, 1906, 1926
5:14—1607B
5:15-22—1924C
5:17—202A, 311A, 1701B
5:22—1710B

2 Thessalonians
2:1-12—1503, 1818, 1906
3:11-13—305B
3:13—1806A

1 Timothy
1:18—1508M
4:2—001
4:6-10—1804A
4:11-16—1803
4:12—1508H, 1825D
5:8—1508J
6:5—1401
6:6-10—1919B
6:10—401K
6:11-21—1508M
6:19—1827

2 Timothy
1:5—1828A, 1904C
1:8—1825C
1:11-14—1813F
2:1-13—1909D
2:8-13—1904A
2:15—1512A, 1708D
3:5—1813I
3:10-17—601
3:15—1813C
3:16-17—305C, 305E, 1706,
    1909C, 1925

Topical Index

Contributor's Index

(WLA)—W. Loyd Allen—305A, 305B, 305C, 305D, 305E, 305F, 401F, 1401,
1607A, 1821A, 1902, 1909F

(PSA)—Penrose St. Amant—401H, 401I, 401J, 401K, 401L, 1508N, 1904A,
1904B

(RB)—Rosalie Beck—203B, 309, 601, 702, 1301, 1604, 1804A, 1808, 1816,
1830

(CDB)—Carolyn D. Blevins—311A, 1302, 1510, 1609, 1822, 1829, 1915

(WRE)—William R. Estep, Jr.—1502, 1503, 1506, 1509

(TG)—Timothy George—1501, 1504, 1508C, 1508D, 1508E, 1508F, 1508G,
1508H, 1511A, 1511B, 1511C, 1511D, 1512B, 1612

(DLH)—D. Leslie Hollon—1813A, 1813B, 1813C, 1814D, 1813E, 1813F,
1813G, 1813H, 1813I, 1813J

(EEJ)—E. Earl Joiner—001, 105, 303C, 311B, 401C, 401E, 1508J, 1602B,
1709A, 1710B, 1810, 1904C, 1904D, 1904E, 1904F

(DML)—Deirdre Madison LaNoue—313, 1314, 1905

(BJL)—Bill J. Leonard—1508A, 1605, 1708A, 1708B, 1820, 1823A, 1823B,
1823C, 1910D, 1923A

(AMM)—Andrew M. Manis—1801A, 1801B, 1801C, 1824A, 1824B, 1824C,
1909E, 1911, 1921, 1923B, 1923C, 1923D

(PRP)—Phyllis Rodgerson Pleasants—203A, 203C, 302, 303A, 303B, 308,
312A, 312B

(WBS)—Walter B. Shurden—1601, 1607B, 1706, 1815

(MAS)—Michael A. Smith—102A, 102B, 104B, 106, 201, 202A, 202B, 204,
401B, 501C

(CDW)—C. Douglas Weaver—101, 103, 104A, 202C, 304A, 306, 701, 901,
1003, 1202A, 1202B, 1202C, 1402, 1512A, 1603, 1606, 1608, 1610, 1614A,
1614B, 1614C, 1614D, 1614E, 1702A, 1703, 1704, 1705, 1707, 1708C,
1804B, 1811, 1814, 1818, 1819A, 1819C, 1821B, 1825A, 1825B, 1825C,
1826B, 1827, 1828B, 1831, 1832, 1903A, 1904G, 1906, 1907C, 1908,
1909A, 1909B, 1909C, 1912A, 1912B, 1913, 1914, 1918, 1923E

(JAW)—James A. Weaver—301, 304B, 307, 310, 401A, 401D, 401G, 402,
501A, 501B, 1001, 1002, 1101, 1201, 1202D, 1203, 1303, 1505, 1507A,
1507B, 1508B, 1508K, 1508L, 1508M, 1508N, 1602A, 1611A, 1613,
1701A, 1701B, 1702B, 1708D, 1709B, 1709C, 1802, 1803, 1805A, 1805B,
1805C, 1806A, 1806B, 1807, 1812, 1819B, 1825E, 1826A, 1828C, 1903B,
1907B, 1909D, 1910A, 1910B, 1910C, 1917A, 1917B, 1919A, 1919B, 1920,
1924C, 1925, 1926

(**DMW**)—Danny M. West—1508I, 1901A, 1901B, 1901C, 1907A, 1916A, 1916B, 1922, 1924A, 1924B

Students of Brewton-Parker College

(**ALC**)—Anthony L. Chute—1809
(**GJC**)—Gregory J. Carroll—1825D
(**TF**)—Terri Farless—1611B, 1710A
(**ARN**)—A. Randy Niswonger—1828A
(**CKP**)—Clarice K. Poland—1817